MW00938254

BLACK NIGHT, GOLD COAST

by Gray George

Black Night, Gold Coast
Copyright © 2015 by Gray George

All rights reserved. With the exception of brief quotations embodied in critical reviews and articles, no portion of this book may be reproduced or used in any manner whatsoever without the express written permission of the author.

First Edition

Cover Design by Streetlight Graphics.

"The boy needed to behave insanely, even though that would probably not change things. His rage was simultaneously blind and planned, berserk irrationality as a means to an end."

Edward Bunker
from *Little Boy Blue*

PREFACE

Home invasions are far from rare in the United States. Between 2003 and 2007, nearly 267,000 Americans were violently attacked each year during home burglaries. [i] Some of these victims were beaten, some of these victims were raped, and some of these victims were murdered. While the specific details of each home invasion are different, the general circumstances are almost always the same: an armed intruder enters an occupied dwelling, accosts the residents, and leaves a trail of violent devastation in his wake. Most home invasions happen at night, and in more than half of cases, the intruder gains access to his victims through an unlocked door or window. [ii] Because home invasions involve deadly weapons, powerful emotions, and direct contact between violent predators and frightened residents, these offenses are considered especially dangerous by law enforcement.

Despite their unsettling ubiquity, a significant number of home invasions go unsolved. In this sense, home invasions share a common bond with other crimes in the U.S. On average, in a given year,

American law-enforcement agencies clear about twelve percent of all burglaries, twenty-nine percent of all robberies, forty percent of all rapes, and sixty percent of all murders. [iii] If crime is a cottage industry in the U.S., then unsolved crime is the industry standard.

This book explores a home invasion that nearly became an unsolved crime. The incident occurred on May 20, 2009, in the small, unincorporated community of Faria, California. I first learned about the Faria home invasion on the morning of May 21, 2009, when I booted up my computer, navigated to the *Los Angeles Times* website, and started skimming the day's stories. According to the *Times*, a wealthy husband and his pregnant wife had been stabbed to death inside their luxurious beachfront home. The attack had also claimed the life of the couple's unborn child. While the explicit facts of the *Times* article were gruesome, it was an implicit detail of the story that immediately grabbed my attention. Specifically, I was intrigued by the fact that the Faria decedents appeared to be extremely low-risk homicide victims.

In terms of victimology, it's highly, *highly* unusual for affluent couples living in gated communities to be murdered in their own homes. It's also worth noting that, in 2009, only thirteen percent of homicides in the U.S. were committed with knives. [iv] The Faria home-invader's choice of victims, coupled with his choice of murder weapon, made the beach-house homicide a real rarity. Statistical anomalies have always piqued my interest, and the circumstances surrounding the Faria home invasion were no exception.

Over the next several days, I followed media coverage of the Faria case very carefully. The Ventura County Sheriff's Department was hinting at a possible connection between the Faria victims and their killer, but based on what I was reading in the press, this seemed unlikely. If a connection had existed between the Faria victims and their murderer, there was a strong likelihood that a suspect would've emerged in days—if not hours—of the killings. This was particularly true given the statistically anomalous nature of the crime. By reading between the lines of the media reports, it was easy to see that Ventura County detectives had no good leads in the case. Eventually, with the investigation at a standstill, press coverage of the Faria murders started to dry up.

A year passed.

On the morning of April 12, 2010, I booted up my computer, navigated to the *Los Angeles Times* website, and started skimming the day's headlines. As my eyes moved across the screen, one headline hit me like a lightning bolt: An arrest had been made in the Faria case. Not only was the Faria suspect in custody, the events leading to his capture were compelling. According to the *Times*, the suspect's DNA had been linked to the Faria murders after he was arrested for an unrelated felony and his genetic profile ended up in the state's DNA database. Science and public policy, not sleuthing or police work, had cracked the Faria case. As I took in the details of the suspect's arrest, I was riveted to my screen.

The more I learned about the Faria suspect's arrest and the DNA legislation leading to his capture, the more fascinated I became and the more questions I had. What were the circumstances that led to the Faria home invasion? What drove the suspect to commit such an unusual, statistically improbable crime? Most importantly, how many violent crimes could arrestee

DNA collection solve—and prevent—in the future? With a myriad of questions swirling through my mind, I knew that I wanted to write about the Faria case. However, I didn't want to churn out a quick, sensational piece of pulp. Instead, I wanted to write a nuanced account of the Faria murders, with an emphasis on the DNA angle. Unfortunately, researching and writing such an account would require patience. The legal proceedings in the case needed to play out first, and that would take time. Back then, I had no idea just how long the wait would last.

When the legal process had finally run its course, I immediately started work on this book. As I delved deeper into my research and became acquainted with some of the key figures in the case, I began to realize that the Faria saga was much more than a regional homicide story or a parable about DNA's crime-fighting utility. In the course of reviewing documents, conducting interviews, and analyzing evidence in the case, it became clear that the Faria murders cut to the core of the American experience. When the Faria murderer invaded his victims' residence, he didn't just take the lives of three human beings. Instead, he attacked the most sacred institutions in our society— the institution of home, the institution of family, the institution of marriage.

At the same time, I came to understand that the Faria murderer himself was a living, breathing symbol of social failure. As I explored the murderer's background in minute detail, it became obvious that his life history offered a bleak and revealing commentary on our dysfunctional schools, our broken mental-health system, and our collective social standards— standards that, all too often, place a higher premium on looking good than being good. Examining these issues and telling the full story of the Faria tragedy are the objectives of this book.

All of the information contained in these pages has been taken from personal interviews, law-enforcement reports, legal filings, school records, medical documents, jail logs, police and sheriff's interview transcripts, and other relevant sources as noted. At certain points in the text, small pieces of dialogue have been added to ensure narrative continuity. However, it should be noted that at least ninety-five percent of the dialogue in this work has been lifted verbatim from law-enforcement reports and interview transcripts. Also, in select cases, I've changed the names of the people involved with this story. All name changes are indicated with an asterisk [*].

Black Night, Gold Coast isn't a story about one-dimensional characters, feel-good bromides, or easy answers. Sanitizing the truth won't stop home invasions, prevent murders, or enhance public safety. To accomplish these goals, we need to face facts, grapple with deeper meanings, and address root causes. To this end, *Black Night, Gold Coast* is a book about complexity and loss and reality. It's a story about the possibilities of science, the fragility of the human condition, and the dark-side of the American Dream.

Gray George
Los Angeles
October 7, 2015

PART I

CHAPTER 1

The motorcycle picked up speed as it roared down the entrance ramp and merged with the river of glass, iron, and fuel-injected steel flowing north on the 101 Freeway. Perched atop the motorcycle was a rider. Because he was dressed in black from head to toe, the rider was barely visible to other motorists as they made their way out of Ventura and onto the long, dark stretch of freeway that leads north to Santa Barbara, Paso Robles, San Francisco, and beyond. The date was May 20, 2009. The time was a few minutes before 10 p.m.

As the motorcycle bobbed and weaved through traffic, the rider leaned into his machine, revved the engine, and threaded his way through the slalom course of cars, light trucks, and big rigs in his path. On the cyclist's right side, the lights of multi-million-dollar homes twinkled in the velvety hills above central Ventura. To the rider's left, the empty void of the Pacific stretched west toward a jet-black horizon. During the day, this stretch of freeway is one of the most picturesque locations on the planet, with crystal-blue waves, jagged mountains, and towering palms augmenting the visual spectacle. At night, however, the roadway's visual grandeur disappears into the darkness. When the sun goes down, the freeway takes on a foreboding quality, and the possibility of an organ-smashing traffic collision or a bone-shattering rollover is never more than a heartbeat away.

Roaring north against the salty Pacific wind, the motorcycle rider bided his time for several miles, then darted into the freeway's right-hand lane. As he approached Exit 72, otherwise known as the State Beaches exit, the rider throttled back on his accelerator, veered off the freeway, and sliced a stealthy path down Exit 72's lightly traveled off-ramp. After rounding a quick curve to the left and going back under the freeway, the rider emerged on an isolated stretch of Pacific Coast Highway. This stretch of PCH serves as both a frontage road for the 101 and a pathway to the public beaches, surfing breaks, RV parks, and oceanfront neighborhoods that dot the exquisite coastline of southwestern Ventura County.

Zooming into the night, the rider watched as the lights of the freeway dimmed, dissipated, and then disappeared entirely. Cool ocean air tickled the flesh on the rider's neck and seeped into the minuscule openings on his black, faceless helmet. With his hands locked tightly around the bike's handlebars and his soul synched with the mechanized growl of the engine, the rider saw only darkness ahead.

* * *

At that same moment, approximately three miles north of the motorcycle rider's location, nine-year-old

Brockie Husted sat in the bright, warm living room of his parents' immaculate beachfront home. Built in 1979, the home was part of an exclusive gated community called Faria Beach Colony. Although many of the houses in Faria Beach Colony served as second homes for out-of-town moguls, the community's spectacular oceanfront location and close proximity to downtown Ventura made it an attractive option for year-round residents as well. Brockie and his family counted themselves among a select group of year-round habitués who called Faria Beach Colony home.

Brockie Husted and his older sister Isabella had lived at 4250 Faria Road since 2005, when their parents purchased the family home for a cool $2.1 million. While the home's price-tag had been steep, the Husteds had no trouble affording it. Moreover, the home's unbeatable location on an ultra-scenic stretch of the Southern California coast meant that the Husteds had definitely gotten their money's worth.

At 1,681 square feet, the Husteds' one-story, caramel-coloured home was a masterwork of intelligent planning. Although the property's design emphasized quality of life over quantity of space, the home still contained everything a family of four could possibly need. In addition to the sizable master bedroom where Brockie's parents slept, the home also contained two smaller bedrooms for the children. The Husteds' bedrooms were tucked away on the northeast end of the house, which offered views of the Santa Ynez Mountains to the east.

While the Husteds' bedrooms were more than adequate, the property's *piece de resistance* was the enormous, beautifully appointed great room at the southwest end of the home. Not only did the great room contain the living room, dining room, and kitchen, it also offered jaw-dropping views of the swirling Pacific, which lay just a few feet beyond the home's rear wall. The great room was encased in large, spotless windows that extended almost from the floor to the ceiling. In the middle of the bank of windows was a door. The door led onto a large sun deck above the beach. If one walks through the door, across the deck, and down the back steps at high tide, he or she will be standing in the cool, blue waters of the Pacific Ocean.

While the location and layout of the Husted home was second-to-none, the interior was equally impressive. Simply put, the home's interior decorating was a study in impeccable taste. Blond hardwood flooring ran throughout the house and served as a perfect compliment to the subdued beige paint on the walls. In the living room, two solid white sofas did a perfect job of picking up the snow-white baseboards that ran around the perimeter of the great room. Between the sofas was a rectangular glass-topped coffee table. A few feet away, a large flatscreen television was mounted above the fireplace, which was framed by a gorgeous maple mantlepiece.

In the kitchen, top-of-the-line stainless-steel appliances provided a modern metallic counterpoint to the ample wooden cabinetry and the emerald-green countertops. The narrow brown veins that ran through the marble countertops were perfectly matched with the stain of the wooden cabinetry. Beneath the cabinets, a five-burner stovetop was situated in the middle of the countertop. A block of sharp, black-handled knives was positioned to the right of the stovetop.

Every facet of the Husted home screamed sophistication, aesthetic refinement, and prosperity.

The Husted home wasn't some soulless, cavernous McMansion tucked away in a generic, quasi-Stepford subdivision. Instead, the Husteds lived in a distinctive, world-class house that made terrific use of every available square inch. At a time when many Americans were struggling to make ends meet after the economic meltdown of 2008, the Husteds were living embodiments of the American Dream.

Although the Husted home was magnificent, the family wasn't planning to live there forever. After Brockie's mother discovered that she was pregnant in early 2009, the family decided to sell the Faria Road property and move into a larger home. On the night of May 20, 2009, as Brockie and his parents sat in their living room watching television, the house where they'd spent so many happy times was on the market for $3.2 million.

Brockie and his parents sat close together as they gazed at the flatscreen television mounted above the mantle. Like 28 million other Americans, the Husteds were watching the Season 8 finale of *American Idol*. That night, the show would score an impressive 10.0 share in the Nielsen ratings, as underdog Kris Allen rocketed to victory over audience favorite Adam Lambert. After the winner was announced, many would agree that Kris Allen won the contest due to his stirring rendition of the song *No Boundaries*. As it turned out, Allen's performance was prophetic; the theme of no boundaries would be a recurring one on May 20, 2009.

The judges announced Kris Allen's victory at 10:07 p.m. Pacific Standard Time. As the Husteds sat in their living room and watched Allen revel in his victory, the wind howled in the darkness beyond their windows and ripping waves pounded the beach below their back deck. Because the moon was a waning crescent, there was little natural light to scrub away the night's many shadows.

Shortly after Kris Allen was named America's newest pop idol, Brockie's father raised himself off the plush white sofa and walked into the brightly lit kitchen, where a marble-topped island separated the refrigerator, stove, and other appliances from the seating area in the living room. Brockie sat with his mother on the sofa, while eleven-year-old Isabella slept in her bedroom at the front of the house. Besides the fact that Brockie was up past his normal bedtime to watch the season finale of *American Idol*, nothing about the night was out of the ordinary. The Husteds were a close, loving family whose existence was grounded in the good life. For the Husteds, comfort was a given and happiness was a foregone conclusion. In fact, life was so comfortable that middling concerns—such as keeping doors locked—were sometimes overlooked.

It all happened so fast that none of them had time to think.

As Brockie sat on the sofa with his mother and his father poked around in the kitchen, the backdoor of their house burst open and a man charged into the great room.

"Get on the floor!" the man shouted at Brockie's father, who stood dumbstruck between the refrigerator and the kitchen island.

Brockie's mind struggled to process the details of what he was witnessing: the man wore a black jumpsuit, black gloves, and a black motorcycle helmet with a visor. The man's outstretched hand grasped a black semiautomatic pistol.

As Brockie's father dropped down behind the kitchen island and proned himself on the polished hardwood, Brockie's mother ordered the boy to get off the sofa and onto the living-room floor. Brockie's mother struggled to lower herself to the floor, but because of the advanced stage of her pregnancy, descending onto the blond hardwood was not a simple task.

The intruder meant business. It had taken a matter of seconds to get the entire family on the floor, and without missing a beat, the black-clad stranger moved over Brockie's father, dropped his knee into the homeowner's back, grabbed a handful of the defenseless man's brown hair, and smashed his face into the varnished hardwood. As blood gushed from the father's face, the intruder started making demands.

"Your money, where is it?" the stranger demanded to know in a deep, menacing bark. He added that he also wanted any jewelry in the house.

Brockie was still on the floor next to his mother in the living room. Because of the great room's layout, Brockie was unable to see his father on the floor behind the kitchen island.

Pinned to the floor, with the stranger's knee shoved painfully into his back, Brockie's father tried to reason with the intruder. His efforts were to no avail. The situation was panicked and confusing and there was no room for getting thoughts out in a coherent manner.

Always a take-charge personality, Brockie's mother attempted to get control of the rapidly deteriorating situation. From her slumped position on the rigid floor, Brockie's mother instructed her son to get her purse from the bedroom. In the same instant, Brockie's father told the boy to get his money clip from the bedroom as well.

Scrambling to his feet and dashing toward the bedroom, Brockie looked behind the kitchen island and saw the black-clad stranger on top of his father. The stranger's right knee was jammed into his father's back. The stranger's left foot was planted flat on the floor, allowing him to control the amount of back-breaking pressure he was forcing into the father's spine. Brockie also noticed the position of the intruder's firearm. It was aimed at the back of his father's head. Brockie had to act quickly.

After running into the bedroom and grabbing his father's bulging money clip, Brockie removed all of the cash from his mother's wallet. Then, acting with what can only be described as incredible courage and poise, Brockie ran back into the great room, rounded the kitchen island, and turned to face the stranger who had pounced on his father's back like a cougar.

With great trepidation, Brockie inched toward the intruder. The motorcycle helmet made it impossible for the petrified boy to get a clear view of the intruder's face. As Brockie approached, the stranger maintained his aggressive posture on the father's back. When Brockie was a couple of feet away from his father and the intruder, he tossed the wad of bills onto the floor. The large pile of crisp cash slid toward his father's face.

The intruder immediately scooped up the money and stuffed it in his pocket. Then, as Brockie retreated into the living room and hid behind the coffee table, the intruder reiterated his demands for jewelry.

Hearing the intruder's words, Brockie's mother struggled up from her position on the floor. Getting both herself and her unborn child into a standing position was an ordeal, but once she was on her feet,

Brockie's mother made her way to her purse and carried it to the intruder. Brockie watched as the intruder snatched the Louis Vuitton purse from his mother's hands and ordered her to lie on the floor beside the kitchen island.

From his position behind the coffee table, Brockie could only see a portion of what was happening. At some point, the situation's malignancy began to overwhelm the boy. The horrifying phantasmagoria Brockie was witnessing inside his once-safe home began to short circuit his senses. Later, Brockie would have trouble piecing together all the details of his fragmented memories for detectives.

What Brockie remembered is this: After snatching the purse and ordering his mother to lie on the floor, the intruder rose to his feet. Brockie heard both of his parents begging the intruder not to harm their children.

Brockie's parents were told to move down the hallway toward the bedroom at the front of the house. Within moments, Brockie could hear footsteps moving toward the bedroom.

Once the intruder had herded the parents out of the great room, down the hallway, and into their master bedroom, Brockie could only hear bits and pieces of what was happening.

There was slamming, banging, and thrashing coming from the bedroom, but Brockie couldn't make out exactly what was occurring. As the heavy slamming reached a violent crescendo, Brockie could hear the intruder's muffled voice exclaiming the words "Fuck, fuck, fuck!" from beneath his motorcycle helmet.

There was more thrashing and more movement in the bedroom, then an eerie stillness. The stillness was absolute. Before Brockie could flinch, he heard his mother let loose a piercing, panic-stricken scream from the master bedroom. It was clear that something awful was happening. Moving swiftly, Brockie scampered from his location near the coffee table into a more secure position behind the far end of the living-room sofa.

Brockie got low to the floor. As he crouched behind the sofa, Brockie heard a single, heavy, and deliberate set of footsteps thundering through the house.

Brockie stayed perfectly still. His eyes were riveted in the direction of the hallway.

Soon enough, Brockie saw the helmeted stranger come into view. Brockie could see that the man in black was was rubbing the fingers and thumb of his gloved right hand together. The intruder's march across the great room seemed to take forever, but eventually, Brockie saw the man standing at the threshold that led to the home's back deck. This was the same door the stranger had burst through just minutes earlier, changing Brockie's world forever.

Not missing a beat, the stranger moved through the door. From his vantage point behind the sofa, Brockie watched as the stranger walked onto the oceanfront deck and dissolved into the darkness.

The interior of the house was deathly still.

Once Brockie was sure that the intruder was gone, he sprang to his feet and raced toward his parents' bedroom. As he moved through his once-placid home, Brockie noticed the intruder's black handgun on the floor of the hallway just outside his parents' room.

What Brockie saw next was almost incomprehensible to his nine-year-old mind.

Moving from the hallway into his parents' brightly lit bedroom, Brockie saw both of his parents crumpled on the floor. Neither parent was moving. Both parents were lying in large pools of bright-red blood. The pool of blood surrounding his mother—who was now topless—was at least five feet in diameter. Brockie moved close to his mother, knelt down, and began shaking her. He wanted her to wake up.

His mother didn't wake. His mother didn't move.

Brockie looked at his father. For a moment, Brockie thought he heard his father making some low, guttural noises. However, when Brockie inched closer to his father—who was still clad in the comfortable cargo shorts and t-shirt he'd worn throughout the evening—Brockie could tell that his father was dead. There was simply too much blood and too much stillness for there to be any other explanation. The pained, contorted, glassy-eyed expression on his father's unmoving face was unmistakable, even to a nine-year-old boy who had no previous experience with violent homicide.

Brockie knew his parents were gone. With nothing left to do for them, his thoughts shifted to his sister Isabella. She'd been asleep in her bedroom when the intruder barged into the house, but once Brockie's parents had been marched out of the great room, several minutes had passed when Brockie couldn't see what was occurring.

Was his sister okay? Was she alive?

Pulling together every iota of his strength, Brockie made his way out of the master bedroom and down the short hallway to his sister's bedroom door. The blond-haired little boy had no idea what he'd find on the other side.

The door swung open in front of Brockie and light from the hallway poured into Isabella's room. Only two years older than her brother, Isabella was incredibly close with Brockie. As light drenched Isabella's bedroom, Brockie had no way of knowing if he'd find his sister in the same condition as his parents.

Fortunately, Isabella was safe and sound in her bed.

Brockie dashed to Isabella's side, shook her awake, and began explaining what had happened to their parents. Such news would be difficult for an adult to process when fully lucid, but for an eleven-year-old girl who had just been roused from a deep sleep, Brockie's story was almost impossible for Isabella to comprehend.

Isabella encouraged Brockie to climb into bed with her. She tried to comfort her brother, but he was inconsolable. As she came fully awake, Isabella recognized her brother's legitimate agitation and started to become alarmed herself. At Brockie's urging, Isabella climbed out of bed and made her way toward their parents' bedroom.

Upon seeing the carnage together, the children's terror reached a new zenith. Trembling, terrified, and not sure what was happening, Isabella grabbed Brockie's hand and pulled him into their parents' bathroom. They immediately locked the door and stood on the cold tile floor, shaking in the blackness of the night.

Isabella knew they needed a plan, but she had no idea what to do. As she tried to think, the eerie silence of the night was replaced by a new and unmistakable noise: footsteps, heavy and deliberate, moving through the house.

Fearing for their lives, the children took refuge in the one place that offered a semblance of protection: the shower. In a desperate attempt to shield themselves from harm, Brockie and Isabella stepped into the shower, pulled the frosted-glass door closed behind them, and got as low to the floor as they possibly could.

The children heard the powerful, thudding footsteps move up the hallway and into their parents' bedroom. With their breath held tight in their lungs, Brockie and Isabella heard the footsteps moving toward the master bathroom.

The children sat frozen in fear.

From their semi-concealed location in the shower, Isabella and Brockie could hear footsteps pounding around in their parents' bedroom. It was clear from the stomping that a single individual was moving around the bedroom in an erratic manner.

After several minutes, the pounding footsteps stopped moving. Then the footsteps changed direction and started to grow softer. Eventually, the house was quiet again.

Isabella and Brockie clung to each other in the frosty night air.

Realizing that they needed to summon help, the children decided to leave the bathroom. Brockie inched the shower door open and stepped onto the cold tile floor. Isabella followed him.

Brockie put his hand on the locked bathroom door and started to press down on the handle. The house was quiet, but the children had no way of knowing whether the intruder was waiting silently on the other side of the door. If their strong, responsible, loving parents had stood no chance against the intruder, what chance would they possibly have?

Displaying tremendous courage, Brockie depressed the door handle and eased the bathroom door open. He peered out from behind the door and looked down the main hallway toward the oceanfront deck. No one was there. However, Brockie did notice one important detail: the black handgun that had been on the hallway floor just minutes earlier was gone.

Brockie and Isabella moved into their parents' bedroom and locked the door to the hallway. While Isabella checked the closets to make sure no one was hiding inside them, Brockie walked through the pool of blood surrounding his mother's body and climbed across the bed. His goal was to access the cordless phone that had been knocked to the floor in the corner of the room. Brockie could see that the phone lay just beyond the reach of his father's cold, dead, outstretched hand. As Brockie climbed across his parents' thick, billowy comforter, his tiny feet left little scarlet blood prints on the comforter's pure-white fabric.

Once Brockie had the cordless phone in hand, he tried to turn it on. It wouldn't work. He tried pushing the phone's power button again. It still wouldn't work. By that point, Isabella had looked through the closets and determined that no one was hiding inside them. Nevertheless, both she and Brockie remained terrified that the intruder would kick down the bedroom door at any moment and massacre both of them, just as he'd done to their parents. With this thought racing through their minds, the children made the best decision they possibly could have under the circumstances: they elected to flee the house.

Brockie climbed off the bed. In his attempt to avoid

the large puddle of blood on the floor, Brockie was forced to step over his mother's lifeless body. He and Isabella then reentered the bathroom and locked the door behind them. From there, they moved to the toilet, which was beneath a window to the outside. Brockie was still clutching the cordless phone.

The children climbed atop the toilet tank and slid the window open. Within seconds, they'd both climbed through the window and dropped the short distance to the pavement outside. As soon as their feet hit the ground, Brockie and Isabella Husted set off running into the night.

CHAPTER 2

Faria Beach Colony, which stretches along the coast for approximately two-tenths of a mile, is bisected by the narrow blacktop of Faria Road. Though much of the community is oceanfront, roughly forty percent of the Colony's properties are situated on the north side of Faria Road, away from the beach. In May 2009, one of the houses on the north side of Faria Road was occupied by a young man named Orion Womack. After shimmying through the bathroom window and fleeing the abattoir of their parents' home, Brockie and Isabella Husted made a beeline for Womack's light-blue, two-story residence.

It was almost a quarter of 11 p.m. when Orion Womack heard the frenzied pounding on his front door. Such a sound would be unsettling in any neighborhood late at night, but in a serene community like Faria Beach Colony—where a stray dog is a newsworthy event—the pounding was particularly worrisome.

Upon opening his door, Womack found the Husted children shivering and terrified on his doorstep. The children tried to explain what had happened, but it was all too much to communicate in a coherent manner. From what Womack could gather, the upshot was that Brockie and Isabella's parents had been badly injured in their home. Womack saw that Brockie was holding a cordless phone. He took it from the boy's hand and attempted to call 911. When Womack pressed the power button, however, he found that the receiver was dead. Undeterred, Womack brought the children into his home and used his own telephone to summon help.

Faria lies in an unincorporated section of Ventura County, just south of the Santa Barbara County line. As a result, the Ventura County Sheriff's Department has law-enforcement jurisdiction over the area. Womack's 911 call was received by the Ventura County Sheriff's Department at exactly 10:44 p.m.

Upon receiving Womack's call, the 911 operator immediately dispatched units to the scene.

In the meantime, Womack wasn't going to stand idly by if he could help neighbors who were in trouble. Through their tears and consternation, Brockie and Isabella told Womack that their parents were dead. Nevertheless, Womack wasn't absolutely sure if this was the case. In the event that his neighbors were still alive, Womack wanted to do whatever he could to help them. Consequently, Womack made a courageous decision to go next door and render whatever assistance he could.

Leaving Isabella on the phone with the 911 operator, Womack grabbed a hammer, locked the Husted children inside his house, and headed next door. Womack made his way across the empty blacktop of Faria Road and down the left side of the Husted home. As he approached the side door (which the Husteds referred to as their front door because of the home's position against the beach), he could see lights on in the great room. When Womack pressed the doorbell, he was greeted with a ghastly stillness from inside the house. After waiting a few beats and detecting no movement from inside the home, Womack decided to try the knob. It turned easily.

Entering the brightly lit residence, Womack made his way into the great room. To his left, a large family portrait hung on the wall. The picture showed the four members of the Husted family sitting together and smiling under a flawless azure sky. A placid beachscape filled the background behind them.

Although the lights were on and the television was playing, something about the home just didn't feel right. For one thing, the eerie stillness of the house seemed menacingly out of the ordinary. For another, the door to the back deck stood wide open.

Making his way down the hall, Womack noticed that the lights were on in Isabella's bedroom. Then Womack's eyes fixed on a dreadful sight: the contents of a brown Louis Vuitton purse were spilled helter skelter across the hallway floor.

Womack lifted his eyes from the purse. They landed on the closed door at the end of the hallway. This was the door to the master bedroom. Gripping his hammer, Womack moved down the hallway toward the master bedroom door. When he reached the door, Womack extended his arm, grabbed the door handle, and pushed down. It was locked.

At that moment, a jolt of fear surged through Womack. The unsettling stillness of the house, the dead phone, the open back door, and the spilled purse were troubling enough, but the locked bedroom door signaled a new level of danger. Womack decided to return to his home and await the arrival of law enforcement.

Years later, the events of that night would still haunt Orion Womack. Speaking of the incident during a brief phone conversation in March 2015, Womack was clear about the lasting impact of that night.

"It was a really bad experience," Womack said in a soft, serious voice. "I've had a lot of trouble dealing with it."

Within minutes of Womack's 911 call, as deputies made their way toward Faria, a California Highway Patrol unit was already surveilling the 101 Freeway. Because Brockie had seen his parents' assailant wearing a motorcycle helmet, the Highway Patrol unit was on the lookout for bikers matching the suspect's description, as well as any other suspicious vehicles.

By 10:54 p.m., Ventura County deputies had arrived on scene at the Colony. Knowing that one or more residents might be seriously injured at 4250 Faria Road, the deputies quickly made entry into the Husted home. Within a few feet of the front door, it became obvious to the deputies that something awful had taken place inside the residence. In addition to the deathly stillness that permeated every corner of the house, the deputies saw signs of a struggle everywhere they looked. There was blood on the kitchen floor, a woman's purple shirt had been tossed on top of the kitchen island, the contents of a purse were spilled all over the hallway, and a woman's black tank top had been thrown on the hallway floor near the purse. To the deputies who were first on scene, the entire house seemed like a gaping wound.

Charging down the hallway, the deputies found the door to the master bedroom locked from the inside, just as Orion Womack had minutes earlier. However, no door was going to stand in the way of citizens in need. After rearing back, cocking his leg, and letting an enormous, highly polished boot fly, one of the deputies buried his heel in the door and sent the wooden barrier torquing back on its hinges.

Even for veteran law-enforcement officers, the brutal scene that greeted them on the other side of the door was shocking. It was obvious that detectives needed to be summoned immediately.

Homicide investigation procedures are firmly established within the law-enforcement community. After arriving at the scene of a homicide, detectives should start at the outside periphery of the crime scene and work their way toward the location of the bodies. Along the way, detectives must keep meticulous notes about everything they're observing. These notes should begin with the detectives' time of arrival, the precise location of the crime scene, and the existing weather and lighting conditions. Once these pieces of information have been recorded, detectives should make a point of talking with the first responders on scene. In turn, the first responders can tell detectives when they arrived at the location, whom they spoken with at the location, what actions they've taken at the location (such as kicking down a locked bedroom door), and any evidence they've observed at the location.

After detectives have received and recorded all of their preliminary information, they should begin making their way toward the victims. In making their approach, whenever possible, detectives should try to

victim had gone for the phone in a desperate attempt to call for help. When this happened, the offender— who had grabbed the biggest butcher knife he could find from the cutlery block in the kitchen—had begun stabbing the male victim ferociously. After that, the knife hadn't stopped ripping, tearing, and plunging until both victims were dead.

In addition to the bloody butcher knife and the severed phone cord, detectives also made another important discovery in the bedroom. Draped across the female victim's right shoulder was a mint-green cotton hand towel. This towel matched a set of mint-green towels that hung on racks in the master bathroom. From what detectives could see during their initial evaluation of the crime scene, the hand towel on the female victim's right shoulder was stained with blood. Coupled with the droplets of blood that led out of the bedroom and into the bathroom, detectives began to theorize that the offender had somehow wounded himself during the course of the attack. As a result, detectives speculated that the offender's blood might be found on the towel. This belief was reinforced when detectives found blood droplets around the bathroom sink. These blood droplets were well beyond the range where the victims' blood could've spewed.

The most intriguing piece of evidence found in the bedroom was almost invisible to the casual observer. As detectives leaned over the male victim—being careful not to damage, contaminate, or destroy potential evidence—one of them noticed something strange under his head. Moving closer, the detectives could see that some sort of plastic object was lodged beneath the male victim's skull. One detective mentioned that the object beneath the male victim's head might be the visor off a motorcycle helmet. When the scene was finally processed and the object was examined at the county crime lab, this theory turned out to be right on the money; the piece of curved plastic resting inconspicuously behind the male victim's head was indeed the visor off a motorcycle helmet.

Once detectives had made their preliminary assessment of the crime scene, another critical step of the investigation commenced: an exhaustive canvass of the neighborhood. As detectives fanned out across Faria Beach Colony to talk to neighborhood residents and potential witnesses, they unearthed a couple of important bits of information. For instance, one neighbor who lived on the north side of Faria Road remembered hearing a motorcycle roar to life around the time of the murders. The neighbor said it sounded like the motorcycle was parked on Pacific Coast Highway. Only a short wall separates PCH from the exclusive, gated confines of the Colony. Although she never saw the motorcycle or any suspicious persons in the neighborhood, the resident was quite confident that she'd heard the motorcycle starting sometime around 10:30 p.m.

While the neighborhood canvass was under way, detectives and crime-scene personnel continued to scour the Husted property and the surrounding area for clues. In the course of their search, a bloody $20 bill was found in the weeds along Pacific Coast Highway. The bill was immediately bagged as evidence. Back at the house, detectives were examining the whirlpool on the Husteds' back deck. As they examined the top of the whirlpool, detectives noticed a brownish-red blood smear on its cover. Detectives surmised that, in his haste to flee the property, the Husteds' assailant had run out of the house, tripped over an object on the darkened deck, and stumbled into the whirlpool where blood from his hand left a mark on the cover. The whirlpool was immediately tagged for processing by the crime-scene unit.

After being questioned by detectives, Brockie and Isabella Husted were taken to the Sheriff's Department headquarters and their relatives were contacted. Detectives also obtained a detailed statement from Orion Womack. He had been the first adult on scene at the Husted home and detectives knew that his information would be essential in piecing the case together.

Atrocities like the Husted homicide don't happen every day, particularly in affluent, low-crime communities like Faria. Between 1998 and 2008, the Ventura County Sheriff's Department investigated an average of 4.4 murders per year. [2] Despite their relative inexperience investigating complex homicides, Ventura County detectives knew how to size up an evidence-rich crime scene when they saw one. Not only did the detectives have the probable murder weapon, possible blood evidence from the offender, and the visor off the offender's motorcycle helmet, they also had a living witness to the Faria crimes. With all of this evidence in mind, it was possible for detectives to begin drawing reasonable inferences about the type of offender who was responsible for the Faria murders.

Based on his use of brute force and carelessness with potentially inculpatory evidence, it was clear that the Faria slayer wasn't a highly sophisticated offender. The individual who had murdered the Husteds wasn't the least bit savvy about evidence, indicating a probable lack of serious involvement with with the judicial system in the past. In addition, it was clear that the offender was physically strong, highly impulsive, and opportunistic. Because there were no signs of forced entry, it was obvious that the offender had stumbled across a soft target, entered through the home's unlocked backdoor, and waylaid victims of opportunity in a hastily planned attack. In his wake, the offender had left a frenzied, chaotic mess. Clearly, the Faria murders were not the work of a mature, methodical, organized offender with an eminently refined modus operandi. In fact, the preliminary evidence at the crime scene indicated that, in all likelihood, the Faria offender was quite young and quite inexperienced with this type of offense. The Faria murderer didn't have the patience or finesse of a good stealth burglar. Instead, the behavioral indicators at the crime scene suggested that the Faria murderer was a strong-armed robber type—a bully, a brawler. Yet, despite the fact that certain educated guessed could be made about the type of young, violent, impulsive suspect they were seeking, detectives were no closer to establishing the offender's identity.

Detectives worked doggedly through the night. As the sun began to rise above the craggy green peaks of the Santa Ynez Mountains, the Pacific became a shimmering glow of gold-flecked brilliance. Light danced atop the early morning waves, and through the misty sea spray on the shore, little rainbows arced above the beach.

The tranquil beauty of the early morning coastline stood as a stark counterpoint to the intense investigation taking place at 4250 Faria Road. As the morning wore on, detectives continued to pour over the crime scene. Though they had plenty of physical evidence, the detectives had no leads on specific suspects. From what detectives could tell, the murders seemed to have occurred in the course of a home-invasion robbery. However, certain aspects of the crime scene were incongruous with the robbery scenario. For example, if the motive of the crime had simply been robbery, there would've been no need for the offender to remove the female victim's shirts, much less escalate the crime to a brutal, blood-soaked double murder. Detectives knew that these signature elements of the crime, which fulfilled a deep-seated psychological need for the offender, would be critical to understanding the murders in context.

Although detectives didn't know the suspect's identity, one thing was absolutely certain: The individual responsible for the Faria murders was extremely dangerous and needed to be taken off the streets immediately. Until the suspect was in custody, detectives knew that the community would not be safe.

Since detectives had no suspects and no leads in the case, they would have to look elsewhere for clues. As the darkness of night gave way to the bright light of morning, detectives decided to take the next logical step: finding out as much as they could about the Faria victims.

CHAPTER 3

According to archeologists, Chumash Indians have inhabited California's Central Coast since at least 2000 BCE. However, it wasn't until the mid-sixteenth century that Europeans laid eyes on the region's coastal mountain ranges, wind-swept beaches, and prime agricultural land.

The first European to explore the area now known as Ventura County was Portuguese conquistador Juan Rodriguez Cabrillo. A highly decorated navigator, Cabrillo spent much of his adult life mapping California's coastline for the Spanish crown. After Cabrillo's ship laid anchor off present-day Ventura in 1542, an exploratory party rowed ashore in a small wooden raft. Stepping off the raft and walking onto the wide, sandy beach, Cabrillo discovered a warm, verdant, palm-studded paradise that rivaled the most alluring ports in his native Mediterranean homeland. Cabrillo dubbed the area around modern-day Ventura *La Tierra del Eterno Verano*—The Land of Eternal Summer.

Over the next two centuries, Europeans continued

to explore, settle, and transform the coastal areas of modern-day California. On March 31, 1782, Father Junipero Serra founded Mission San Buenaventura. Father Serra's mission, which was the last of his nine settlements, would eventually grow into a thriving center of seaside commerce and industry.

One of the watershed moments in Central Coast history occurred on March 22, 1872, when Ventura County split from neighboring Santa Barbara County. The city of San Buenaventura, which was already being referred to by the informal monicker Ventura, was declared the seat of the newly formed county. Around the same time, the last boards were nailed into place on the Ventura Pier. Stretching 1,958 feet into the Pacific, the Pier was an icon of nineteenth-century life on the Central Coast. At the time, Ventura ranked as the second-busiest port on the West Coast after San Francisco. The Pier symbolized the burgeoning city of Ventura's prosperity, vitality, and significance as a maritime powerhouse.

During the twentieth century, the population of Ventura County exploded. When President James A. Garfield was assassinated on September 19, 1881, the population of Ventura County stood at just over 5,000 residents. By the time of President John F. Kennedy's assassination on November 22, 1963, more than 200,000 people lived in Ventura County. Much of the area's population growth was due to the discovery of oil in 1914. The county's largest oil-extraction facility was the Ventura Avenue Oil Field. Positioned just north of the Ventura city limits, the Ventura Avenue Oil Field pumped out almost 3 million barrels of crude a month during its heyday. The oil brought large sums of money to the county, the money brought jobs, and the jobs brought people. This cycle—money, jobs, people, money, jobs, people—continued to repeat itself over the coming century.

By the spring of 2009, the population of Ventura County had swelled to more than 840,000 residents. The majority of those residents lived in the county's four largest cities: Oxnard, Thousand Oaks, Simi Valley, and Ventura respectively.

By mid-morning on May 20, 2009, Ventura County detectives were wrapping up their preliminary work at 4250 Faria Road. As soon as their work was complete, the detectives wheeled out of Faria Beach Colony, jumped on the 101 South, and made their way back to Sheriff's Department headquarters. Located next door to the county's Hall of Justice on Victoria Avenue, the Sheriff's headquarters is a modern facility situated just east of downtown Ventura.

As detectives made their way back to headquarters, they passed through downtown Ventura. An attractively manicured city of 108,000 residents, Ventura is large enough to have every amenity one could want, while still retaining the intimate, cohesive character of a small town. The streets of Ventura are clean and well-kept, and although the downtown storefronts are replete with upscale restaurants, boutiques, and bookstores, the city has a relaxed, down-to-earth vibe. There's not a hint of ostentation in Ventura's sea-clean air, but neither is there a hint of decay. Despite Ventura's undeniably upscale sensibility, there's nothing stuffy or pretentious about the city. Walking through the downtown area at midday, one will encounter senior citizens relaxing on park benches, businesspeople in smartly tailored suits, punk rockers with Day-Glo pink mohawks, grizzled hitchhikers sleeping beneath gleaming mosaic wall art, and girls on longboards being dragged along smoothly paved sidewalks by smiling, tongue-wagging dogs on leashes. To the outside observer, Ventura seems to strike an effective balance between live-and-let-live acceptance and decorous propriety.

After making their way through downtown Ventura and arriving back at Sheriff's Department headquarters, detectives started digging into the backgrounds of the Faria murder victims. By that point in the morning, the victims had been positively identified as Brock Edward Husted and Davina DeBoni Husted. They were both forty-two years old. The Faria homicide had also claimed the life of the Husteds' unborn son, whom they were planning to name Grant. Grant's death meant that, per the state Penal Code, the detectives were now investigating a triple murder.

Brock Edward Husted was born in the ultra-affluent community of Hidden Hills, California, on July 15, 1966. In March 2009, *Bloomberg Business* listed Hidden Hills as one of the wealthiest towns in the United States, with residents earning an average household income of almost $320,000. It was against this backdrop of money and privilege that Brock Husted (who was nicknamed Gus) came of age.

The youngest of seven brothers and sisters, Brock Husted enjoyed a close, loving relationship with his family. For grade school, Brock Husted attended a private academy called Saint Mels Catholic School in Woodland Hills. While Brock was still in grade school, his family left Hidden Hills and moved to Moorpark, an upscale suburb in southeastern Ventura County.

After attending Saint Paschal Babylon School in Thousand Oaks for junior high, Brock Husted matriculated into Ojai's exclusive Villanova Preparatory School for high school. Founded in 1924 and set against a spectacular backdrop of green mountains and chaparral thickets, Villanova Prep is known for balancing rigorous academics with a healthy respect for the Catholic faith. As the school's mission statement indicates, Villanova Prep students are conditioned to "...think, judge, and act in ways that are sound and in keeping with the teachings of Jesus Christ."

Villanova Prep has a strong track record of placing its graduates at prestigious colleges and universities, including Cornell, Notre Dame, Stanford, and the University of Chicago. However, after graduating from Villanova Prep in 1984, there's no indication that Brock Husted ever attended college. (Brock's brother, John Husted, did not return phone calls and e-mails seeking clarification for this book.)

While it appears that Brock Husted might have eschewed a formal education after graduating from high school, there's no doubt that he continued learning, cultivating his professional skills, and growing as a person. After leaving Villanova Prep, Brock Husted began refining his skills as a metal worker. Through this work, he found his calling in life. Eventually, Brock Husted became an artist and master craftsman, whose highly prized wrought-iron work was featured in magazines. [3]

During the late 1980s and early '90s, Brock Husted

worked diligently to perfect his professional skills. Around the same time, his older brother Scott went to work at a Ventura County bank. One of Scott Husted's co-workers at the bank was a stunning, statuesque blond named Davina DeBoni. Sensing that the dazzling Davina might appreciate his enterprising younger brother, Scott played matchmaker and introduced the two in 1990. By 1993, Brock Husted and Davina DeBoni were engaged to be married.

———————

Davina Marie DeBoni was born in Ventura County on July 31, 1966, just two weeks and two days after her future husband Brock. The daughter of David John and Allane DeBoni, Davina's roots ran deep in Ventura County.

After Davina DeBoni's great-grandparents immigrated to the United States from Italy, her paternal grandfather, Tranquillo "Tad" DeBoni, was born in Oxnard in 1912. By 1931, Tad DeBoni had started his career as a lima bean farmer in the small agricultural town of Somis. Blessed with miles of thick, loamy, nutrient-rich soil, the land around Somis is some of the richest on the North American continent. Today, a drive through the back roads around Somis leads one through a maze of fecund farmland and citrus orchards, where mounds of bright yellow lemons collect in towering piles under fruit-laden trees and freshly watered crops glisten for miles in the fields. It was within this pastoral environment that Davina's grandfather cultivated his expertise as a farmer.

As he explained to the *Los Angeles Times* in 2003, Tad DeBoni was a tried-and-true lima bean man. At one time, lima beans were the most abundant crop in Ventura County, and the Oxnard Plain was the number one lima bean producer on the planet. [4] However, starting in the 1950s, Ventura County farmers shifted away from lima bean production when the prices of other commodities spiked. Nevertheless, Tad DeBoni stayed the course with his beloved lima beans. By the time he finished building his family's spacious, scenic home in 1961, Tad DeBoni was regarded as one of the foremost lima bean farmers in the region.

Constructed above the sun-kissed fields of Somis, Tad DeBoni's home offered sweeping views of the avocado and citrus orchards in the valley below. It was within this bucolic milieu that Davina DeBoni, who was often called Vina, spent her childhood years.

Davina DeBoni's parents married in 1963, and the life they made for their children appears to have been a Middle-American masterpiece. In addition to working on the family farm, Davina's father was also employed by the Berylwood Mutual Water Company. As a popular member of the community, David DeBoni was elected Exalted Ruler of the Oxnard Elk's Club in 1973 when Davina was in grade school at Mesa Union Elementary.

Childhood friends remember Davina as a happy, loving child who adored her older brother Vincent and tried to adopt every stray dog and cat she could find. Davina's innate concern for the well-being of others was a theme that would repeat itself throughout her life.

After graduating from Oxnard's Rio Mesa High School in 1984, Davina attended Moorpark College. Later, she transferred to California State University-Northridge. Eventually, with her sights fixed firmly on a career in business, Davina finished her education at the Sawyer School of Business. Around the same time, she earned both a real-estate license and a brokerage license.

While Davina DeBoni showed a strong aptitude for business, her interests extended well beyond escrow disbursements, principal balances, and revolving debt. To wit, Davina DeBoni was a ravishing knockout who had an interest in beauty pageants. When Davina competed in the Miss Oxnard pageant in 1987, she won handily. This victory paved the way for Davina's participation in the Miss California pageant of 1987.

The Miss California pageant is the final contest before the Miss America pageant, one of the most prestigious beauty competitions in the world. On February 12, 1987, Davina was in Orange County for that year's Miss California pageant. Despite a strong performance, Davina lost to Lori Dickerson of Lodi, who ended up losing to Miss Tennessee in the national competition.

With the Miss California pageant behind her, Davina began modeling and appearing in commercials. The poise and confidence she learned from these jobs proved valuable in her later endeavors. After Davina's passing, her friends and acquaintances continued to comment on her polished speaking abilities and sterling personal presentation. There's little doubt that Brock Husted noticed and admired these same qualities when he was introduced to Davina in 1990.

From all indications, Brock Husted and Davina DeBoni hit it off right from the start. He was an ambitious, up-and-coming craftsman from a wealthy family and she was a stunning beauty with powerful people skills. Friends described the couple as "dynamic."

Brock and Davina Husted tied the knot on September 9, 1995. Soon thereafter, the couple moved into a spacious luxury home in the upmarket neighborhood of Ventura Keys. Located within the city limits of Ventura, the Keys is a unique residential community. In addition to its beachfront location, most of the homes in Ventura Keys come with their own boat docks and mooring areas. With an average lot size of 4,500 square feet, most properties in the Keys sell for multiple millions of dollars. When Brock and Davina Husted purchased their home at 2917 Seaview Avenue, there's little doubt that they recognized the property's investment potential.

Two years later, in 1997, Isabella was born. It was clear to everyone that the birth of his first child changed Brock's life. In interviews given after his murder, friends indicated that Brock became much more serious about work and business when Isabella was born. [5] After Brockie was born in 1999, Brock Husted started his own metal-fabricating business. It was called Couture Concepts.

Headquartered on an industrial stretch of Garden Street in Santa Barbara, Couture Concepts provided unique metal designs to high-end clientele. These metal designs included gates, window frames, and railings. In the early years of the business, Davina kept Couture's books while Brock focused on the design and fabrication end of the business. Because of the exceptional quality of Brock's work, his reputation as a master metal craftsman spread quickly. Within a few years of its founding, Couture Concepts was handling major metal projects for celebrities like Suzanne Somers, Mel Gibson, and Oprah Winfrey.

Both the personal and financial fortunes of the Husteds were surging upward by the mid-aughts. However, the family did have one problem: They'd outgrown their home in Ventura Keys. As a result, in 2005, Brock and Davina Husted purchased their beachfront home at 4250 Faria Road. The Keys property was retained as a rental unit.

Brock worked long and hard to make Couture Concepts a success. At the same time, Davina was establishing herself as a major player in the local charity world.

In the years after her marriage to Brock, Davina took a job as an administrative assistant at a charitable organization called Good Sam. Eventually, through her hard work and dedication, Davina parlayed her work at Good Sam into a position with the National Charity Junior League of Ventura, where she was eventually elected president. As the local charity's leader, Davina spearheaded a number of high-profile and extremely lucrative charity initiatives. While Davina worked doggedly to raise money for a wide variety of charitable causes, her favorite charity was the Children's Cancer and Blood Disease Program. Using her keen intelligence and magnetic personality, Davina was able to raise more than $300,000 for this organization. However, Davina's commitment to healthcare fundraising didn't stop there. Just a week before her murder, Davina presented a check for $82,500 to Ventura County Medical Center on behalf of the National Charity Junior League.

After her passing, friends and business associates remembered Davina as an extraordinarily accomplished woman with a deep concern for others. Perhaps the most extraordinary facet of Davina's personality was that—despite her beauty, brains, and personality—she never let her blessings go to her head.

As one acquaintance put it, "If you spoke to Davina (on the phone), you'd never know about her beauty or personal wealth."

While Brock and Davina Husted were both hard workers with steadfast commitments to their professional lives, they always made time for their children. The Husteds were regular parishioners at Our Lady of the Assumption in Ventura, and just before their murders, they had enrolled their children in Cotillion classes. In addition, Davina was actively involved as a volunteer at Pierpoint Elementary School, where Isabella and Brockie were enrolled as students. When Isabella and Brockie were out of school, their father spent time teaching them to surf, fish, dive, and boat. These were pastimes that Brock adored, and by all accounts, he loved nothing more than sharing them with his children.

When they weren't spending time at work or with their children, Brock and Davina Husted made time for themselves. Sometimes they'd brave the traffic into downtown Los Angeles to watch the Lakers play at Staples Center. On other occasions, they would take exotic vacations. Not long before they were murdered, the Husteds' travels took them to locations as disparate as Costa Rica and France. Regardless of where Brock and Davina Husted chose to spend their time, they always made an impression.

"When they walked into a room, everyone noticed," Monica White, a long-time friend of the Husteds, told the *Ventura County Star*. "They were our rock-star friends."

After carefully probing the personal histories of the Faria murder victims, Ventura County detectives were left with more questions than answers. From what detectives could tell, Brock and Davina Husted were solid citizens who worked hard, loved their children, had no enemies, and lived to make the world a better place. In short, the Husteds were extremely atypical homicide victims.

The preliminary inquiry into the Husteds' backgrounds offered few investigative avenues for detectives to pursue. The overwhelming majority of murders are predicated on conventional motives like anger, jealousy, and revenge. This ensures that, in most cases, there's a link between the offender and the victims that can be traced. While this link might not be obvious from the outset, detectives in most homicide cases have some means of connecting victim to killer, or vice versa. After examining the Husteds' backgrounds, however, detectives could find no connections to potential suspects. Nevertheless, Ventura County detectives were committed to identifying the person responsible for the Faria murders.

With the miasma of blood still thick in the air and their once-vibrant victims lying on cold steel slabs at the morgue, detectives knew they needed to work swiftly to establish the identity of the Husteds' murderer. Brock, Davina, and baby Grant had already lost their lives. Detectives shuddered when they thought about who could be next.

CHAPTER 4

Terror spread like a plague in the weeks after the Husted murders. Community members were shocked that the successful, attractive couple had been snuffed out so swiftly, so violently, and so ruthlessly in their own home. Many feared that the same fate could befall them. Like an early morning marine layer rolling in off the Pacific, dread began to blanket the genteel coastal communities of greater Ventura.

While local residents purchased burglar-alarm systems, installed deadbolts, and loaded their Mossbergs with double-aught buck, the county medical examiner was completing his autopsies on Brock and Davina Husted. The medical examiner concluded that Brock Husted had been stabbed and sliced at least twenty-five times with a butcher knife. Brock's injuries included multiple stab wounds to the upper chest and several deep slash wounds to the neck. As for Davina Husted, the medical examiner determined that she'd been stabbed no less than forty-one times. Her wounds included eight stab wounds to the neck, eleven stab wounds to the back, five stab wounds to the chest, and four stab wounds to the head. One of the head wounds had gone through Davina Husted's ear. Another had gone through her once-smooth cheek and opened a sickening gash inside her mouth. In addition, the medical examiner found thirteen defensive stab wounds on Davina Husted's arms and hands. These wounds indicated that Davina had fought valiantly to protect herself and her unborn son Grant. As prosecutors would later write in their Statement In Aggravation, "The word 'overkill' does not being to describe what (the offender) did, which was far more than necessary to accomplish the killings." [6]

In keeping with standard autopsy protocols, the medical examiner took swabs from the victims to determine whether a sexual assault had occurred. Sure enough, one of the swabs taken from Davina Husted's mouth revealed a quantity of semen. This discovery indicated that Davina Husted had been forced to perform oral sex on her murderer as Brock lay dying in the corner of the bedroom and their nine-year-old son hid behind the sofa in the living room.

Details of the Faria murders began to trickle out to the public. These details exacerbated the alarm that was already festering in the community. The daylight hours were fairly calm, but when the sun dropped behind the turquoise horizon, fear took hold of the community. Before the Faria murders, many Ventura residents were lackadaisical about locking their doors. After the murders, when the blackness of night spread across the land, Gold Coast residents began barricading themselves inside their luxury homes.

Although the public was unaware of it at the time, detectives had made no progress with their investigation of the Faria murders. The case was a top priority for the Ventura County Sheriff's Department, but as the days passed, detectives were unable to come up with any solid leads. Before long, theories about the Faria slayer's identity started swirling through the community.

Early in the investigation, it was theorized that the Husteds might have been murdered by a transient living along Pacific Coast Highway. Considering the unusual socioeconomic dichotomy that exists along the highway, this theory was more than plausible.

While the coastline of southwestern Ventura County is dotted with high-end residential communities like Faria Beach Colony, the area is also a well-known haven for full-time RVers, van-dwellers, drifters, and other individuals with no permanent roots in Ventura County. On any given night, the stretch of Pacific Coast Highway between Faria and La Conchita is lined with miles of RVs, vans, and other vehicles converted for nomadic living. By parking along empty stretches of PCH, nomadic vehicle-dwellers can enjoy the same mild weather and oceanfront views as residents living in million-dollar houses nearby. The shoulder of PCH offers a free and primitive home for anyone willing to live inside a vehicle. The practice is known as boondocking.

Not every vehicle-dweller who makes Faria his temporary home lives along the shoulder of Pacific Coast Highway. The highway is peppered with small RV lots that offer electrical hook-ups, bathrooms, and assigned parking spaces for a nominal nightly fee. One of these oceanfront RV lots is called Faria Beach Park.

Lying flush with the sand and offering parking for forty-two vehicles, Faria Beach Park abuts the western end of Faria Beach Colony. Only a chain-link fence separates the county-run RV lot from the neighborhood where the Husteds were murdered. Along the beach, there's no barrier preventing entry into the Colony. If one walks through Faria Beach Park and onto the sand, he will be standing about fifty yards west of the former Husted home. At night, with waves crashing against the shore and darkness shrouding the beach, it would be very easy for a black-clad prowler to enter the Colony from Faria Beach Park and mount an attack on the community's unsuspecting residents.

With all of this in mind, detectives scoured Faria Beach Park for clues or witnesses in the days after the Husted murders. The detectives were looking for anyone who'd seen a man in a jumpsuit, a motorcycle rider, or any other suspicious persons on the night of the homicide. Despite their best efforts, detectives came up empty-handed. None of the highly mobile denizens of Faria Beach Park had seen or heard anything out of the ordinary on the night of the murders.

Meanwhile, detectives were also probing deeply into the backgrounds of Brock and Davina Husted. The detectives were looking for any shady dealings, any outstanding debts, any connections to known criminals, or any other life circumstances that might shed some light on the baffling murders that had left two children orphans. After their parents were murdered, Brockie and Isabella Husted had gone to live with relatives. Detectives were committed to giving the Husted children justice for the loss of their parents and unborn baby brother.

Countless man-hours were spent pouring over every aspect of the Husteds' lives. The deeper detectives dug, however, the more convinced they became that the Husteds were not murdered over a personal vendetta.

Brock and Davina Husteds' personal and financial dealings were clean, they had no criminal records, and they didn't associate with unsavory individuals. In fact, based on all of the information detectives had gathered, it was clear that Brock and Davina Husted were solid citizens whose lives revolved around their children, their professional endeavors, their families, and their friends. All of this led to an unavoidable conclusion: the Husteds had been murdered by a stranger. The more this realization sank in for detectives, the more unsettled they became. Stranger murders are notoriously difficult to solve. For this reason, detectives quickly recognized that they faced an arduous, uphill battle in their attempt to identify the Faria murderer.

Despite the challenges involved with investigating the Faria murders, detectives worked hard to generate leads and restore calm in the community. Law enforcement was committed to achieving justice for the victims, their traumatized family members, and society. However, all of the detectives' efforts were of little comfort to community members. Citizens were on edge. They wanted answers about the Husted case. They wanted reassurances about their own safety. Sensing that public fear was reaching a boiling point, the Ventura County Sheriff's Department scheduled a community meeting for the evening of May 28, 2009. The meeting was held at Fire Station Number 25 in Rincon Beach, an oceanfront community located eight miles up the coast from Faria.

As citizens and media representatives crowded into the fire house on the night of the meeting, officials with the Ventura County Sheriff's Department attempted to assuage the community's mounting fears. Commander

Dennis Carpenter told the assembled crowd that, because a suspect had not been identified in the Husted case, few details could be released during the meeting. Sergeant Billy Hester, a major-crimes detective who was assigned to the Husted investigation, told residents that he and his team were sifting through evidence in an attempt to locate the Husteds' killer.

Such general statements provided little solace to the anxious, agitated crowd in the fire house.

One woman stood up and demanded to know why the Sheriff's Department had scheduled a community meeting if it couldn't release more information about the Faria case. Another woman rose to her feet and told the detectives that she no longer felt safe in her own home. These comments gave way to a torrent of statements by other frustrated community members who feared for their lives and longed for some peace of mind. One gentleman in the audience pointed out that, because the wealthy residents of Faria paid a disproportionate share of local taxes, members of his community should be able to expect greater responsiveness from law enforcement. The gentleman added that, on the night of the Husted murders, it had taken an inordinate amount of time for deputies to respond to Orion Womack's 911 call.

Sheriff's Captain Mike Aranda addressed this issue head on. Aranda pointed out that, on the night of the murders, deputies had been on scene in Faria within ten minutes of Womack's call. Aranda also pointed out that a California Highway Patrol unit was scanning the 101 for suspects within five minutes of Womack's call. [7]

Despite their technical accuracy, these statements did little to stem the rising tide of discontent among community members. Locals who attended the fire house meeting began clamoring for a Sheriff's Department substation to be built in Faria. In the meantime, Sergeant Hester cautioned residents to keep their doors locked, communicate with neighbors, and remain vigilant about their personal safety. With a brutal murderer still on the loose, both law enforcement and community members recognized that no one was safe.

———————

Sheriff's officials hoped that the May 28 meeting in Rincon would calm community fears. As it turned out, the meeting seemed to have its intended effect. Over the coming days, tensions in the community began to ease. Although Faria residents remained diligent about securing their homes and watching out for suspicious persons, the palpable sense of fear in the community seemed to subside. This allowed detectives to get on with the laborious task of identifying and eliminating suspects in the Faria murder case.

One week later, a bombshell dropped.

On June 3, 2009, Ventura County residents awoke to news that a sixty-one-year-old licensed therapist had been hacked to death in her Ventura Keys bedroom. The victim's name was Wendy Di Rodio. At the time of her murder, Di Rodio was sleeping in a first-floor bedroom at her parents' home. As the gull flies, the Di Rodio residence at 2833 Sailor Avenue is less than 100 yards from the Husteds' former home on Seaview Avenue.

News of another bedroom knife murder thrust the community back into a state of terror.

Unlike Faria, the Keys neighborhood lies within the city limits of Ventura. Therefore, the Ventura Police Department had jurisdiction over the Di Rodio case. From what Ventura detectives could tell, Di Rodio was asleep in her bed when she was accosted by a knife-wielding attacker. Di Rodio's body was found by her mother, Florence Di Rodio, around 3 p.m. the following day.

After conducting a careful analysis of the Di Rodio murder scene, Ventura detectives made some significant preliminary findings. For one thing, detectives found that there were no signs of forced entry into Di Rodio's bedroom. Furthermore, it appeared that Di Rodio had been attacked in bed, indicating that she might have known her murderer.

Like the Husteds, Wendy Di Rodio's victimology profile placed her in a very low-risk category for becoming a homicide victim. In addition to her therapy practice, Di Rodio was also a self-help author. Her 2005 book, entitled *The Magic of Animals: Living Happier & Healthier with Pets*, encouraged people to find joy through a love of animals. Friends described Di Rodio as a happy, outgoing woman who loved socializing and swing dancing in her free time. At the time of her murder, Di Rodio was temporarily living with her parents while she closed escrow on a home of her own.

Community turmoil reached a fever pitch after the announcement of Wendy Di Rodio's murder. Although local law enforcement denied a link between the Husted murders in Faria and Di Rodio's murder in Ventura Keys, the public continued to wonder if the two crimes were somehow connected. In both cases, affluent members of the community had been savaged in their own bedrooms by a violent, knife-wielding predator. Neither case had an apparent motive and neither case appeared to be anything more than purely random. Perhaps most disturbingly, no suspects had been named in either the Faria murders or the Di Rodio homicide.

Law enforcement could offer little solace to the community. As the spring of 2009 gave way to summer, Ventura County detectives had exhausted their paltry set of leads in the Husted case. Old-fashioned detective boot leather had produced zero results in the triple murder of May 20, 2009, and detectives were growing frustrated. They had no suspects, no leads, and no conclusive theories about the Faria crime. Although detectives doubted that the Husted murders were connected to the Di Rodio slaying, they had no way of proving this definitively.

The detectives' dilemma underscored one of the dirty little secrets about law enforcement: without a connection between victims and offenders, detectives are often unable to make meaningful progress with their investigations. The Husted and Di Rodio cases were not exceptions. Leads are the lifeblood of investigations, and with no way to generate leads, detectives are often rendered helpless.

Despite the herculean task they were facing and despite their dearth of leads, the investigative team assigned to the Husted case did have an ace up its sleeve. When the Husted home was processed after the murders, technicians had discovered significant forensic evidence that linked the Faria killer to his crime scene. This forensic evidence came from a variety of sources. For instance, when Brock Husted's autopsy was performed, his fingernails were scraped. These fingernail scrapings uncovered genetic material from an unknown individual. In time, this genetic material was amplified into a DNA profile of the Faria murderer.

From what detectives could gather, Brock Husted had attempted to fight back against his assailant on the night of the murders. When this occurred, Brock Husted ended up with the offender's DNA under his fingernails. Brock Husted's resistance also provided detectives with another crucial clue; it appeared that during his fleeting struggle, Brock Husted had dislodged the visor from his attacker's motorcycle helmet. When the visor was processed at the county crime lab, scientists found breath droplets on its inside surface. These breath droplets were used to develop a second DNA profile, which was eventually matched to the DNA recovered from the fingernail scrapings.

The fingernail scrapings and breath droplets weren't the only pieces of forensic evidence recovered from the Husted home. When detectives initially examined the crime scene on May 20, 2009, they noticed blood drops leading from the Husteds' bedroom to the bathroom sink. Based on the pattern of these blood drops, as well as the position of the butcher knife behind Davina Husted's back, detectives drew a penetrating conclusion: In the course of the stabbings, the Faria murderer's hand—slick with the blood of his victims—had slipped off the knife's handle. When this occurred, the offender had cut himself on the knife's long, serrated blade. Detectives theorized that, with his hand gashed open and dripping blood, the offender had darted into the bathroom to wash his wound. In the process, he'd left a blood trail along the floor and on the bathroom countertop. This theory also squared with one of Brockie Husted's memories about the night of the murders: the killer rubbed the fingers of his right hand together as he fled the scene.

One of the most critical pieces of evidence recovered from the Husted crime scene was a green, blood-stained towel that had been dropped on Davina Husted's back by the killer. This towel constituted a proverbial mother lode for detectives. Blood samples recovered from the green towel were matched to both Davina Husted and the unknown offender. In addition, the bottom edge of the towel contained traces of spermatozoa from the unknown offender. The spermatozoa indicated that the offender had used the towel to dry himself after committing his sexual assault against Davina Husted.

Detectives didn't know the name of the Husteds' slayer, but they had his DNA profile. The detectives knew that one solid lead was all they needed to identify a suspect, collect a sample of his DNA, compare it to the forensic evidence recovered from the Husteds' home, and solve the case. With all of this in mind, Ventura County detectives had no intention of allowing their forensic evidence to remain static. After the county crime lab completed its work on the Faria suspect's DNA profile, detectives sent the profile to the California Department of Justice Lab.

Located in the East Bay suburb of Richmond, the Department of Justice Lab is California's central processing center for genetic profiles. When DNA is recovered from a crime scene in any of California's fifty-eight counties, it is sent to Richmond and entered into the state's Combined DNA Index System, otherwise known as CODIS. Similarly, when DNA is collected from arrestees and convicts in California, it is sent to the Department of Justice Lab. After arriving in Richmond, all DNA samples are assigned numeric sequences that serve as unique genetic identifiers. Once these numeric sequences are entered into CODIS, the computerized database searches for matches between unknown-suspect DNA and known-offender DNA.

When the Faria murderer's DNA profile was sent to Richmond, Ventura County detectives hoped that it would trigger a "hit" in CODIS and give them the lead they so desperately needed. Unfortunately, the Faria murderer's DNA profile did not trigger a hit in CODIS and the Husted homicide investigation remained at a standstill.

In the meantime, residents of Ventura County remained fearful that the Faria killer would emerge from the darkness to claim more victims. After sunset, dead-bolted doors and motion-sensored lights provided little comfort to the people of Ventura.

Fear was in the air.

CHAPTER 5

As Ventura County detectives struggled to generate leads in the Faria investigation, detectives with the Ventura Police Department were laboring under their own burden of difficult cases. Not only were Ventura homicide detectives actively pursuing Wendy Di Rodio's murderer, the department's robbery unit was chasing an elusive serial bandit who was terrorizing small businesses throughout the city.

From what detectives could piece together, the robber's crimes started on September 3, 2009, when he ripped off a Shell gas station on Harbor Boulevard. According to the Shell station's clerk, a gunman dressed in black burst through the gas station's doors without warning and demanded money. The robber had brandished a black semiautomatic handgun. After forcing the Shell clerk to the floor and emptying the cash register, the gunman had fled the scene. Although the clerk was able to describe the robber as a white male dressed in black, the clerk was unable to glimpse the robber's getaway vehicle.

The following night, a robber matching the same

general description and utilizing the same M.O. struck an Arco gas station located at 2259 East Main Street in Ventura. The Arco station, which is situated across the street from Ventura High School, is only a mile north of the Shell station on Harbor Boulevard. In describing the stick-up to police, the Arco's on-duty clerk described the robber as a white male in his early to mid-twenties wearing dark clothing and carrying what appeared to be a black semiautomatic pistol.

A few days later, on September 10, 2009, a young, white, black-clad robber targeted the Dairy Queen at 7770 Telegraph Road in Ventura. According to Dairy Queen employees, the robber accosted a cashier around 8:20 p.m., flashed a black handgun that was tucked into the waistband of his jeans, and demanded cash. After cleaning out the till, stuffing his pockets with loot, and sprinting through the restaurant's doors, the robber disappeared into the night.

Four days later and four blocks west of the Dairy Queen, a robber matching the same description ripped off College Liquors on Telegraph Road. Waving a black handgun and barking commands, the robber ordered the liquor-store clerk to the floor. The robber then loaded his pockets with cash and ran from the store. According to the clerk, the robber was a white male in his twenties wearing dark-coloured clothing.

After College Liquors was robbed on September 14, 2009, the hold-ups came to an abrupt halt. Each of the robberies had occurred within the Ventura Police Department's jurisdiction, but detectives made little progress in identifying the perpetrator. All detectives knew for certain was that their young suspect dressed in black, carried a handgun, wore gloves, and pocketed easily accessible cash. Detectives also knew that such a brazen criminal was, by nature, quite dangerous.

Weeks passed. As the summer of 2009 gave way to fall, crime was booming across the United States. More than 408,000 robberies were committed in the U.S. in 2009, and because these robberies were often stranger-on-stranger crimes, the vast majority went unsolved. [8] One of these robberies was committed on the evening of September 23, 2009. The location was a Thrifty gas station on the outskirts of Santa Barbara.

Situated on an isolated stretch of roadway in an unincorporated area of Santa Barbara County, the Thrifty gas station at 4069 State Street made an excellent target for robbery. Few homes or businesses were located near the station. In addition, the gas station was positioned near the entrances to two freeways, ensuring an easy getaway for would-be bandits.

Just before 9:30 p.m. on September 23, 2009, the Thrifty's nighttime cashier, Azael Pinzon, was waiting for his shift to end. Before going home for the night, Pinzon was required to empty the trash, close up the Thrifty's small snack shop, and lock the fuel pumps in front of the business.

The weather was warm that evening, with a mild sea breeze causing the cypress trees along State Street to sway gently against the nightscape. An occasional car drove past the Thrifty, but for the most part, the street in front of the station was still and silent.

With no customers in the store and no vehicles at the fuel pumps, Pinzon began his end-of-shift duties.

Just before 9:40 p.m., Pinzon stepped outside the station to empty the trash. Upon exiting the snack shop, Pinzon noticed an SUV parked beside the station. Pinzon didn't recognize the vehicle, but as he made his way through the warm, pleasant evening, he didn't give the SUV much thought.

After disposing of the trash and reentering the station, Pinzon spent a few minutes straightening the front-counter area around the cash register. By the time he finished straightening, there were still no customers in the snack shop and no cars had pulled into the station for fuel. With business at a standstill and his shift drawing to a close, Pinzon went outside to lock the fuel pumps. The chirpy, melodic door chimes echoed behind Pinzon as he pushed through the station's entryway.

As he approached the first row of fuel pumps, Pinzon noticed a man walking toward him from the darkened edge of the Thrifty parking lot. The man moved with quick, deliberate steps. As the man drew closer and moved into the light, Pinzon recoiled. It wasn't the man's modest height, slight build, or rapid footsteps that gave Pinzon pause. Instead, it was the fact that the black-clad man had a bandana tied across his face bandito-style. Only the man's empty eyes and a hint of his pale forehead were visible above the menacing mask. A moment later, Pinzon saw the gun.

"Get inside!" the stranger shouted at Pinzon while raising his arm and jamming his firearm in the terrified clerk's face.

Pinzon stumbled backwards with his hands raised. Following the robber's directions, Pinzon pushed through the station's glass doors and reentered the snack shop.

"Get down on the ground!" the robber commanded in a menacing bark.

Pinzon immediately proned himself on the white tile floor.

"Don't move motherfucker," the robber ordered as he stepped over Pinzon's body and darted behind the counter.

Not knowing if he was going to live or die, Pinzon heard the cash register opening and bills being removed. Within seconds, the robber had cleaned out the register's cash tray. All and all, the score turned out to be penny-ante kid's stuff; the robber was only able to pocket about $100 from the register.

Dissatisfied with his meager haul, the robber demanded that Pinzon give him the key to the store's safe. Pinzon explained that he didn't have a key to the safe.

Saying nothing, the robber moved into the Thrifty's back office, where loud thrashing and banging could soon be heard.

Seconds ticked by.

Pinzon remained proned on the floor, fearing for his life.

Finally, the robber emerged from the Thrifty's back office. Pinzon watched as the robber moved toward him with speed and confidence. As the robber passed the Thrifty's front counter, he grabbed Pinzon's Verizon Voyager cell phone and stuffed it in his pocket. The robber then moved toward Pinzon, hovered over the terrified clerk's back, and with the speed of a master pickpocket, snatched the wallet from the back pocket of Pinzon's jeans.

The robber opened the wallet and read the information on Pinzon's identification card aloud.

"Azael Pinzon," the robber recited in a low, soulless voice. "You know I know where you live, Azael. You know that, right?"

Fearing for his life, Pinzon responded in the affirmative.

"You better not tell anybody about this, understand?" the robber said, aiming his weapon directly at Pinzon's head. "You'd better not call the police. Remember, I know where you live."

The fact that the robber was warning Pinzon not to call the police was a promising sign. It suggested that Pinzon might just make it through the encounter in one piece.

"Don't say shit to anybody," the robber added one last time. "And don't forget, I know where you live."

With that, the robber stood up, stepped over Pinzon's proned body, walked to the Thrifty's exit, and pushed through the doors. The friendly, welcoming door chimes added a chilling touch to the frightening encounter.

Pinzon remained on the floor with his hands out to his sides and his face flat against the cold tile. When he was convinced the robber was gone, Pinzon lifted his head and looked outside the store. There was still no traffic on State Street and nothing was moving. Not knowing if the robber would return, Pinzon sprang to his feet and maneuvered behind the counter as quickly as he could.

Disregarding the robber's warning, Pinzon immediately seized the phone and used the Thrifty's landline to call 911. Within minutes, Deputy Anthony Kouremetis of the Santa Barbara County Sheriff's Department was on scene at the Thrifty. Although Pinzon was badly shaken by the encounter, he'd kept a level head during the robbery and was able to provide Deputy Kouremetis with an excellent description of his attacker.

Pinzon described the robber as a young white man between the ages of twenty and thirty. He estimated the robber's height at 5'8" and his weight at 180 pounds. In addition to describing the robber's black-on-white face bandana, Pinzon also told the deputy that his assailant wore a black hoodie, black jeans, and black gloves. Pinzon added that the robber's voice betrayed no trace of a regional accent. [9]

Pinzon also told the deputy that the robber had stolen his personal cell phone and wallet.

As luck would have it, in the moments after the robbery, customers had begun driving into the Thrifty parking lot to purchase fuel. Two of the customers saw a vehicle leaving the scene as they maneuvered their car toward the fuel pumps. In speaking with Deputy Kouremetis, the witnesses described the vehicle as a silvery SUV. One witness thought the vehicle might be a Chevy Trailblazer. The other witness added that the SUV had turned west on State Street after leaving the Thrifty.

Keying his radio, Deputy Kouremetis immediately relayed this information to dispatch. Within seconds, a be-on-the-lookout (BOLO) alert was broadcast to all units in the area. The BOLO described the robbery, the suspect, and the SUV that was seen leaving the Thrifty parking lot.

A few blocks west of the Thrifty, a patrol deputy spied a silver Chevy Trailblazer matching the description of the suspect's vehicle. The deputy fell in behind the Trailblazer and began following the vehicle at a short distance.

It's no secret that nighttime traffic stops can be perilous duties for law-enforcement officers. As an officer approaches a strange vehicle, he never knows if an armed, violent, desperate suspect is waiting inside. Despite extensive training and experience on the streets, law-enforcement officers always use caution when performing traffic stops, particularly when they're dealing with potential felons who might have nothing to lose.

Following the silver Trailblazer and watching the driver carefully for any unusual movements, the deputy illuminated his blue lights, hit his siren, and began to execute the traffic stop. The Trailblazer pulled slowly toward the curb, its amber turn signal flickering in the darkness. From what he'd heard in the BOLO alert, the deputy knew that the Thrifty robber had been carrying a firearm. Although the Trailblazer's driver wasn't making any furtive movements, the deputy had no way of knowing if a fusillade of bullets would come flying his way at any moment.

As it turned out, the patrol deputy's encounter with the Trailblazer was a mix of good news and bad news.

The good news was that the Trailblazer's female driver posed no threat and knew absolutely nothing about the Thrifty robbery.

The bad news was that the Thrifty robber was still on the loose.

CHAPTER 6

As the night of September 23, 2009, wore on, the investigation into the Thrifty robbery continued. A few miles from the gas station, a man named Javier Espinoza was busy dialing his best friend's cell-phone number. For the past hour, Espinoza had been trying to reach his best friend, Azael Pinzon, but Pinzon wasn't answering. This was quite unusual. Typically, during his night shifts at the Thrifty, Pinzon was quick to take calls from his best friend. Intrigued by Pinzon's reticence to answer the phone, Espinoza went on with his evening.

At 10:12 p.m., roughly forty minutes after the Thrifty robber fled the scene of his heist, Javier Espinoza's cell phone began to ring. When Espinoza checked his caller ID, he saw that Pinzon had finally decided to call him back. Flipping open his phone, Espinoza was eager to find out why his friend hadn't answered his calls from earlier in the night.

"*¿Que paso?*" Espinoza asked as he placed the phone to his ear.

"Hey Javier," said the deep, cold, unaccented American voice on the other end of the line.

"Yeah, who's this?" Espinoza asked.

"Listen Javier, and listen good," said the ice-cold voice. "You tell Azael that if he says anything about what happened tonight, I'm gonna kill him and his family. You understand?"

Terrified and mystified by the caller's words, a mortal chill ran down Espinoza's spine. Had his friend Azael been hurt? Who was the person on the other end of the line? How had this white guy obtained Azael's phone and how did he know Javier's name?

"You still there, Javier?" the calm, threatening voice asked. "Tell Azael that if he says anything, I'm gonna kill him. And I'm gonna kill you too."

The line went dead.

With the silent phone still pressed against his ear, Espinoza sat wide-eyed in his living room. Espinoza deduced that the caller must've somehow stolen Pinzon's cell phone and found his number in the contact list. Espinoza was immediately afraid to leave his house. He worried that the mystery caller might be waiting for him outside, hiding in the darkness. Locking his doors tightly and barricading himself inside his home, Espinoza tried to decide what he should do next. The fact that the caller had used Espinoza's first name was particularly unsettling.

An hour or so later, as Espinoza sat terrified inside his home, his phone started ringing again. Dreading the prospect of more death threats from the mystery caller, Espinoza was reluctant to answer. There was something about the white guy's voice that chilled Espinoza to his core. Nevertheless, Espinoza wanted to find out if Pinzon was alright. With great trepidation, Espinoza answered his phone.

Hearing Pinzon's voice on the other end of the line sent a wave of relief through Espinoza. Pinzon told his friend about the Thrifty robbery, the masked gunman, and the theft of his cell phone. Then, with unmistakable horror in his voice, Espinoza described the call he'd received from Pinzon's stolen cell phone at 10:12 p.m. Pinzon told Espinoza that he'd spoken to the Sheriff's Department and given deputies a full description of the robber. Pinzon also told Espinoza that he'd pass his name along to detectives.

A few hours later, at approximately 3:30 a.m., Detective Ray Gamboa of the Santa Barbara County Sheriff's Department was notified about the Thrifty hold-up. After receiving the robbery notification, Detective Gamboa contacted the deputies who'd responded to Pinzon's 911 call. The deputies described their preliminary investigation and gave Gamboa an overview of the crime.

By 5:40 a.m., with his investigation of the Thrifty robbery already underway, Detective Gamboa met with Azael Pinzon at the Sheriff's Department headquarters near Goleta. After confirming the events of the robbery, Pinzon described his cell phone and the contents of his wallet for the detective. The contents included several credit cards, a Bank of America debit card, multiple receipts, and an identification card issued by the Mexican Consulate.

"Do you know if any of your bank cards have been used since the robbery?" Detective Gamboa asked.

"No," Pinzon answered. "You want me to check on that?"

Detective Gamboa told him that he did. Pinzon promised to check his bank and credit card accounts when he returned home.

News of the Thrifty robbery circulated through the Sheriff's Department headquarters like chilled air through the ventilation system. In discussing the Thrifty hold-up with his colleagues, an astute Santa Barbara County detective recalled hearing about a series of robberies in the nearby city of Ventura. From what the detective recalled, police in Ventura were looking for a young, white robber who dressed in dark clothing and carried a black semiautomatic handgun while robbing small businesses. Not only did the Thrifty robber use the same M.O. as the Ventura crook, he displayed the same reckless indifference for public safety. Considering that Ventura was only thirty miles down the coast from Santa Barbara, detectives knew they needed to dig into the possibility of a link between the cases. Soon, calls were being made to robbery detectives in Ventura.

Meanwhile, Detective Gamboa made contact with Javier Espinoza and took a statement about the threatening call from the previous night. Then, at about 8:45 a.m., Pinzon called Detective Gamboa to report on the use of his credit and debit cards. After returning home and checking his bank accounts, Pinzon discovered that one of his credit cards had been used the previous night at an In-N-Out Burger in Ventura. Pinzon also stated that, minutes before the In-N-Out transaction, someone had attempted to use his Bank of America debit card to withdraw cash from an ATM in Ventura.

Gamboa thanked Pinzon for the information and promised to follow up soon. The detective knew that the first forty-eight hours of an investigation are crucial in developing leads and identifying suspects. Because Pinzon had been diligent about checking his bank accounts and communicating with the detective, momentum was building in the case. Whether he knew it or not, the noose was tightening around the Thrifty robber's neck.

Since the 1970s, multiple studies have found that large numbers of crimes are committed by a small, hardcore group of offenders. [10] Such offenders are rarely satisfied with committing a single type of offense. The shoplifter, the car thief, and the fetish burglar are often one and the same. More disturbingly, these poly-aberrant deviants often escalate to more serious offenses, such as kidnapping, rape, and robbery. Sometimes they escalate to murder. For this reason, getting versatile, hardcore offenders off the streets is a top priority for all law-enforcement agencies.

Little did they know it at the time, but on the morning of September 24, 2009, Azael Pinzon, Javier Espinoza, and Detective Ray Gamboa had just played pivotal roles in taking a hardcore offender off the streets and resolving several brutal crimes along the coast. One of those crimes was a still-unsolved triple murder from the previous spring.

CHAPTER 7

While Detective Gamboa continued to work his end of the Thrifty robbery in Santa Barbara, his colleague, Detective Mike Scherbarth, drove down the coast to Ventura. The purpose of Scherbarth's trip was straightforward: follow up on robbery leads and collect evidence linked to the Thrifty hold-up.

Cruising south on the 101, Detective Scherbarth passed through some of the most magnificent scenery on the planet. Jade mountains jutted toward the sky, sparkling waves licked the rocky coastline, and well-heeled beachfront neighborhoods sprouted from the terrain like chaparral. Amidst such beauty, it was hard to believe that residents in small coastal communities could fall prey so quickly and so easily to brutal predators. Crossing the Ventura County line, Detective Scherbarth drove through a corner of Faria. In the fall of 2009, with the Husted murders still unsolved, a drive through Faria was a stark reminder that tragic crimes could occur anywhere, anytime, and without warning.

Arriving in Ventura, Detective Scherbarth wheeled

off the 101 and drove to the In-N-Out Burger where Azael Pinzon's credit card had been used on the night of the Thrifty robbery. Located on a commercial stretch of Harbor Boulevard, the In-N-Out chosen by the Thrifty robber for his nighttime snack was across the street from the Shell gas station that had been robbed on September 3, 2009. As far as police could tell, the Shell stick-up marked the beginning of the robber's crimes in Ventura.

After obtaining a surveillance video from In-N-Out's management, Detective Scherbarth made his way east. His destination was the Bank of America branch on Victoria Avenue. There, he collected a video from one of the branch's exterior ATMs. Ironically, this Bank of America branch is located less than a block south of the Ventura County Hall of Justice, the Sheriff's Department headquarters, and the county jail.

With the In-N-Out and Bank of America videos in hand, Detective Scherbarth sat down to watch the footage. At first glance, it didn't appear that the In-N-Out video offered much in the way of clues. Scherbarth watched as patron after patron cruised up to In-N-Out's drive-thru window, exchanged money for sacks of grease, then drove away into the night. Soon enough, however, the suspect's vehicle entered the frame. Because Detective Scherbarth had a time-stamp from Pinzon's credit card company, he was able to tell exactly when the suspect's SUV entered the drive-thru. As the Thrifty witnesses had indicated, the suspect's vehicle was a late-model Chevy Trailblazer. Although Detective Scherbarth was unable to catch a glimpse of the driver, he did notice an important detail about the SUV: there was no license plate affixed to its bumper. [11]

When Detective Scherbarth finished watching the suspect's Trailblazer pass through the In-N-Out parking lot, he shifted his focus to the ATM video from Bank of America. The ATM video showed a young, white male strolling confidently toward the cash machine. When he reached the ATM, the young man pulled Azael Pinzon's debit card from his pocket and shoved it into the digitized cash dispenser. Wearing a brown zip-up jacket, a blue and white t-shirt, a black baseball cap, and sunglasses with white trim, the youthful suspect in the ATM video didn't betray a hint of shame about the felony he was committing.

Around the same time that Detective Scherbarth was viewing the In-N-Out and Bank of America videos, his colleagues in Santa Barbara County were reviewing surveillance footage from the Thrifty's security cameras. This footage gave detectives their best view yet of the Thrifty suspect.

Analyzing the Thrifty surveillance video with eagle-eyed attention, detectives saw the bandana-masked intruder force Azael Pinzon to the floor at gunpoint, move behind the Thrifty's front counter, and clean out the gas station's cash register. Detectives watched carefully as the robber got on top of Pinzon's back and pointed his weapon at the clerk's head. Everything in the video happened just as Pinzon had described. However, Santa Barbara County detectives noticed something in the surveillance footage that Pinzon had missed from his prone position on the floor: the robber had stolen a single pack of Kamel Red Filter cigarettes from the gas station's counter. The detectives immediately recorded the lot number of the cigarette pack so it could be traced, if and when a suspect was identified.

With their robbery investigation in full swing and the momentum of justice continuing to build, Santa Barbara County detectives seized the moment. Based on all the evidence he and his colleagues had collected, Detective Gamboa put together an attempt-to-identify poster regarding the Thrifty robbery. Such posters allow far-flung law-enforcement agencies to share critical information about wanted suspects and high-status investigations. By sharing information and working together, law-enforcement agencies can synergize their resources and enhance the probability that dangerous offenders will be apprehended.

Detective Gamboa's attempt-to-identify poster listed critical information about the suspect who had ripped off the Thrifty and terrorized Javier Espinoza via cell phone. The poster included details about the suspect's height, weight, age, race, clothing, and M.O. It also featured information about the suspect's Chevy Trailblazer and its missing license plate. When the poster was complete, Detective Gamboa disseminated it to law-enforcement agencies across the state.

After the attempt-to-identify poster was released, detectives were hopeful that it would generate a solid lead in the Thrifty case. However, as the days passed and the phones remained silent, detectives with the Santa Barbara County robbery detail watched as the pace of their investigation slowed to a crawl. Clues had been exhausted in the case, and with no information forthcoming, the detectives shifted their focus to other matters. Despite their diligence, attention to detail, and hard work, the detectives knew the realities of investigating stranger-on-stranger crimes: Without a DNA link or some good old-fashioned luck, such crimes often go unsolved.

Luck is an intangible commodity that's impossible to create, demand, or issue. Worst of all, luck is usually scarcest when it's needed most. Sometimes, however, luck comes along at just the right moment. When this happens, luck tends to pay off enormous dividends.

Exactly one week to the day after Azael Pinzon was robbed at the State Street Thrifty, detectives caught an extremely lucky break.

While patrolling their beat on September 30, 2009, two uniform officers with the Ventura Police Department noticed a Chevy Trailblazer speeding through the city. The speeding Trailblazer matched the vehicle description from Detective Gamboa's attempt-to-identify poster. Knowing that the Thrifty bandit was also suspected of multiple hold-ups in their city, the observant Ventura patrol officers decided to take action and stop the speeding Trailblazer.

Unlike the Trailblazer in the In-N-Out surveillance video, the Trailblazer that was seen speeding on September 30, 2009, had license plates affixed to its bumpers. As blue lights lit up the night and the prowl car guided the speeding Trailblazer to the curb, one of the officers read the plate number number, 6JTG282, into the radio.

With the Trailblazer stopped on the curb, the officers proceeded with caution. Unsure if they were approaching an armed felon, the officers weren't taking any chances. However, as it turned out, the young man behind the wheel of the speeding Trailblazer offered no resistance. From what the officers could tell, the young driver wasn't tall, but he had a compact, sinewy, athletic toughness to his physique. Upon request, the Trailblazer's driver immediately handed over his license and proof of insurance.

Studying the motorist carefully, the patrol officers could tell that—at least on the surface—the driver matched the physical description of the serial robber who had eluded authorities since the beginning of the month. The officers also noted the date of birth on the speeder's license, which indicated that he'd turned twenty on September 21, 2009, just nine days earlier.

With no articulable suspicion that the young driver had committed a crime, the patrol officers issued him a speeding ticket, kicked him loose, and proceeded with their nightly duties. However, as the Ventura patrol officers watched the Trailblazer's tail-lights grow smaller on the streetscape, they made note of one crucial detail: the driver's name.

It was Joshua Graham Packer.

CHAPTER 8

By the fall of 2009, the Faria homicide investigation had reached a dead end. Ventura County detectives had worked diligently to follow up on tips and generate leads in the Husted case, but despite their best efforts, detectives were no closer to making an arrest than they had been on the night of the murders. A dangerous predator was on the loose, and with zero progress being made in the investigation, the community remained on edge. It didn't help that Wendy Di Rodio's murder was still unsolved.

More than ever before, it was becoming clear that the Husteds had been murdered by a stranger. And, because suspects in stranger-homicides are so difficult to identify, there was an unspoken concern that the Faria murderer might escape justice. As the fall of 2009 gave way to winter, some detectives were increasingly concerned that the Faria murders might join the list of high-profile California crimes that have gone unsolved for eternity. Such crimes are as well known within the law-enforcement community as the ridges and grooves on a tarnished badge.

One of California's oldest and most infamous unsolved crimes is the 1947 slaying of twenty-four-year-old Elizabeth Short. Better known as the Black Dahlia, Short grew up in a broken, lower-middle-class home in Medford, Massachusetts. As a child, she dreamed of moving away from the biting New England cold and making it big as a Hollywood movie star. Unfortunately, Short's hard-scrabble existence was at odds with her grandiose ambitions. Although she was superficially attractive and attempted to dress in fashionable attire, Elizabeth Short was a sickly young woman whose asthma prevented her from finishing high school. In an attempt to improve her health, Short moved first to Miami Beach, then to Northern California, where her father worked on a military base in the Bay Area. Eventually, Short drifted south to Santa Barbara, where she took a job at Camp Cooke (now Vandenberg Air Force Base). The job at Camp Cooke paid very modest wages, but it plugged Short into the local social scene. During her free time, Short took to running with a wild, raucous crowd. On September 23, 1943, Short was arrested by the Santa Barbara Police Department for underage drinking. She was nineteen years old.

Working a menial job at Camp Cooke wasn't Elizabeth Short's dream in life, so in the summer of 1946, she moved to Los Angeles. Entering the noirish world of Old Hollywood, Short lived in a succession of rooming houses and hung out at downtown diners. Though her exterior appearance—which by this point included lots of black clothing and black lipstick—conveyed a sense of glamour and mystique, records indicate that Short was living at or slightly below California's poverty line during her stint in Los Angeles. According to *Severed*, author John Gilmore's outstanding book on the Black Dahlia case, Short financed her meager lifestyle by relying on the generosity of others. Sometimes this generosity amounted to couch-surfing at friends' apartments. Other times, however, Short's dependence took on a much darker complexion. According to Gilmore, Short was known to trade oral sex for shoes, clothing, a place to stay for the night, or even just a meal. From her desperate ploys to earn money to the ersatz glamor of her wardrobe to the candle wax she used to camouflage the abscesses in her rotting teeth, Elizabeth Short's aimless party-girl lifestyle was a study in pathetic desperation.

In December 1946, Elizabeth Short travelled to San Diego. After arriving there, Short spent time living with a local family that found her sleeping in a twenty-four-hour movie theatre downtown. In early January 1947, having worn out her welcome with the San Diego family, Short caught a ride back to Los Angeles with a traveling salesman named Robert "Red" Manley.

On the afternoon of January 9, 1947, Manley dropped Elizabeth Short at the Biltmore Hotel in downtown Los Angeles. According to a statement Manley later gave to detectives, Short said that she wanted to contact her sister, whom she claimed was living at the Biltmore. Hotel staff observed Elizabeth Short sitting in the Biltmore's lobby during the late afternoon of January 9, 1947. However, at some point in the early evening, Elizabeth Short walked out the front doors of the Biltmore and turned south on Olive Street. She was never seen alive again.

Six days later and six miles west of the Biltmore, a Leimert Park housewife named Betty Bersinger loaded her three-year-old daughter into her stroller and took her for a walk around their neighborhood. Located just south of Hollywood, Leimert Park was an up-and-coming neighborhood in the post-war years, with many new bungalow homes lining its carefully gridded streets. However, not every lot in Leimert Park had been developed in January 1947. Many lots stood empty and overgrown, waiting for buyers to develop them.

As Betty Bersinger made her way through Leimert Park on the sunny morning of January 15, 1947, she turned north on Norton Avenue from 39th Street. Approaching the middle of the block between 39th and Coliseum streets, Bersinger saw a strange-looking object in a weed-infested lot beside the sidewalk. She thought the object was a department store mannequin that had been separated into two parts. Drawing closer, Bersinger was shocked to discover that it was actually the bisected corpse of a young woman. The nude victim's arms were stretched above her head and her legs were pried apart at a grotesquely revealing angle. Grabbing hold of her daughter's stroller and hurrying from the scene, Bersinger used the phone at a nearby home to call the police.

When detectives from the Los Angeles Police Department arrived at the body-dump location on Norton Avenue, they were horrified by what they discovered. Not only had the victim's body had been cut in half at the waist, detectives also noticed that the victim's face had been slashed viciously with a large knife. It appeared that the killer had placed his knife in the corners of the victim's mouth and ripped outward toward her ears, creating two savage face wounds that looked like a repugnant parody of a smile. Later, when an autopsy was performed, the medical examiner found that the murderer had tortured his victim by cutting a large chunk of flesh from her thigh. The medical examiner also found bruising on the victim's ankles, suggesting that she'd been suspended upside down while being tortured. Bruising on the right side of the victim's scalp indicated that she'd suffered a powerful blow to the head prior to death. Ultimately, the medical examiner concluded that the victim's cause of death was blood loss due to the lacerations on her face. The manner of death: homicide.

Fingerprints were lifted from the severed victim and sent to FBI headquarters in Washington, D.C. Within hours, the feds were able to match the victim's prints to a set of prints collected three years earlier after a delinquency arrest in Santa Barbara. The prints belonged to Elizabeth Short.

Pulling out all the stops and assigning an army of detectives to the case, the Los Angeles Police Department worked hard to identify Elizabeth Short's murderer. However, because Short lived a transient lifestyle, consorted with a multitude of men, and had no fixed address, solving her murder was like trying to capture smoke in a bottle. Clues were unearthed in the case and tenuous leads were established, but few solid suspects were ever identified. After being investigated at length, Red Manley was cleared of suspicion in the case. Other suspects were similarly cleared as the months, years, and decades passed.

Eventually, Elizabeth Short's sad existence and brutal demise faded from the headlines, receded into the past, and all but disappeared from public memory. Her case stands as a stark reminder that some murders—and particularly stranger murders—

go unsolved forever if connections aren't established between crimes and killers.

Southern California doesn't have a monopoly on the unsolved-murder business. In the late 1960s, when the psychedelic zeitgeist held Northern California firmly within its lysergic thrall, a lovers' lane serial killer began attacking couples in the Bay Area.

The first attack took place around 11 p.m. on December 20, 1968, when high-school sweethearts David Faraday and Betty Lou Jensen were gunned down on an isolated stretch of roadway between the North Bay cities of Benicia and Vallejo. Both victims were seventeen years old.

Seven months later, on the Fourth of July 1969, another couple, nineteen-year-old Michael Mageau and twenty-two-year-old Darlene Ferrin, was assailed by an unknown gunman while sitting in Ferrin's parked car near a Vallejo golf course. Ferrin perished from her injuries, but despite suffering several gunshot wounds to his head and body, Mageau survived the attack. When questioned by detectives, Mageau described his attacker as a young, heavy-set white man who had shined a flashlight in the couple's eyes before opening fire. The bullet-riddled youth also described how the killer had parked his vehicle behind Ferrin's car prior to the attack.

Armed with the suspect description and shell casings from both shootings, detectives from the Solano County Sheriff's Department and the Vallejo Police Department worked with stolid determination to identify their mystery murderer. Because the M.O.

in both cases was identical—young couples shot while sitting in parked cars in lovers' lanes—authorities took little time in linking the attacks. However, despite their eyewitness description and physical evidence, no suspects were identified in the linked cases.

Then, on August 1, 1969, three bizarre letters were received by three Bay Area newspapers: the *San Francisco Chronicle,* the *San Francisco Examiner,* and the *Vallejo Times-Herald.* In the letters, a mystery writer took credit for the lovers' lane attacks in December 1968 and July 1969. The writer also revealed details of the crimes that, at the time, were known only to law enforcement. Along with his macabre missives, the killer also included a cipher composed of arcane symbols, letters, and numbers. Demanding that the ciphers be published on the front pages of the three newspapers, the mystery writer threatened to "...go on a kill rampage..." if his demands weren't met. The newspapers acquiesced to the letter writer's demands, and when the ciphers were published, a school teacher and his wife cracked the code. What they uncovered is one of the most disturbing messages in the annals of American crime.

In his published cipher, the killer claimed that he hunted people because "...man is the most dangerous game of all..." The killer went on to state that he was murdering his victims in order to collect slaves for his afterlife.

The decoded cipher rocked the Bay Area like an earthquake and sent law enforcement on high alert. Couples were told to stay out of lovers' lanes and parks were monitored carefully after dark. As these precautions were being implemented and detectives worked overtime to identify a suspect in the case, more of the killer's letters poured into local newspapers. In his second letter to the *Examiner*, the killer gave himself a nickname: Zodiac. At the end of his letter, the killer signed off with a very distinctive symbol: a circled cross. As each letter was reported on by the media, local terror grew to near hysteria.

Responding to the public terror, law enforcement redoubled its efforts to identify the killer. However, Zodiac was far from stupid. By September 1969, he had refined his M.O. in an effort to evade capture.

On September 27, 1969, college students Bryan Hartnell, age twenty, and Cecelia Shepard, age twenty-two, took a day trip to Lake Berryessa. Located in an isolated portion of Napa County, Lake Berryessa is approximately fifty miles north of Vallejo. Lying in the tall golden grass and gazing out across Berryessa's calm waters, Hartnell and Shepard didn't have a care in the world. As they lay side by side on a blanket, talking about school and life, Shepard saw a man approaching them from a line of trees. As the man drew closer, Shepard could see that he was dressed in a black outfit with a black executioner's hood pulled over his head. Soon, both Shepard and Hartnell saw the man's gun.

"I want your money and your car keys," the armed man said in a calm, firm, monotone voice as he marched toward the couple, his semiautomatic firearm pointed directly at them.

Complying instantly, Hartnell tossed his car keys and wallet onto the blanket.

The masked man told the couple that he needed to tie up them up. Hartnell and Shepard lay facedown on the blanket. During the binding process, the man in black told the couple that he was an escaped convict from Deer Lodge, Montana, and that he was on his way to Mexico. By that point in the late afternoon, the sun was starting to set and an early autumn chill was creeping into the air.

With both victims bound on the blanket, the assailant holstered his firearm and pulled a large, bayonette-style knife from the belt of his black outfit.

Stating that he couldn't bare to watch Shepard being stabbed, Hartnell asked to be stabbed first. Within seconds, the stranger began pounding his knife into the helpless man's back. When the knife stopped falling, Hartnell had suffered eight stab wounds.

With his male victim out of the way, the killer turned his attention to Shepard. Shredding her delicate flesh to ribbons, the killer stabbed the screaming girl more than twenty times in the back, arms, and abdominal area as she writhed on the blanket.

When he was done stabbing his victims, the heavy-set stranger stood up, sheathed his blade, and walked away from the blood-soaked crime scene.

After hiking back to the roadway, the killer stopped long enough to scrawl a horrifying message on the passenger door of Hartnell's white Volkswagen Karman Ghia. The message read:

Vallejo
12-20-68
7-4-69
Sept 27-69 - 6:30
by knife

Leaving no doubt as to the vandal's identity, a large circled cross was drawn above the message.

Zodiac had committed a heinous crime along the

golden-grassed shores of Lake Berryessa, but it wasn't a perfect crime. In his haste to target the female victim, Zodiac failed to deliver fatal wounds to Bryan Hartnell. As a result, the strong, athletic young man was able to free himself from his bindings and drag his oozing body to the road. That's where he was found by law-enforcement officers, who rushed him to an emergency room in the city of Napa.

Cecelia Shepard wasn't as fortunate. Although she was still alive when law enforcement reached her location on the lake shore, she expired two days later from blood loss and shock.

Eager to identify a suspect, detectives from the Napa County Sheriff's Department questioned Bryan Hartnell as he recovered at the hospital. Hartnell described his attacker as a stocky white man in his late twenties or thirties with a bulging gut. Hartnell went on to say that the man was dressed in black with a black hood over his head. According to Hartnell, the Zodiac's trademark symbol, a circled cross, was emblazoned on the portion of the black hood that hung over the assailant's chest.

Armed with their eyewitness description of Zodiac, law enforcement worked tenaciously to solve the attack on Bryan Hartnell and Cecelia Shepard. As usual, though, their efforts were to no avail. Stranger murders are extremely difficult to solve under the best of circumstances, but when detectives are dealing with an organized, sophisticated offender like Zodiac, identifying and eliminating suspects can be next to impossible. Lacking an effective means of developing leads in the case, detectives in Napa and Solano counties spun their wheels in a vain attempt to identify Zodiac.

Relishing in the success of his hideous crimes and gloating over law enforcement's inability to identify him, Zodiac bombarded the media with letters. Judging from the contents of these letters, Zodiac fancied himself an outlaw celebrity.

Within three weeks of the Lake Berryessa attack, Zodiac had refined his M.O. once again. By October 1969, with cold Pacific winds sweeping through the streets of San Francisco, Zodiac set his sights on the big city.

Around 9:45 p.m. on October 11, 1969, cab driver Paul Stine picked up a fare near Union Square in downtown San Francisco. According to Stine's log book, the fare asked to be driven to a prosperous residential neighborhood in Presidio Heights. After arriving at the destination, the fare asked Stine to drive one block west and park on the street. The cab rolled forward a block and pulled to the curb. Once the cab was in park, the fare withdrew a 9-mm pistol from the pocket of his parka, pressed the barrel against Stine's head, and squeezed a bullet into the driver's brain. The cabbie was dead before his body had slumped across the seat.

With the cab driver dead, the homicidal fare reached over the front seat and ripped a piece of fabric off Stine's shirt. The fare then hustled from the cab and set off in the direction of a nearby park.

Little did the fare know it, but Stine's murder had been witnessed by a small group of teenagers in a house across the street from the death scene. The teens watched in horror as the executioner emerged from the cab and walked northbound on Cherry Street. Within moments, the teens were on the phone with police.

Two officers with the San Francisco Police Department were on routine patrol in the area when the report of the cabbie shooting went out over the radio. Unfortunately, because the radio alert was garbled, the patrolmen were told to be on the lookout for a black male adult with a handgun. Consequently, when the patrolmen passed the stocky white man on Cherry Street in the moments after the murder, they didn't stop him. Instead, from the warm interior of their prowl car, the officers asked the stocky white man if he'd seen any suspicious people in the neighborhood. Obliging the officers like any good citizen, the stocky man coolly replied that he'd seen a man with a gun running in the opposite direction. The officers roared south on Cherry. The stocky man in the parka hustled north into the darkness and disappeared forever.

Days later, a Zodiac letter showed up at the *San Francisco Chronicle*. It contained a tattered scrap of Paul Stine's bloody shirt. Over the next few years, more letters containing pieces of Stine's shirt showed up in the *Chronicle's* mail room. Every time a letter arrived at the newspaper, SFPD inspectors would examine it carefully. However, despite taking credit for several more murders and disappearances during the 1970s, no other crimes were ever definitively linked to Zodiac after Paul Stine's murder.

Zodiac's last confirmed letter was received by the *Chronicle* in late January 1974. By then, his trail had gone cold and detectives throughout the Bay Area had tacitly given up on the case. In 2002, using the latest DNA technology, the SFPD lifted a genetic profile from an envelope containing one of Zodiac's letters. The profile was compared to DNA from a prime suspect in the Zodiac case.

The DNA profiles didn't match.

With no other suspects and no other DNA samples to compare, the SFPD closed the books on Zodiac, conceding a humiliating defeat in one of the most infamous murder cases in state history.

Zodiac is a terrifying figure in California crime lore, but from the standpoint of threat assessment, Zodiac was more bark than bite. As some contemporary experts have pointed out, Zodiac probably got as much of a thrill from sending his letters to newspapers and chiding law enforcement as he did from his actual murders. Although Zodiac posed a lethal threat to young couples in isolated lovers' lanes and luckless cab drivers, he posed little threat to random members of the public who were safely ensconced in their own homes. Unfortunately, not every unidentified predator in California has been so benign.

Beginning in the summer of 1976, a shrewd, organized, and highly sadistic serial rapist began striking in the suburbs east of Sacramento. Most of the rapist's crimes conformed to a very specific pattern: he would make silent entry into a single-family suburban home, confront the sleeping residents at gunpoint, and bind them with soft ligatures he'd brought to the scene. Once the residents were bound and immobilized, the offender would rape the female victims. Sometimes the offender would place knife blades to his victims' throats or gun barrels to their heads as he taunted them with death threats. In many cases, this psychological torture went on for several hours.

When the Sacramento rape series began, the offender was only attacking female victims who were home alone or at home with small children. Eventually, the rapist became emboldened and started invading the homes of male-female couples. In the course of his attacks, the rapist proved himself to be an expert stealth burglar, an accomplished knot tier, and a complete sadist with a penchant for kinky bondage fantasies. Because most of the offender's early crimes occurred on Sacramento's east side, the press nicknamed him the East Area Rapist.

By 1977, the East Area Rapist had move beyond the parameters of his original hunting grounds on the east side of Sacramento. At first he travelled to nearby population centers like Stockton, Modesto, and Davis to find fresh victims. Then, in 1979, he moved to the Bay Area, where he began invading the homes of upscale suburbanites. All totaled, the East Area Rapist is suspected of committing at least forty-five home-invasion rapes in Northern California between mid-1976 and mid-1979.

In the summer of 1979, the East Area Rapist's reign of terror ended in the Bay Area. Some detectives believed that the rapist had been imprisoned for an unrelated crime. Other detectives thought that he'd died in some sort of accident. Still other detectives believed that the rapist had simply moved out of the area and continued his criminal career elsewhere. It would take more than two decades to resolve this debate, but in the end, the latter group's cynicism would be proven correct.

In November 1996, a forensic scientist with the Orange County Sheriff's Department in Southern California began typing DNA from three unsolved rape/murders. Each of the rape/murders had taken place in the early to mid-1980s and each had involved a similar set of circumstances: a highly skilled burglar had broken into upscale suburban homes in the middle of the night, waylaid the residents in their bedrooms, bound them with soft ligatures, and raped the female victims. At some point, after the sexual assaults were complete, the intruder had bludgeoned his victims to death with unknown clubs. Because the offender was extremely evidence savvy, both the clubs and the bindings had been removed from the crime scenes. In all, four victims were claimed in the Orange County murders: Keith and Patrice Harrington, who were murdered in Dana Point on August 18, 1980; Manuela Witthuhn, who was murdered in Irvine on February 5, 1981; and Janelle Cruz, who was murdered in Irvine on May 4 or 5, 1986. Despite being murdered five years apart, Witthuhn and Cruz lived less than two miles from each other in the Northwoods section of Irvine.

Serological evidence left inside the Orange County rape victims was used to develop three DNA profiles. When the forensic scientist compared the DNA profiles, she was astonished to find that they came from a single unidentified male suspect. Detectives were notified immediately and a cold-case task force was assigned to reexamine the Harrington, Witthuhn, and Cruz murders.

Realizing that a previously unidentified serial killer had been operating in their jurisdiction, Orange County detectives began exploring the possibility that their unknown offender had claimed additional victims in other parts of the state. In exploring this theory, it didn't take long before the detectives hit pay dirt.

As they started to examine unsolved rape/murders

from the early 1980s, the cold-case detectives came across a Ventura homicide that bore eerie parallels to the Orange County crimes. In the Ventura case, a prominent attorney and his wife had been bludgeoned to death in the bedroom of their tony hillside estate. The male victim, who was a former prosecutor with the Ventura County District Attorney's Office, was forty-three-year-old Lyman Smith. The female victim was thirty-three-year-old Charlene Smith. At the time of the Smith murders on March 13, 1980, Lyman Smith was waiting to be sworn in as a Superior Court judge.

Evidence found at the Ventura crime scene revealed that the Smiths were confronted in their bedroom as they slept. They were then bound with soft ligatures and Charlene Smith was raped. Before the offender departed the scene, he used a large log from a wood pile in the Smiths' yard to beat both victims to death. The log was left at the foot of the Smiths' blood-saturated bed after the crime.

Because Lyman and Charlene Smith were a high-profile couple, Ventura detectives were convinced that they'd known their killer. However, after thoroughly investigating the Smiths' backgrounds, detectives were unable to generate any solid leads in the case. Eventually, with the local political establishment in an uproar, Ventura detectives arrested one of Lyman Smith's business associates for the bizarre, fetishistic murders. The detectives' evidence: a single fingerprint found on a wine glass in the Smiths' kitchen.

For his part, the business partner readily admitted that he was a frequent guest at the Smiths' home. He also admitted drinking wine with the Smiths in the days before the homicide. Although the business partner was cooperative with detectives, he was arrested and charged with the Smith murders. However, before the business partner could be tried for the murders, the charges against him were dropped. Eventually, the business partner was eliminated as a suspect, and by 1982, the Smith murders had gone cold.

In 2001, using long-stored biological evidence from the Smith crime scene, a DNA profile was developed of the Ventura killer. When the DNA profile of the Smiths' killer was compared to the DNA profile of the Orange County serial killer, it turned out to be a perfect match.

The forensic link between the Smith murders and the Orange County cases didn't just energize detectives in Southern California. As word of the Ventura-Orange County link spread, detectives in other parts of the state began to wonder if the Southern California serial killer—who had been dubbed the Original Night Stalker—was responsible for attacks in their jurisdictions as well. In particular, detectives in Sacramento County wondered if the East Area Rapist, who had vanished in 1979, had migrated south. Before long, a DNA profile was developed from biological evidence left at the East Area Rapist's crime scenes. When the East Area Rapist's DNA was compared to the Original Night Stalker's DNA, it proved to be a perfect match. In one fell swoop, astute law-enforcement officers and crime-lab scientists had linked a single unidentified offender to six murders and at least fifty home-invasion rapes.

Sacramento County detectives weren't alone in their curiosity about a potential link between the East Area Rapist-Original Night Stalker and unsolved crimes in their jurisdiction. Authorities in Santa Barbara County also wondered if a bizarre series of unsolved home-invasion murders from the late 1970s and early 1980s was the work of the same offender. Santa Barbara County detectives tagged three cases that bore the depraved hallmarks of the Original Night Stalker's other crimes.

The first Santa Barbara County home invasion occurred in Goleta on October 1, 1979. Around 2 a.m. that morning, a sleeping couple was confronted in their bedroom by a masked intruder brandishing a knife. After binding the couple with soft ligatures, the intruder moved the female victim into the living room and began to examine her nude body with his flashlight. Several minutes later, when the offender went to check on the male victim in the bedroom, the female struggled to her feet, escaped from the home, and began screaming for help from her driveway. As luck would have it, an FBI agent happened to live next door to the victimized couple. When the FBI agent heard his neighbor screaming for help, he rushed downstairs and into his yard. As the FBI agent was about to enter his neighbors' driveway, he saw the intruder fleeing the scene on a bicycle. The FBI agent ran to his car and chased the intruder, but the suspect was able to escape. Although the home-invader's bicycle was recovered (and identified as stolen), his identity was never established.

Eleven weeks later, on December 30, 1979, a Goleta physician and his girlfriend were murdered inside the doctor's condominium after being confronted in bed by a late-night burglar. The male victim was Dr. Robert Offerman, age forty-four, and the female victim was Dr. Debra Alexandria Manning, age thirty-five. Offerman lived half a mile south of the home that was invaded on October 1, 1979.

After doctors Offerman and Manning were murdered, the Goleta crimes came to a stop for two years. Then, in the summer of 1981, the murders resumed with brutal intensity.

On July 27, 1981, a thirty-five-year-old mother named Cheri Domingo was spending the night with her ex-boyfriend, twenty-seven-year-old Greg Sanchez. Domingo's Goleta home was located half a mile south of Dr. Offerman's condominium. At some point in the night, Domingo and Sanchez were confronted in bed by an armed intruder carrying a .38 special. After the initial confrontation, Domingo and Sanchez were bound with soft ligatures and Sanchez was shot in the face. Before making his getaway, the intruder bludgeoned both victims to death with an unknown club.

With a forensic link established between the Smith murders in Ventura, the Orange County homicides, and the Northern California rapes, debate raged about whether the murders in Santa Barbara County were connected to the East Area Rapist-Original Night Stalker. On May 16, 2011, the debate was finally settled.

Using the latest DNA technology, scientists at the California Department of Justice Lab developed a genetic profile from semen left on Cheri Domingo's bedding in 1981. The DNA found on Domingo's bedding was a perfect match with the East Area Rapist-Original Night Stalker's DNA.

In the mid-to-late 1970s, the East Area Rapist's victims described him as a white male, twenty to thirty years old, about 5'10" tall with a medium build. The victims also told detectives that the rapist always wore a mask and spoke to them through clenched teeth with an unaccented voice. Despite these physical descriptions, the DNA links, and the large sums of money that have been spent investigating the case, the East Area Rapist-Original Night Stalker has never been identified.

———— ·•·◄ ————

Between 1976 and 1986, the East Area Rapist-Original Night Stalker committed at least fifty rapes and ten grisly murder in nine counties. Not every unidentified offender in California has been so prolific or so mobile.

Around 7:45 a.m. on April 12, 1981, a fourteen-year-old girl named Sheila Sharp returned home after spending the night at a friend's house. Sheila lived with her mother and four siblings in the former resort community of Keddie, California. Located high in the Sierra foothills, Keddie was, at one time, a thriving vacation destination. By the early 1980s, however, the Keddie resort had fallen into disrepair and its cabins were permanently occupied by low-income families. When Sheila's mother, thirty-six-year-old Glenna "Sue" Sharp, moved to Keddie with her brood of five children, they were assigned to live in Cabin 28.

On the morning of April 12, 1981, nothing appeared amiss as Sheila Sharp walked toward Cabin 28. However, as Sheila stepped inside the cabin, she was met by an unthinkably horrific sight. Lying on the living-room floor, covered in blood, were Sheila's mother, Sheila's fifteen-year-old brother Johnny, and Johnny's friend, seventeen-year-old Dana Wingate. All three were dead. Surprisingly, Sheila's two younger brothers—ten-year-old Ricky and five-year-old Greg, as well as their friend Justin—were unharmed in one of the cabin's back bedrooms. On a more menacing front, Sheila's twelve-year-old sister Tina was missing from the cabin.

When deputies from the Plumas County Sheriff's Department arrived in Keddie to investigate the murders, they were shocked by the brutality they found inside Cabin 28. Sue Sharp, Johnny Sharp, and Dana Wingate were bound on the floor of the cabin's living room. All three had been bludgeoned severely with a hammer. In addition, Sue and Johnny Sharp had both been stabbed numerous times, while Dana Wingate had been manually strangled. All three victims lay in large pools of blood.

In many homicides, there's a single piece of evidence that serves as a gruesome metaphor for the entire case. In the Keddie murders, this piece of evidence was a mangled steak knife. Because the steak knife been plunged into the victims with such heartless, homicidal intensity, its blade was bent to a twenty-five degree angle.

Detectives interviewed Sheila Sharp, her brothers Ricky and Greg, and their sleepover friend Justin. The boys stated that they'd slept through the murders, although years later, Justin claimed to have witnessed some of the carnage after getting out of bed in the middle of the night.

While the children were unable to provide detectives with any useful information about the crimes, evidence inside the small, rundown cabin told the awful story of what had occurred there. Large quantities of blood were found on the walls and floors. Blood was also found on the door knob to the younger boys' bedroom, indicating that the killer or killers had looked inside.

Similarly, blood smears were found in the bedroom of Tina Sharp, who was missing from the scene.

Significant resources were invested in solving the Keddie murders and locating Tina Sharp. However, because the Plumas County Sheriff's Department was a tiny, rural law-enforcement agency, it had neither the resources nor the expertise to handle such a complex investigation. Detectives from Sacramento were sent in to provide support with the case, but their assistance failed to produce any viable leads.

Detectives learned that Sue Sharp had moved to Keddie just six months before the murders. With five children and no husband, Sue Sharp's existence in the small, remote, rundown cabin seemed unimaginably bleak. However, based on the information gathered by detectives, there was nothing about Sue Sharp's lifestyle that made her a particularly high-risk homicide victim. On the other hand, her son Johnny and his friend Dana Wingate were known to dabble in marijuana and hitchhike around the rural county. Both of these activities elevated their risk for victimization.

Unable to produce any leads in the Keddie case and desperate to find Tina Sharp, law enforcement went to the media. The Keddie murders were featured on an episode of *California's Most Wanted* and composites of two strange men were developed, but the case quickly went cold. In 1984, a portion of Tina Sharp's skull was found in a park thirty miles southeast of Keddic. No other clues ever surfaced in the case.

In 2004, with the Keddie murders still unsolved and detectives unable to move forward with their investigation, Cabin 28 was razed to the ground.

***

As they struggled to produce leads in the perplexing Faria murders, Ventura County detectives hoped that the Husted case wouldn't join the list of high-profile California homicides that have gone unsolved forever. Delivering justice to Brock and Davina Husteds' family members and restoring a sense of calm in the community were top priorities for the Ventura County Sheriff's Department. However, with no good suspects and no promising leads, Ventura County detectives were stuck.

In the meantime, detectives in another jurisdiction were having significantly greater success with one of their ongoing investigations.

After Josh Packer's Trailblazer was stopped by Ventura police officers on September 30, 2009, his name was passed along to robbery detectives in Santa Barbara County. From there, it didn't take long before Josh Packer emerged as a serious suspect in the Thrifty hold-up. By that point, Detective Gamboa and his colleagues had traced the threatening phone call that had been made to Javier Espinoza on the night of the robbery. As it turned out, the call to Espinoza had originated from Josh Packer's neighborhood in Ventura. Santa Barbara County detectives weren't going to make an arrest in the Thrifty case without extremely compelling evidence, so they decided to learn more about Josh Packer.

The deeper detectives dug into Josh Packer's background, the more intrigued they became. From what detectives could tell, Josh Packer's life was a sordid tale of abandonment, abuse, and aggression. These biographic details didn't prove that Josh Packer had robbed the Thrifty or leveled terrorist threats against Javier Espinoza. However, as Santa Barbara

County detectives delved deeper into Josh Packer's background, a clear and compelling picture began to emerge of their prime suspect in the Thrifty hold-up.

CHAPTER 9

To understand Josh Packer, it's necessary to understand the fractured and tumultuous circumstances of his youth. In particular, it's important to understand the background of his mother, Terri Williamson.

Growing up in the Cincinnati suburb of Milford, Ohio, Terri Williamson's early years were fraught with trauma. Though she was raised by two loving and well-intentioned parents, Terri's life started to get off track when her mother and father separated in 1978. The Williamsons' break-up was anything but amicable. When Terri's father learned that his wife was leaving him, he grabbed a gun, held it to his head, and threatened to pull the trigger. Terri, who was nine years old at the time, witnessed the entire episode.

Though the suicide attempt left an indelible impression on Terri's psyche, she steadfastly maintains that her father was a good man who did his best to raise her right. For that matter, Terri speaks highly of both her biological parents. Today, Terri describes her parents as salt-of-the-earth people who regularly took her to church at their Southern Baptist congregation and worked diligently to instill her with solid values.

"As fucked up as my childhood was, I was raised with good morals," Terri said of her formative years. "My parents tried really hard to teach me right from wrong."

Although he only had a third-grade education, Terri's father, Floyd Williamson, was a hard worker who loved his daughter deeply. When he wasn't earning a living as the head custodian for the Milford School District, Floyd Williamson always made ample time for Terri. Today, Terri's best memories of childhood are the times she spent with her father when she was small.

After her parents divorced, Terri tried to make the best of her less-than-ideal situation. Terri did well in elementary school, often bringing home all-A report cards. Within a year of her parents' divorce, however, Terri's problems started to intensify. According to Terri, most of her problems were centered around her father's decision to remarry. At the time of his second marriage, Floyd Williamson was in his mid-forties. Terri's new stepmother was in her mid-twenties. Once Floyd Williamson and his new bride had exchanged nuptials, Terri's home became a powder keg of tension.

Terri was less than enthusiastic about the changes in her household. However, it didn't take long before a new, unfathomable horror would supplant all of Terri's other problems.

"One day when I was walking home, I got raped by this group of guys," Terri said, adding that she was eleven years old at the time.

When Terri arrived home and told her father what had happened, he went berserk. According to Terri, her father threatened to kill the boys who'd attacked her. However, neither Floyd Williamson nor his new wife called the police or sought trauma counseling for Terri. According to Terri, the incident was simply shelved and not discussed within her family. From that point on, Terri's world began to unravel. Terri explained that, before the rape, she was regarded as one of the top students in her class. After the rape, Terri's life began to spiral out of control. It was a downward spiral that ended up lasting almost two decades.

With her problems mounting and her self-esteem deteriorating by the day, Terri started looking for destructive outlets for her inner turmoil. One day, Terri picked up a library book at school and wrote "fuck you" inside the front cover. School authorities quickly identified Terri as the vandal and dragged her into the office. Although her vandalism was a trifling matter in the grand scheme of things, getting caught was terribly traumatic for Terri.

"I was so ashamed about getting caught for that," Terri said, her voice strained with emotion. "The way my parents looked at me afterwards...just terrible."

Terri added that, after the vandalism incident, she started to feel like a problem child within her family. Up to that point, Terri's parents had always considered her a good kid with excellent grades and a high IQ. After the vandalism incident, however, Terri feared that her parents didn't think as highly of her. This phenomenon can be explained through labeling theory, which holds that an individual's actions are dictated in large measure by how she *thinks* other perceive her. Because Terri started to see herself as a problem kid, she began living down to her parents' expectations.

After the vandalism incident, Terri became sullen, withdrawn, and rebellious. Before long, Terri started experimenting with soft drugs. From that point on, Terri's problems snowballed.

Reacting to Terri's adolescent rebelliousness with great concern, Floyd Williamson attempted to intervene. When Terri's behavior became unmanageable, she was placed in a residential psychiatric facility and a series of group homes. None of the institutions had any impact on Terri's increasingly rebellious behavior. However, during her confinement at the residential psychiatric facility, Terri made the acquaintance of another patient. He was a cool, good-looking guy who was two years older than Terri. His name was Randall "Randy" Packer. As it turned out, Terri's chance encounter with Randy Packer would end up shaping the rest of her life.

Recognizing that the psychiatric facility and the group homes had done little to curb Terri's aberrant behavior, her father and stepmother looked for other alternatives. It would be wrong to condemn Terri's parents for doing what they thought was right at the time, but in attempting to help their daughter, the Williamsons made one of the worst decisions possible: They enrolled Terri in an aggressive, experimental, and unorthodox drug-treatment program called Straight, Incorporated.

Emphasizing physical punishment, rigid rules, and a cult-like adherence to the program's ideology, Straight served as an quasi-prison/indoctrination center for its teenage participants. Straight's enrollees, who were known as Straightlings, were removed from their parents' homes, taken out of school, placed with host families, deprived of contact with the outside world, and required to participate in grueling "therapy" sessions that lasted from ten to twelve hours each day. During the arduous therapy sessions, groups of thirty to fifty teens would gather in large auditoriums filled with stiff plastic chairs. Not only were Straightlings expected to divulge the most intimate details of their personal lives during group therapy sessions, they were also expected to conform to Straight's sadistic physical dictates. For example, during the long, tedious group therapy sessions, Straight's teenage participants were not allowed to sit back in their chairs. If a Straightling's back touched the chair, he or she would be singled out for punishment. This punishment, according to Terri and other Straight survivors, often turned physical.

Ironclad seating rules weren't the only unconventional aspect of Straight's regimen. Instead of hiring board-certified psychologists or trained mental-health professionals to conduct the group therapy sessions, Straight used teenagers from its own ranks to run the meetings. Straight's hierarchical model required its teenage participants to go through "phases" in order to progress in the program. Once a Straightling reached a certain phase, he or she would be asked to lead group meetings. This model resulted in fourteen, fifteen, and sixteen-year-old children meting out punishment against one another when Straight's inflexible rules weren't followed. The results were often brutal.

Straight's abusive tactics didn't end when the daily therapy sessions were finished. At night, Straight's participants were required to lodge with other group members who were further along in the program. When a Straightling in the lower phases of the program went "home" at night, he or she was locked inside a secured and alarmed bedroom until morning. The child received no reading materials and was physically barred from having any contact with the outside world. If the captive Straightling had to use the bathroom, he or she would be watched the entire time by a member of the host family. Privacy, personal dignity, and proper education were non-existent for the children of Straight.

Between 1976 and 1993, Straight operated "treatment" centers in nine states. Since the program was shuttered in the early '90s, many of Straight's former participants have gone public with their stories of abuse, neglect, and deprivation of rights. During the 1980s, however, Straight was touted by the Reagan Administration as a model of youth reform. First Lady Nancy Reagan was a particularly vociferous supporter of Straight. [12] According to the former first lady, Straight was an integral part of her "Just Say No" campaign, as well as the larger War on Drugs. Despite the Reagan Administration's unwavering support for Straight, strong evidence suggests that the program was little more than glorified, socially sanctioned abuse. Strong evidence also suggests that the program was highly lucrative for Straight's operators. [13] In the years since Straight went out of business, several of its former participants have reportedly committed suicide and many more have had ongoing psychological problems. [14] While a handful of former Straight participants have prevailed in lawsuits against the program's operators, a class action has never been pursued. Today, Straight's scarred participants are considered little more than collateral damage in the War on Drugs. According to many former Straightlings, the irony of their situation is egregious: Straight did far more damage to its participants than adolescent drug experimentation or youthful indiscretions ever could have.

When Floyd Williamson first learned about Straight in 1982, he was reluctant to enroll Terri in the program. Floyd Williamson recognized that Terri needed help, but he wasn't sure if Straight was the solution to her problems. For her part, Terri admits that she had issues as a young, rebellious, traumatized teenager.

"I was no angel and my father did what he thought was right to help me," Terri said. "But you have to understand that that program (Straight) destroyed my life. Everything changed for me after that."

In examining her adolescence today, there's little evidence that Terri's problems were substantially different from those faced by countless other teens throughout history. However, like many victims of physical and sexual abuse, Terri struggled throughout her teenage years. While Terri probably would've benefitted from talking to a trained, empathetic, and reputable therapist, her new stepmother pushed hard for Terri to enter Straight. Because Floyd Williamson's insurance through the school district paid for Terri's enrollment in the program, she was taken out of school and placed with a host family from Straight's Cincinnati chapter. Terri was thirteen years old at the time.

Terri's first day in Straight was a nightmare. Not long after she was locked into her first group therapy session, one of the female group leaders confronted Terri about her hair. The group leader, who was two years older than Terri, claimed that Terri's long bangs made her "too proud." Before Terri knew what was happening, the older girl had thrown her to the floor.

Moments later, several male Straightlings converged on Terri and pinned down her limbs. While Terri was immobilized on the floor, the female group leader grabbed a pair of scissors and cut Terri's bangs all the way down to her scalp. Terri's Straight experience just got worse from there.

As she slogged through the rigid and often violent world of Straight, Terri was forced to exercise to the point of collapse, physically attacked by group members, locked in a room at night with only a mattress on the floor, and prevented from using the bathroom without higher-ranking Straight participants or their parents watching her. Today, Terri says that one of the worst parts of Straight was seeing other kids being harmed by the program's group leaders. During the years she was in Straight, Terri says she saw countless children being beaten, bashed, spit on, and publicly humiliated during group therapy sessions. Over time, witnessing such events began to undermine Terri's belief in the goodness of other people.

Being young, impressionable, and highly vulnerable, Terri eventually adapted to Straight's sordid routine of multi-hour therapy sessions, host families, zero privacy, and constant threats of physical abuse. Though she always hated Straight and recognized that she and the other kids were being mistreated, some of Terri's experiences in Straight made the program seem legitimate. For example, Terri and her fellow Straightlings were sitting in a group therapy session one day when men in black suits began flooding into the secured Cincinnati auditorium where the meeting was being held. Some of the men wore earpieces with little wires curlicuing into their shirt collars. While the men spread out across the room, the Straightlings in Terri's group were told—in no uncertain terms—that they'd better not misbehave. Soon, First Lady Nancy Reagan breezed into the auditorium, flanked by a phalanx of Secret Service agents.

"The group totally changed when (Nancy Reagan) came in the room," Terri recalled. "Nobody acted like they usually did. When she was there, we had to act like everything was just totally normal."

Nancy Reagan's visit made Straight seem slightly more legitimate in Terri's thirteen-year-old eyes, but she still loathed the program. Every day was a living nightmare, and like her fellow Straightlings, Terri never knew when she might be physically attacked by group leaders or humiliated in front of her peers. Discipline in Straight was erratic, unpredictable, and inconsistent. During their daily group meetings, Straightlings were required to "motivate" if they wanted to speak. To motivate, a child would throw her or his arms in the air and flail them wildly for several seconds while remaining completely silent. Failure to motivate hard enough would be met with swift punishment. Straight's participants were often thrown to the floor and restrained by other kids in the program. Sources indicated that male Straightlings were often punched, kicked, or slapped while being pinned to the floor. According to Terri, female Straightlings were often groped, fingered, or otherwise sexually battered while being pinned to the floor. In an attempt to protect herself and make the best of her circumstances—circumstances over which she had absolutely no control—Terri conformed to Straight's dictates.

Eventually, Terri made it past First Phase and began working her way up the Straight hierarchy. Over the next three years—years when she was missing out on school, friends, and anything approaching a normal life—Terri worked her way to the level of group leader. While Terri enjoyed the limited freedom that came with being a group leader, she was unsettled by one key aspect of her new leadership role: per Straight's design, sadism was part and parcel of being a group leader. Straightlings were expected to confess their "drug sins" during group therapy meetings. If a Straightling wasn't confessing, it was the group leader's job to extract a confession by providing "the proper encouragement." From what Terri could tell, some group leaders enjoyed humiliating and terrorizing lower-level Straightlings, many of whom had done nothing more than smoke a couple of joints or drink a few beers before entering the program. Terri despised the sadistic expectations of her new leadership position, but lacking good options, she did what she had to do to survive.

As she moved up through the ranks of Straight, Terri was given more privileges and more personal latitude. After she was appointed group leader, Terri was given her own bedroom and allowed to use the bathroom without being watched. Terri was also given limited access to the outside world. By that point, according to Terri, Straight's administrators were convinced that her personal resolve had been worn down and that her brainwashing was complete. It was widely believed that a veteran group leader in Straight was incapable of exercising independent judgment.

One day Terri obtained some nail polish. Though body decorations were strictly *verboten* in Straight, Terri liked the way the nail polish accentuated her fingers. As a group leader, Terri believed that a minor violation of Straight's rigid protocols would be tolerated. Terri was wrong.

When Terri showed up to group therapy wearing nail polish, a hysterical coterie of her fellow Straightlings went ballistic. According to the true believers, Terri's minor breach of the prescribed decorum could only mean one thing: she was using drugs. Before long, as Straightlings crowded around Terri's colourful hand to gawk at her "druggy behavior," one histrionic girl accused Terri of having a "coke nail." Within seconds, Terri was bombarded with a torrent spurious accusations that she was on drugs. Considering that Terri had been given little access to the outside world over the previous couple of years, it was unclear how she would've obtained any drugs. Nevertheless, like their counterparts in seventeenth century Salem Village, the hysterical Straightlings didn't need evidence of guilt. Instead, unsubstantiated accusations of drug use were enough to inflame the passions of Straight's Kool-Aid drinkers. When the group started to get physical with Terri, she grew frightened. Although she was able to get out of that day's meeting without serious consequences, Terri feared what might happen if she stayed in the program. As a result, Terri made the decision to escape.

The previous year, a boy from Straight's Cincinnati chapter had been removed from the program by his parents and taken back to his home state of Michigan. Because Terri had always liked the boy, she decided to seek him out after her escape.

Late one night, Terri slipped out of her host family's

house, obtained a car, fled Cincinnati, and made her way to Michigan. After tracking down her friend, Terri and the boy began drifting. It didn't take long before the teenage duo ran out of options. A couple of weeks after Terri and the boy went on the lam, their car got stuck in the snow in Marion, Ohio. Broke and out of options, Terri called her father. Floyd Williamson picked Terri up in Marion and took her back to his house. However, he didn't allow her to stay there for long. Terri was scared of being returned to Straight, but despite her protests, her father and stepmother opted to re-enroll her in the program.

Instead of being returned to Straight's Cincinnati chapter, Terri was shipped to Florida, where she was placed in Straight's St. Petersburg chapter. Terri's situation in Florida was even worse than it had been in Cincinnati. Terri was constantly afraid of being attacked physically by other group members and the conditions in her host family's home were revolting.

"That place was absolutely disgusting!" Terri remembered. "There was just dirt and filth everywhere in that house, clothes all piled up. And they had the biggest cockroaches I've ever seen. As soon as I'd been there two days, I knew I had to get out of there."

Terrified that she would endure further abuse in Straight and nauseated by her living conditions with the host family, it didn't take long for Terri to hatch her next escape.

"One night I went out a window," Terri described. "So when I was running down the street, one of the people (from the host family) saw me and tried to chase me down. Right about that time, I saw a cop and started screaming for him to help me. The cop looked over and saw me and I told him that the people in the house were abusing me and that I was from Ohio and that I needed help."

Recognizing Terri's fear, the St. Petersburg police officer refused to return her to the Straight host family. Instead, Terri was taken to a homeless shelter for teenagers and assigned a bed.

Compared to the twisted, violent, and unpredictable world of Straight, the St. Petersburg homeless shelter was a welcome relief for Terri. She spent several days in the shelter before calling her mother and asking if she could return home. After receiving the call, Terri's mother immediately flew to Florida, picked up her daughter, and returned her to Ohio.

Terri was profoundly traumatized by the things she'd seen and experienced in Straight. Although she would never be returned to the program, Terri continued to fear that she would be snatched from her bed while she was sleeping, dragged out of her mother's house, and placed with another host family. Even decades later, Terri continues to be tormented by her experiences in Straight.

"Straight put me on a totally different path in life," Terri explained. "It totally numbed me. Other things I saw later in life didn't seem as bad because of what I'd experienced in that program."

Though she was out of Straight, Terri was horribly distraught at her mother's home. Every day, Terri worried that Straight's administrators would find her and force her back into the program. Eventually, Terri moved into her father's house and took a job as a nurse's assistant at a convalescent home.

Despite her new job and her stable living situation, Terri continued to fear that she would be placed back in Straight. If she was returned to the program, Terri knew that she would be demoted to First Phase—the most physically brutal and psychologically demeaning phase of the program. Terri didn't feel comfortable in her own skin; she was incapable of relaxing. Terri was sixteen years old and desperate.

Terri loved her father, but she also recognized that he was the one who'd placed her in Straight. Terri longed to get out of her father's house and achieve some peace of mind. As Terri brainstormed ways to protect herself from the threat of Straight, her thoughts drifted back to Randy Packer, the good-looking young man she'd met three years earlier in the residential psychiatric hospital. Terri knew that Randy Packer had mental-health issues, but by that point in her young life, the abnormal had become normal for Terri Williamson. After experiencing the depredations of Straight for three years, it was easy for Terri to look past Randy's idiosyncrasies. Terri was constantly anxious about returning to Straight. With her anxiety reaching a fever pitch, Terri contacted Randy Packer and they made plans to meet.

It didn't take long for Terri's relationship with Randy to become extremely intense. In a desperate bid to escape her Straight-related anxiety, Terri hatched a plan: She would marry Randy Packer, emancipate herself from her parents, and attempt to restart her life.

When Terri floated the idea to Randy, he was on board with it. On June 26, 1986, just five weeks after her seventeenth birthday, Terri wed Randy Packer.

Today, when she describes the early years of her relationship with Randy, Terri doesn't mince words.

"He was really nice at first, but it didn't last," she said. "I was married with bruises on my wrists."

Having missed out on high school because of her involvement in Straight, Terri was lacking in both basic educational skills and basic life skills.

"I never learned how to cook, I never learned how to do anything," Terri lamented. "When I moved in with Randy, the first time I tried cook at our apartment, I started this huge grease fire while I was trying to make French fries. I'd missed out on so much that I really didn't know how to do any of the normal things you need to know to survive."

Terri's problems ran much deeper than troubles in the kitchen. Not long after they exchanged their wedding vows, Randy's mental illness became more acute. According to Terri, as Randy's psychological condition deteriorated, he became increasingly abusive to her. Through it all, though, Terri stayed with Randy. She was a helpless and desperate teenager, and she knew that her marriage to Randy—no matter how bad it became—would shield her from the horrors of Straight.

In early 1987, Terri learned that she was pregnant. However, news that his young wife was expecting did little to diminish Randy's volatility. According to Terri, Randy continued to beat her while she was pregnant. Fortunately, the beatings didn't have an adverse impact on Terri's delivery. On August 11, 1987, Terri gave birth to a healthy baby girl, whom she named Shauna.

Despite having a new baby at home, Straight never strayed far from Terri's mind. Day and night, Terri worried that Straight administrators would kidnap her, place her with another host family, and make her restart the program in First Phase. The thought of returning to Straight was bad enough, but the thought of being separated from Shauna was absolutely unbearable for Terri.

The more she thought about it, the more Terri realized that she wanted— *needed*—to get out of Ohio. The streets of Cincinnati were a constant reminder of the abuses she'd suffered in Straight and Terri longed to get as far away from her hometown as possible. Randy was also up for a change of scenery, so in late December 1987, they bundled up Shauna, cranked up their 1974 Chevy Impala, and hightailed it out of Ohio. Their destination: California.

Two weeks later, Terri and Randy rolled into Ventura with an empty gas tank, a blown muffler, a hungry baby, and $1.50 in their pockets. The fact that the Packers ended up in Ventura was pure chance.

"We didn't really know where we were going when we came out here," Terri explained. "Ventura is just where our car broke down."

The day they arrived in Ventura, the Packers drove through the downtown area en route to the beach. As Terri piloted the aging Impala along Poli Street, a police car appeared in her rearview mirror. It didn't take long for the blue lights to start flashing.

Terri cranked the steering wheel toward the sidewalk and the Impala limped to the curb. Terri had no idea why they were being stopped. Because the Impala was in such abysmal mechanical condition, Terri knew that she hadn't been speeding. Once the officer arrived at Terri's window, he quickly explained why he'd pulled her over: the shotgun mounted in the Impala's back window.

Terri told the officer that, in Ohio, it was legal to carry rifles and shotguns in the back windows of cars. Probably recognizing that the young family was from out of state and in a bad situation, the officer decided not to press the issue. He told Terri and Randy to secure the shotgun in the trunk, gave them a warning, and went about his business.

While they were stowing their shotgun in the Impala's trunk, Terri and Randy were approached by two good samaritans from the Church of the Foothills. Sensing the young couple's desperate circumstances and asking nothing in return, the church members took Terri, Randy, and Shauna to the homeless shelter operated by their ministry. Terri and Randy spent the next few weeks exchanging menial labor at the church for room and board. Soon thereafter, the church found cleaning jobs for the Packers, as well as a small trailer where they could live. By the end of 1988, Terri and Randy had amassed enough money to move out of the trailer and rent a small apartment on Kalorama Street near downtown Ventura.

Around that time, the *Ventura County Star-Free Press* ran an article on Terri, Randy, and Shauna. The article focused on the good work of the Church of the Foothills rescue mission and how it had helped the young homeless family from Ohio. In the article, the Packers were referred to as the "Wolfe" family.

"We had warrants out at the time, so we couldn't use our real last name," Terri explained when asked about the family's fictitious name in the article.

When asked for more details about the warrants, Terri elaborated.

"It was nothing really serious," Terri said. "I think the warrants were for forged money orders, something like that."

A year and a half after the Packers arrived in Ventura, Terri became pregnant again. By then, Terri,

Randy, and Shauna were living in a rented house on McFarlane Street. Though the Packer family was still intact, their household was anything but stable.

"Randy was very abusive to me," Terri said of that time period. "He was diagnosed as a paranoid schizophrenic with multiple personality disorder. They don't give that diagnosis anymore, but that's basically what they said about him at the time. We just...it was bad."

The Packers' problems went well beyond mental illness and domestic violence. The Packers were also in dire financial straits and unable to provide for their basic needs.

"The day I went into labor with Josh, our electricity got cut off," Terri recalled. "So while I was in labor, before I went to the hospital, I wanted to make sure there'd be electricity when I got home. So I went in the backyard and pried the cover off the electric box and started pulling those little plastic covers off the power switches so I could turn on the electricity. So while I'm pulling them off, I get zapped big time—I mean I really got shocked."

Despite the electric shock, Terri's delivery was not marred by any major complications. On September 21, 1989, Joshua Graham Packer was born at Ventura County Medical Center.

According to Terri, the year after Josh's birth was a living hell. As Randy descended further and further into mental illness, his behavior became increasingly abusive. Eventually, in an attempt to escape Randy's unpredictable wrath, Terri began spending time with one of their McFarlane Street neighbors. The neighbor's name was Barry Rossman.

Rossman was the department manager of a local

thrift store that benefitted battered women. According to Terri, when she first met Rossman, he was a stable, emotionally balanced presence in her life. Although their friendship started out as platonic, Terri's relationship with Rossman soon turned romantic. In early 1990, Terri left Randy and moved to Casitas Springs with Rossman and the children.

Situated along the winding mountain highway between Ventura and Ojai, Casitas Springs is a small town that was even smaller when Terri, Rossman, Shauna, and Josh lived there. Though their home was far from a Rockwell masterpiece, Terri remembers her life in Casitas Springs as far more stable than her life with Randy. Unfortunately, the stability wouldn't last.

On February 20, 1990, Randy showed up at the Casitas Springs house where Terri lived with Rossman and the kids. By that point, Randy was living in Oak View, another small town between Ventura and Ojai. Randy had gotten wind of the fact that Terri—who was still his legal wife—was involved in a romantic relationship with Barry Rossman. When Randy showed up on their doorstep on that fateful February afternoon, it didn't take long for the situation to descend into total chaos.

Storming into Terri's house and confronting her about her relationship with Rossman, Randy was loud, irate, and ready for battle. As the shouting and screaming escalated, Randy grabbed a baseball bat that Terri kept hidden behind her front door. Stomping around the main room and shouting at the top of his lungs, Randy swung the bat wildly. Terri sensed that something bad was about to happen, so she attempted to push Randy out the front door. Randy refused to leave at first, but after several minutes of profanity-laced shouting, he finally walked out the front door and into the parking lot beside Terri's house. Josh was still an infant at the time, but at age two, Shauna was old enough to toddle after her daddy. As Randy stormed into the parking lot, still wielding the baseball bat, Shauna ran after him. According to Terri, as Shauna approached her father from behind, Randy pivoted around, wrenched back his shoulders, and swung the bat as hard as he could. The baseball bat missed Shauna's tiny head by inches.

According to Terri, she'd endured a lot of abuse at Randy's hands by that point. However, when she saw Randy swing the baseball bat at Shauna's head, Terri couldn't take it anymore. Enraged, Terri broke into a full sprint, rushed Randy, and plowed into him at maximum speed. What ensued after their collision was a grunting, bare-knuckled, no-holds-barred brawl in the parking lot beside Terri's house. The violent spectacle attracted significant attention from neighbors.

With two-year-old Shauna and five-month-old Josh inside the house with Rossman, Terri and Randy clawed and screamed and spit and pounded on one another as slack-jawed neighbors looked on in disbelief. Soon, both Terri and Randy were bloodied, bashed, and soaked in sweat, with Terri taking the brunt of the physical punishment. Though she suffered a severe beating that afternoon, Terri feared for the safety of her children and was determined to keep Randy out of her house. Eventually, as Terri and Randy grappled with each other on the ground, Terri was able to wrestle the baseball bat away from her estranged husband and get to her feet. As soon as Randy realized that his wife was armed, he sprang from the ground and sprinted across the parking lot at full tilt as Terri chased after him, baseball bat in hand. With nowhere else to hide, Randy dove into his car and locked the doors. By that point, Terri was beyond furious. Incensed by the beating she'd just suffered—as well as all the other beatings she'd endured at Randy's hands—Terri's rage was like a locomotive barreling down the tracks. As Randy cowered inside his vehicle, shrieking and begging for mercy, Terri was just getting warmed up.

Using the baseball bat as a demolition device, Terri began smashing in the windows of Randy's car and cursing him with every breath. By that point, neighbors had already called 911.

When deputies arrived on scene, Terri was arrested for vandalism and Randy was arrested for battery. Shauna and Josh were left in Barry Rossman's care while their parents were transported to jail. After that, Randy's contact with Terri and the children began to evaporate.

In the months after the parking-lot brawl, Randy continued to live in Oak View, where he found work at Scrubby's Car Wash. However, Randy didn't stay local for long. By the time Terri formally filed for divorce on March 3, 1993, Randy had moved out of Ventura County and was living in Bakersfield. Soon thereafter, Randy severed all contact with his children and returned to Cincinnati.

With two small children, few job skills, and limited education, Terri was barely able to survive. In the divorce paperwork she filed with the court, Terri described her situation in stark, succinct language.

Community property: none.
Obligations: none.
Assets: none.

In her Income and Expense Declaration, which was filed on December 29, 1993, Terri wrote, "...I have not received any child support for the duration of our separation..." [15] This was particularly problematic because, at the time, Terri's relationship with Barry Rossman had grown unstable. Terri and the kids bounced from house to house as she found new friends and new boyfriends with whom she could live. If it hadn't been for the $607 a month Terri was receiving from Aid to Families with Dependent Children, she and the kids would've been living on the streets.

In time, after briefly living with an evangelical Christian zealot who tried to drown Shauna in the bathtub, Terri got back together with Rossman. By that point, Terri's divorce from Randy had been finalized. Strictly as a formality, the judge awarded Terri full custody of the children and signed the dissolution of marriage order on July 22, 1994. Two months later, Josh Packer turned five years old.

By the time her divorce from Randy had been finalized, Terri's life was regaining some much-needed equilibrium. She and the children were living with Rossman in a rented house on Olive Street in Ventura, she'd landed a job at one of the county-run homeless shelters, and she was volunteering at Josh and Shauna's school. In addition, Terri had purchased a classic 1968 Pontiac Ventura, which was "...stock green and ran great." For the first time in many years, things seemed to be going well for Terri.

Then, in late 1994, Terri's relationship with Rossman started to unravel. According to Terri, it all started when Rossman lost his job as department manager at the thrift store. In a case filled with bizarre events and surreal asides, the circumstances surrounding Rossman's termination from the thrift store—as described by Terri—are a blunt reminder that facts are truly stranger than fiction.

One day, while managing the thrift store, Rossman was approached by an aspiring adult filmmaker. The filmmaker told Rossman that he was interested in using the thrift store as the set of his next pornographic masterpiece. Evidently, the filmmaker believed that a backdrop of used clothing racks and aging furniture would whet the erotic appetites of viewers. Sensing an opportunity to make some fast cash, Rossman reportedly jumped at the filmmaker's offer. Rossman even agreed to let the producer put his name in the thank-you credits at the end of the picture. As a result, on the appointed day, the actors appeared at the thrift store and disrobed. Surrounded by racks of discarded clothing, age-spotted lamp shades, and Eisenhower-era appliances, the thespians reveled in their sensual glory as cameras rolled.

There was only one problem: Rossman didn't own the thrift store. Consequently, when the actual owners learned that their shop had been used as a porno set, Rossman was promptly sacked from his job.

At the time, Terri, Rossman, Shauna, and Josh were living a couple blocks off an industrial strip on the west side of Ventura. The industrial strip is known formally as Ventura Avenue, but most locals refer to it simply as "The Avenue." Lined with auto-body shops, liquor stores, and low-income apartment buildings, Ventura Avenue has been partially gentrified in recent years. However, when Terri and the kids lived there in the mid-'90s, the neighborhoods around The Avenue were mostly rundown barrios that attracted all manner of disreputable characters. After Rossman lost his job at the thrift store, these characters began to play a larger role in Terri's life.

By late 1994, Terri's relationship with Rossman was crumbling quickly. When Terri and Rossman finally broke up, Terri took the kids and moved into a motel with a man named Jimmy*. As it turned out, Jimmy was a hardened criminal who had once led authorities on a high-speed chase all the way from Ventura to Los Angeles. Jimmy's rampage was finally brought to an end when his car ran out of fuel and he attempted to escape from police on foot. As he sprinted away from his disabled vehicle, officers sicced a K-9 on Jimmy, who was taken to the ground in a frenzied flash of snapping teeth, clenched jaws, and lukewarm German shepherd saliva.

By the time Terri and the kids moved in with Jimmy in late 1994, the cumulative dysfunction in Terri's life was reaching critical mass. Between Straight's brainwashing, Randy's brutality, and Rossman's boorishness, Terri explained that she'd been through hell and was desperate for an escape. When Terri communicated this to Jimmy, her new paramour claimed to have just the cure she needed. One night, while they were sitting around their motel room with the kids, Terri allowed Jimmy to inject her with crystal meth. As the speed flowed into her mainline, Terri's brain ignited and her life underwent a powerful, instantaneous change.

"I'd *never* felt anything like that before," Terri remembered. "The rush, it was just...it was like nothing I'd ever experienced. I locked the kids in the kitchen and we just had sex for days."

When Shauna and Josh got hungry, they began to cry out for Terri to feed them.

"The kids were hungry and I didn't even do anything for them," Terri recalled with unmistakable sadness creeping into her voice. "I figured that if I wasn't hungry, they weren't hungry. You know, we'd get high and I'd just stay up for days and I got really, really skinny. I never even thought that (Shauna and Josh) might be hungry."

Eventually, Shauna and Josh began looking elsewhere to have their basic needs satisfied. In particular, they were fond of an old woman who lived in a nearby home. Whenever Shauna and Josh would go to the old woman's house, she would feed them, play with them, and generally look after them. Terri was vaguely aware of the old woman at the time. In those days, however, Terri's first priority was crank. As a result, Terri didn't think much about Shauna and Josh when they were out of sight.

Tragically, the old woman's house was anything but a safe haven for Shauna and Josh. The old woman was being cared for by her adult son, who was in his sixties at the time. According to Terri, the son ended up sexually assaulting five-year-old Josh during one of his visits to the old woman's house. Though no arrests were made and Josh was never given any treatment for his abuse, it was becoming apparent to members of the greater Ventura community that Shauna and Josh were living in an unsafe environment. In early 1995, as Terri's life spiraled dangerously out of control, Shauna and Josh were removed from her custody by Child Protective Services and placed in a residential facility for abused and neglected children. The facility was called Casa Pacifica.

Once the Packer children arrived at Casa Pacifica, their basic needs were met and they were cared for by responsible adults. However, the bond the children—and particularly Josh—shared with Terri was unbreakable.

A couple of weeks later, Shauna and Josh were taken out of Casa Pacifica and placed in the custody of Barry Rossman. By that point, Terri was completely consumed by her drug addiction. Homeless and hooked, Terri was living in the river bottoms near the mouth of the Santa Clara River.

Terri's life was an unmitigated disaster zone in early 1995. She'd lost custody of her children, she'd severed contact with her family in Ohio, she was addicted to methamphetamine, she was homeless, and she was consorting with a wide array of degenerates. When asked whether her experiences in Straight had an impact on her thinking and judgment during that time period, Terri didn't hesitate with her answer.

"What I went through in Straight had a huge impact on my thinking!" she declared. "Straight affected everything in my life! I didn't know what it meant to be normal after Straight! I had no family, no support, no childhood. All I knew was my experience getting mistreated in that program."

Just thinking about Straight made Terri furious. As she talked about the toll Straight had taken on her life and her parenting skills, Terri seethed with anger.

Finally, Terri took several deep breaths and calmed down.

"I've made a lot of bad decisions as a parent," she said in a calm, despondent voice. "I've made a lot of really bad decisions and I'm not trying to make excuses for myself. But the thing is, back then, I'd never been in a place were I could learn to make good decisions. What that must've been like for Joshua and Shauna—I don't even know."

Once Shauna and Josh were removed from Terri's custody by Child Protective Services, she didn't see them for more than two months. After that, Terri would occasionally stop by Rossman's house to briefly visit with the kids before drifting away to rejoin her drug cohort. Unfortunately, Terri's visitations in those days were anything but heartwarming.

"When I'd stop by to see the kids, I'd take them out and teach them how to steal," Terri admitted. "Now, looking back, I can't believe what I did, but I'd take Josh to the laundromat and we'd steal socks out of the dryers. Or I'd take him over to Vons (supermarket) and we'd steal penny candy from the display, then run back to the bathrooms and eat it before we got caught."

As she explained this, Terri's voice became softer and softer. After she was finished, Terri got very quiet. When she spoke again, her voice sounded broken.

"When I look back on all that now, it's like I'm looking at a different person," Terri said with tears in her voice. "I just really failed Josh and Shauna."

By her own admission, Terri was far from a perfect parent. She abandoned her children, she taught them to steal, and she exposed them to hardened criminals. However, according to Terri, Shauna and Josh faced other types of negligence in Barry Rossman's care.

Between 1995 and 1998, as Terri ran with her rough crowd and breezed through Ventura periodically to see her children, Josh suffered two significant injuries while in Rossman's custody.

The first injury occurred when Josh was six years old. At the time, Rossman lived in a converted garage with a concrete floor. Josh's sleeping area was in a second-floor loft above the garage floor. There was no railing around the loft. One night, while he sleeping on the floor of the loft, Josh began tossing and turning. Eventually, Josh rolled to the edge of the loft, tumbled over the side, and fell more than fifteen feet to the floor below. Josh smashed into the unyielding concrete headfirst. The impact split his skull open and left him wailing on the floor.

Instead of calling for an ambulance, Rossman hurried Josh to his car and drove him to the emergency room. When they arrived, Josh was treated for a major head injury and a serious concussion. Before Josh left the hospital, one of the physicians told Rossman that Josh needed to return for follow-up care. It was the doctor's opinion that, as a result of the fall, Josh might have suffered major neurological trauma. As the doctor reportedly explained to Rossman, Josh's condition needed to be monitored carefully. According to Terri, Rossman never took Josh back to the hospital for any follow-up care.

It didn't take long before Josh suffered another catastrophic injury while in Rossman's custody. In 1997, when Josh was eight years old, Rossman took him to a yard sale. As it happened, the yard sale was being held at a clubhouse for the local chapter of the Hell's Angels. Unsupervised and on his own, Josh wandered away from the yard sale and made his way into a garage at the back of the property. While he was playing near a tall, adult-sized table, Josh accidentally dislodged a large anvil. Before Josh knew what was happening, the anvil was plummeting to the floor. Josh attempted to grab the anvil, but he wasn't strong enough to hold it. When the falling anvil finally smashed into the concrete, it severed the tips on two of Josh's fingers.

For the second time in two years, Rossman rushed the screaming boy to the emergency room, where a trauma team was unable to reattach Josh's fingertips.

Despite the serious injuries Josh suffered in Rossman's care, it would be unfair to heap too much blame on Rossman. By her own admission, Terri abandoned her children in the mid-1990s so she could indulge her drug habit. When Terri made this choice, Barry Rossman stepped up to the plate and assumed responsibility for two children who were not his biological offspring. Although his track record as a guardian was less than perfect, Rossman deserves some credit for attempting—however ineptly—to fill the parental void in Shauna and Josh's lives.

By the time Josh's fingers were severed, Terri was living away from her children most of the time and running with a very dangerous crowd. An article that appeared in the *Los Angeles Times* on July 20, 1998, reveals just how far Terri had fallen in the years after her divorce from Randy. According to the article, Terri and three of her friends were wanted for multiple crimes across Ventura County. Terri was wanted for drug possession and theft, while her acquaintances were wanted for crimes ranging from sexual assault to drug trafficking to armed robbery. [16]

In late 1998, Terri finally hit rock bottom. Realizing

that she needed to change her life, Terri broke away from her criminal associates, stopped using drugs, and returned to her children in Ventura. Terri's decision to give up her criminal lifestyle was based on a very pragmatic rationale.

"One night, while I was sitting in the living room of this house where I was staying, I saw somebody get murdered," Terri explained. "It really shook me up, you know—seeing this person get killed right in front of me. After that, I just decided I'd had enough."

Although she'd extricated herself from her criminal lifestyle and returned to her children, Terri found herself overwhelmed by the circumstances of her new existence. Between the challenges of her recovery and the needs of her kids, Terri was at her wit's end in early 1999. As a result, when a well-spoken man approached Terri and said that he wanted to serve as Josh's mentor, Terri was eager to take the man up on his offer.

The man's name was Robert Miller*. A college-educated youth counselor, Miller met ten-year-old Josh at the Ventura Boys and Girls Club, where Josh was participating in programs at the time. Terri was ecstatic that a caring, upstanding member of the community had taken an interest in her son. She was in desperate need of help, and Miller's offer seemed like a godsend. Before long, Josh was spending lots of time with his new mentor, whom he called "Uncle Bob."

Around the same time, Josh started to experience major problems at school. While Josh's kindergarten-through-third-grade years had been free of major disciplinary issues, everything started to fall apart in fourth grade. According to records maintained by the

Ventura Unified School District, Josh was involved in at least five fights during fourth grade. The last fight resulted in a one-day suspension for Josh. It would not be his last.

CHAPTER 10

By the time Terri stopped using drugs and associating with criminals, her life had been out of control for three years. Although she worked hard to become a better mother for Shauna and Josh, a significant amount of damage had already been done. By that point in his young life, Josh had witnessed countless incidents of domestic violence, experienced molestation at the hands of at least two men, learned how to steal under his mother's tutelage, suffered a major head injury after falling from an unrailed sleeping loft, and watched as two of his fingers were severed by a falling anvil. As Josh's school records indicate, his aberrant childhood had a devastating impact on his behavior in the classroom.

On January 28, 2000, during his fifth-grade year at E.P. Foster Elementary School, Josh began brawling in the classroom with two other children. Fighting among school-age kids is far from unusual, but Josh exhibited signs of rage that are rare even among hardened adults. At one point during the fight, as one of his classmates flailed at him, Josh seized a pencil off his desk and stabbed the other child in the neck. When the stabbing victim attempted to retreat, Josh pounced on the boy's back and continued jabbing him in the neck with his pencil. Another child tried to intervene in the violent attack by knocking the pencil out of Josh's hand and attempting to subdue him. Instead of calming down, Josh placed the second child in a headlock, grabbed his pencil, and tried to stab the peacekeeper in the stomach. [17] Eventually, the melee ended when Josh was retrained by a school administrator. Ventura Unified School District records don't list the extent of the students' injuries, but the records do make clear that Josh was given a lengthy suspension for the incident.

If administrators at E.P. Foster Elementary School believed that a couple of suspensions would chasten Josh, they were sorely mistaken. Josh was being raised in a home where problems were solved with anger and violence, not calm, dispassionate reflections on cause and effect. More importantly, as Terri readily acknowledges, she contributed to Josh's aggression.

"We lived in a neighborhood where Josh was one of the only white kids and he took a lot of shit for it," Terri said. "I told Josh to handle his business in the neighborhood if people were messing with him."

Evidently, as a traumatized fifth grader who'd been raised around violence and crime for most of his life, Josh missed the implicit subtext of Terri's message: Handle your business *in self-defense.*

When asked if Josh might've had difficulty distinguishing between self-defense in the neighborhood and wanton aggression at school, Terri thought for a second, then said "I don't know." A moment later, she attempted to clarify her answer with a story.

"One day Josh went down to the local skatepark and a bunch of kids started giving him a hard time. They were hassling him and throwing things at him, so Josh left and when he got home he told me about it. I put him in the car and we drove around until we found the kids. I got out of the car and confronted them and told Joshua to get out of the car too. He didn't want to get out, but I made him. I asked him which kid had been picking on him. The whole group was made up of kids of all ages—kids whose ages really didn't even belong together. Josh pointed to one of the kids and I told (the kid) that he and my son were going to fight. That other kid looked at me like I was crazy and Josh said, 'Come on Mom, let's go,' but I said 'No!' You know, Joshua seemed kind of embarrassed by the whole thing but I wanted them to have a fair fight, so I went around to the back of my car and got this big rubber stick out of the back. That stick could've seriously hurt somebody, but I wanted to make sure I could keep the fight fair. I told the kid that if he wanted to fight my son, he better do it right there, but this little kid and the group just walked away, so Josh got back in the car and we left."

Bullying, molestation, and violent experiences with other children weren't the only disturbing episodes Josh endured during his pre-adolescent years.

In 2000, when Josh was eleven years old, he was living with Terri, Shauna, and Rossman in a rented house on Cedar Street in Ventura. One night, Terri and Rossman were awakened after midnight by blood-curdling screams coming from Josh's bedroom. Leaping from bed and running to check on Josh, Terri heard the front door of their house slamming shut. When she entered Josh's bedroom and turned on the light, Terri saw Josh sitting in bed crying. Terri could tell that Josh's eye was red and badly swollen. Josh explained that, as he was sleeping, a man had climbed through his window, dropped down onto his bed, and smashed him in the eye. Terri immediately called the police.

When officers arrived, they found foot impressions outside Josh's bedroom window. After discovering the foot impressions, the officers told Terri that they'd received reports about a prowler in the neighborhood. Despite a search of nearby yards, officers were unable to locate the suspect who had attacked Josh.

A few nights later, less than two blocks from Terri's house on Cedar Street, the Ventura Police Department arrested a prowler as he attempted to break into a bedroom occupied by two little girls. Although the prowler was in custody, Josh continued to fear for his safety at night. Eventually, Rossman's landlord agreed to install bars on Josh's bedroom window. After the bars were installed, the entire matter was dropped, and for all intents and purposes, the attack on Josh was forgotten.

Speaking of the incident years later, Terri was horrified that she hadn't done more to address Josh's psychological needs in the wake of the bedroom attack.

"We should've sought treatment," Terri said. "We should've sought treatment for a lot of things, but we never did."

Such was the darkly surreal and pitifully negligent world of Josh's childhood.

Within days of entering sixth grade at De Anza Middle School, Josh was already in trouble. Some of his behavioral problems were standard fare for middle-school kids. He received behavioral citations for jumping around when he was supposed to be standing in line, failing to cooperate in class, and acting disrespectfully toward his teachers. After each of these incidents, Josh was counseled by one of De Anza's assistant principals. However, not all of Josh's behavioral problems were so innocuous.

On September 5, 2000, just days after starting middle school, Josh was suspended for punching another child during nutrition. The suspension had no impact on Josh's behavior. After he returned to class, Josh regularly ended up in the assistant principal's office for rudeness, failing to follow directions, and cursing out his teachers. Despite all of this, it wasn't until February 9, 2001, that Josh was given another out-of-school suspension. Once again, the suspension was precipitated by a fight in the classroom.

According to school district records, Josh was exhibiting highly aberrant behavior for an eleven-year-old child. During the first six months of the 2000-01 school year, Josh received no less than fifteen referrals to the office. These referrals, coupled with Josh's resistance to normal discipline, should've signaled two things: 1) Josh was a child with serious problems and 2) Josh was desperately in need of psychological intervention. Nevertheless, there's no indication that school administrators attempted to provide Josh with any sort of psychological help. Instead, the records indicate that De Anza officials utilized one of two strategies when Josh got in trouble: he would be counseled by an assistant principal or he would be suspended.

Neither strategy was effective.

Josh's behavioral problems intensified.

Officials with the Ventura Unified School District did not return phone calls seeking comment for this book.

Josh started seventh grade at De Anza Middle School in the fall of 2001. Right from the start, he was back in trouble. After being sent to the office for disrupting class and acting disrespectfully to teachers, Josh was given more "counseling" by the assistant principal. Days later, Josh injured a female classmate when he flicked her with a keychain. Yet again, Josh was suspended from school.

As always, the suspension changed nothing and Josh's seventh-grade year morphed into a case study in adolescent dysfunction. Fighting, office referrals, in-school suspensions, and problems with teachers were the norm for Josh during the first half of the year. When the second semester started, Josh's behavior took an even darker turn.

On February 27, 2002, Josh began harassing two of his female classmates. At first the girls played along with Josh's cajoling, but they soon became alarmed by his aggression. Josh teased and taunted the girls until they were good and worked up. Then, according to school district records, Josh reached out and pulled down one girl's shirt. [18] The girl wrenched away from Josh and promptly reported the incident. Relying on their usual strategy of suspend-and-attempt-to-forget, De Anza's administrators gave Josh a five-day vacation. There's no indication that school administrators sought any sort of psychological help for the clearly troubled boy.

Immediately after returning to school on March 3, 2002, Josh was sent to the assistant principal's office for running around the classroom and calling one of his female classmates a "bitch." There's no indication that school administrators sought any sort of psychological help for the clearly troubled boy.

The following month, on April 25, 2002, Josh was suspended from De Anza for spitting on two girls. [19] There's no indication that school administrators sought any sort of psychological help for the clearly troubled boy.

On Terri's thirty-third birthday—May 16, 2002— Josh was again suspended from De Anza for fighting. There's no indication that school administrators sought any sort of psychological help for the clearly troubled boy.

Problems with authority, sexually charged encounters with girls, and violent outbursts were the defining features of Josh's career at De Anza Middle School. The combination of unquenchable hostility, resistance to normal discipline, sexual misconduct, and violence should've been major red flags for school administrators. Still, as Josh's seventh-grade year dragged on and the suspensions piled up, there's no indication that school administrators sought any psychological help for the clearly troubled boy, whose personal demons were metastasizing by the day.

School officials weren't the only ones who were failing to help Josh during his middle-school years. Around this time, Josh was spending more and more time with his mentor, Robert "Uncle Bob" Miller. Based on Josh's school record, it's clear that Miller's mentoring had a less-than-stellar impact on Josh's life.

A clue to Josh's growing instability might have manifested on May 24, 2002, during the closing days of his seventh-grade year. Only a week after Josh was suspended for spitting on the two girls, he once again found himself in the assistant principal's office. This time he was accused of bullying a classmate. Josh was suspended for the bullying incident, but the suspension itself isn't all that significant. Instead, the incident is noteworthy because of Josh's choice of words to the bullying victim. According to Josh's permanent record, Josh repeatedly called the boy "gay" during his verbal tirade. [20] Such taunts are not uncommon among middle-school students. However, if a perceptive administrator had delved deeper into Josh's choice of epithet, it's possible that Josh's sexual abuse might've been uncovered. If this had occurred, psychological intervention could've been obtained and the underlying causes of Josh's bad behavior could've been addressed. Tragically, this opportunity was missed. De Anza's assistant principal simply rubber-stamped a suspension and sent Josh home to skateboard for a few days. When the suspension had run its course, Josh was allowed to return to school to finish out the year.

If De Anza's administrators thought that one more suspension was going to improve Josh Packer's behavior, they were dead wrong. After returning to class from the bullying suspension, Josh began peppering his female classmates with such endearing lines as "Are you a dyke?" and "Do you lick my butt?" [21] These queries earned Josh a two-day suspension. The day he returned to class—June 4, 2002—Josh marched up to one of his classmates and slugged him in the face. [22] The resulting suspension rounded out Josh's seventh-grade year.

———————————

Things only went downhill for Josh during the first half of eighth grade. Some of his classroom antics, such as making cat sounds and talking out of turn, were normal enough for a middle-school student. However, some of Josh's other behaviors were indicative of much deeper problems. Not only was Josh regularly involved in violent outbursts, he was showing a greater aptitude for planning his attacks on classmates and demonstrating a growing indifference to consequences.

One day, at the start of his eighth-grade year, one of Josh's classmates showed up in De Anza's main office seeking help. The boy claimed that Josh was bullying him. In describing his torment to school officials, the boy stated that he was scared and wanted Josh's harassment to end. It's not clear how, but Josh got wind of the boy's trip to the office.

Exhibiting great cunning, Josh approached his teacher and explained that he needed to go to the office. Not suspecting that anything was amiss, the teacher gave Josh an office pass.

According to Ventura Unified School District records, the boy who'd sought help was sitting near the assistant principal's office when Josh entered the main office. The boy watched in horror as Josh marched past the adults in the room and quietly confronted him for squealing. All of this was done subtly and surreptitiously, so that Josh's continued bullying wouldn't noticed by the adults in the room. Eventually, someone got wise to the fact that a student was being terrorized in the middle of De Anza's main office. [23] Josh was whisked into the assistant principal's office for more counseling. The results were predictable.

Two days later, after the dismissal bell brought the school day to a close, Josh cornered the boy he'd terrorized in the office and challenged him to a fight. Before the boy had time to blink, Josh smashed him in the eye. Josh was given a three-day suspension. A few days after he got back to school, Josh punched a female student. That attack earned him a five-day suspension. [24]

Something had to give and De Anza's administrators knew it. Every day seemed to bring another office referral and every week seemed to bring another violent outburst from Josh. In an attempt to get Josh under control (or at least pass the buck of responsibility to another group of educators), Josh was transferred to Cabrillo Middle School in 2003. As it turns out, this transfer was probably the best thing that could've happened to Josh at that point in his life.

After transferring to Cabrillo, the changes in Josh's behavior were rapid and dramatic. At De Anza, Josh was frequently off task. At Cabrillo, Josh buckled down and his grades went up. At De Anza, Josh was constantly in trouble. At Cabrillo, Josh never had any significant discipline problems. At De Anza, Josh behaved like a violent criminal. At Cabrillo, Josh never displayed any signs of violence. These results mirrored a pattern that would define Josh's life for years to come: When he was surrounded by good, wholesome influences and lots of structure, Josh flourished.

Much of the credit for Josh's turn-around undoubtedly lies in the culture of Cabrillo Middle

School. While De Anza is located an economically disadvantaged area off The Avenue, Cabrillo is located in a well-heeled neighborhood in Midtown Ventura. While 100 percent of De Anza's students qualify for free or reduced-price lunches, only thirty-eight percent of Cabrillo's students qualify for the government lunch program. While thirty-five percent of De Anza's parents never finished high school, nearly sixty percent of Cabrillo's parents hold a bachelor's degree or higher. And while De Anza's API scores place it in the fortieth percentile of schools statewide, Cabrillo is recognized as a California Distinguished School with a reputation for firm discipline and rigorous academics. [25]

It would be unfair to blame De Anza's teachers and administrators for Josh's problems during middle school. De Anza faces a unique set of challenges in educating its student population. Moreover, Josh came from a particularly brutal background, and his problems went well beyond those of most middle-school students. However, there's no doubt that Josh thrived in Cabrillo's no-nonsense environment.

Despite the progress he made at Cabrillo Middle School, Josh never exorcised the demons that tormented him. With the benefit of 20/20 hindsight, it's clear that Josh needed much more help than conscientious administrators, caring classroom teachers, and well-behaved peers could provide. Unfortunately, Josh never received this help. Josh's circumstances improved after he transferred to Cabrillo Middle School, but he remained a wounded animal, a tortured soul, and a kid on the wrong path.

CHAPTER 11

Detectives had learned a lot about Josh Packer's background, but they wanted to learn more. In particular, detectives were curious about Josh's experiences in high school.

———————

By the time Josh Packer entered Ventura High School in the fall of 2003, his life story was fraught with darkness. Notwithstanding the severe behavioral problems he'd exhibited at De Anza Middle School, Josh had been abandoned entirely by his father and abandoned sporadically by his mother. In addition, Josh had suffered a major head injury, lost two digits, witnessed extreme domestic violence, and endured sexual abuse on multiple occasions. Josh's psychological wounds were both deep and untreated.

Through it all, though, Josh never succumbed to bitterness or debilitating cynicism. When asked about Josh's adolescent years, Terri recalls him as a happy, loving kid with lots of friends and a passion for sports. In particular, Josh loved football, wrestling, and skateboarding. By the time he was a freshman in high school, it was clear to everyone that Josh was an extremely gifted athlete. Lithe, strong, and quick on his feet, Josh could perform complex skateboarding tricks just as easily as he could work with teammates to achieve victories on the football field.

Unfortunately, not everything came as easily to Josh as his athletic gifts. As a child, Josh lacked deep, consistent connections with other people. With the exception of Terri and Shauna, Josh had little contact with other family members. Terri's parents visited from Ohio a couple of times when Josh was a kid, and Terri's mother would always send Shauna and Josh cards on their birthdays and at Christmas. However, in terms of deep interpersonal connections, Josh, Shauna, and Terri were on their own.

"On Christmas mornings, it would be just me and the kids and maybe whoever I happened to be dating or married to at the time—if he'd actually get his ass out of bed," Terri explained. "There was no one else, and that's why we became so close. We were the only ones we could ever count on."

While Josh's family connections were extremely circumscribed, he was good at making friends and finding opportunities to socialize within the community. Around the time he was entering high school, Josh learned about a Christian youth organization from a friend. The organization was called Young Life. As Young Life's website states, "We believe in the power of presence. Kids' lives are dramatically impacted when caring adults come alongside them, sharing God's love with them. Because their leader believes in them, they begin to see that their lives have great worth, meaning and purpose."

Getting involved with Young Life was an extremely positive experience for Josh. Growing up around The Avenue generally and in his negligent home specifically, Josh had been exposed to violence, crime, and depravity from a very early age. Young Life opened Josh up to a whole new world. Young Life's ministry was built on a foundation of virtue, spiritual goodness, personal responsibility, and compassion. By and large, the kids involved with Young Life came from good, stable homes where all-American values were the norm. By all accounts, Josh loved Young Life and made tremendous progress as a result of his involvement in the program. Young Life provided Josh with opportunities to meet nice kids, engage in wholesome activities, and travel. On one occasion, Josh and his Young Life group traveled to Mexico to help paint a church. The ministry also took other out-of-state trips. Pictures taken during these trips show Josh as a happy kid with an irrepressible, ear-to-ear smile on his face. There's nothing unusual about Josh in these pictures. If one wasn't aware of the horrific circumstances of Josh's childhood, one would never guess that the smiling, outgoing boy in the pictures came from a background of pure horror.

When Josh wasn't participating in Young Life activities or attending school, he spent much of his time working. Despite his behavioral problems in middle school and his turbulent home-life, Josh always exhibited a strong work ethic and an impressive commitment to upholding his professional obligations.

"From the time he was fourteen, Josh always had a job," Terri said of her son. "He always earned his own money and he hardly ever asked us for anything."

During his high school years, Josh worked in a

skateboard shop, a water store, and a Coffee Bean location. None of the jobs paid much, but by all accounts, Josh did good work and proved himself to be a committed and reliable employee.

As he moved through his high school career, not everything in Josh's life was so positive. By the time he entered ninth grade, Josh was still spending a considerable amount of time with Robert "Uncle Bob" Miller, his mentor from the Ventura Boys and Girls Club. Although Miller was in his mid-thirties at the time, he still lived at home with his mother. When Josh turned fifteen, Miller asked Terri if Josh could live with him for a while at his mother's house. In retrospect, Terri wishes that she had told Miller no and kept Josh at home. At the time, though, Terri agreed to let Josh stay at the Millers' house. According to Terri, Josh underwent a serious personality change as a result of his stay with Miller, which lasted from late 2005 through the middle of 2006.

"When Josh went to live with (Miller), he was a kid who wouldn't even touch a cigarette," Terri said. "When he came back home, he'd gone from an anti-drug kid to a pot smoker."

Besides turning into a recreational dope smoker, Terri says that Josh also underwent other changes during his stay at Uncle Bob's house. One day, while she was standing in the front yard of her new home on Lafayette Street, Terri saw a strange car driving down her block. Before she knew it, the car turned into her driveway and Josh's head popped out the driver-side window like a jack-in-the-box. Terri was baffled. Josh was only fifteen at the time, he had no driver's license, and there was no one else in the vehicle with him.

"Where'd you get this car?" Terri asked.

"Uncle Bob got it for me!" Josh beamed. "Awesome, right!"

Terri couldn't understand why a grown man in his mid-thirties would give a car to a fifteen-year-old kid. Bob Miller was supposed to be mentoring Josh, not contributing to his delinquency by giving him age-inappropriate gifts. When Miller had first approached Terri about serving as Josh's mentor, she was desperate for help with her children and appreciated Miller's offer of assistance. The more she thought about the car, though, the more concerned Terri became about Miller's involvement in her son's life. Terri demanded that Josh take the car back and not drive again until he was licensed. However, Terri wasn't ready to jettison Miller from her life. By that point, Miller had become a friend of the family. Therefore, when Miller's mother kicked him out her house not long after the car incident, Terri allowed him to move into her home. Miller ended up living with Terri and her family from 2006 through 2008. Like a dolphin caught in a fishing net, Josh's relationship with his mentor grew increasingly tangled.

Through it all, Josh managed to get by in school, where his talent for sports was starting to pay off significant dividends. By the end of his freshman year at Ventura High School, Josh's athletic gifts had earned him spots on both the varsity football and wrestling teams. Once he was on the varsity teams, it didn't take long for Josh to distinguish himself as a star. Whether he was charging across the gridiron as a defensive back or marching onto the mat to pin an opponent, Josh was a tough, relentless, and fearless competitor. As one of Josh's acquaintances explained, "Josh didn't care how big the other guy was. He had no fear. He'd just crush (the other guy) when they went up against each other."

From one end of Ventura to the other, Josh's athletic prowess was drawing lots of attention. At one point, Josh was offered a full football scholarship to Saint Bonaventure High School, an exclusive private school in Midtown Ventura. After the scholarship offer was extended, Terri and Josh discussed the possibility of him attending the Catholic school. Though Josh was flattered by the offer and considered Saint Bonaventure a terrific school, he decided to stay a Cougar and remain at Ventura High.

"Saint Bonaventure pays to put its team together, Mom" Josh said. "I just wanna stay where I am. We have a real team."

Never one to question her son on major life decisions, Terri went along with Josh's reasoning.

For a kid who had endured a hellish upbringing, high school turned out to be the high point of Josh's life. From all accounts, he was a gregarious, popular, and well-respected student-athlete. Every once in a while, though, Josh's volatile side would get the better of him. When this happened, things could go south quickly.

One day before football practice, Josh was in the locker room dressing down with his teammates. As the players adorned themselves in jerseys, pads, and helmets, two of Josh's teammates began wrestling with each other. The players weren't intending to hurt each other. Instead, they were testing each other to see who would tap out first. It didn't take long for the playful wrestling match to move into the center of the locker room. When it did, the rest of the team gathered round to watch the grappling.

The pseudo-wrestling match lasted for a couple of minutes, then broke up. However, the brief violence in the locker room had ignited something inside Josh. After the two wrestling players broke it up and walked away from each other, one of the boys headed toward the locker-room exit. Josh stepped into his path.

"Move," the boy told Josh.

"No," Josh told him. "Get back over there and keep going."

Josh hadn't been involved in the original fight, so the other boy was confused by Josh's order. When the boy tried to push past Josh, he was met with a stinging physical rebuke. Without warning, Josh drew back his arm and smashed his teammate in the eye.

"Keep fighting!" Josh commanded.

Recoiling from Josh's powerful, unprovoked blow, the young man stumbled backwards in a daze. Moments later, several varsity football players converged on Josh and pinned him against a row of lockers. [26] It's unclear what the varsity players said to Josh or how justice was meted out for his breach of locker-room etiquette, but one thing is clear: Josh never had another outburst in the locker room again.

Josh's locker-room violence was a one-time event, but his sporadically violent temper continued to rear its head from time to time. Although Josh's reputation as a fighter was well known in the hallways of Ventura High School, not all of Josh's activities roused his aggressive impulses. By all indications, Young Life always brought out the best in Josh. Discussions about faith, lessons about personal responsibility, and wholesome group activities seemed to do Josh a world of good.

In the winter of 2005, the members of Young Life

took a snowboarding trip to Utah. The goal was for Young Life's members to spend time on their spiritual development, as well as on the slopes. When they arrived at their lodging in the snow-covered mountains of the Beehive State, Young Life's members were separated into different rooms. One of Josh's roommates was a young man named Kyle Frawley. Kyle's older sister, Elizabeth, was also a member of Young Life. Kyle and Elizabeth Frawley came from a different world than Josh Packer. Not only was their stepmother one of Young Life's adult leaders, their father, Mike Frawley, is the Chief Deputy District Attorney of Ventura County. Josh and Kyle weren't close friends, but to the extent that they roomed together during the snowboarding trip, the boys got along with one other.

According to Terri, Josh had an outstanding time on the snowboarding trip. Not only was Josh able to participate in the kinds of high-octane outdoor sports he loved, he was also able to attend several Bible-study meetings. At one point, Josh claimed that he'd made a spiritual breakthrough as a result of his experiences in Young Life. Josh went on to explain that, for the first time in his life, he understood the loving salvation of Jesus Christ. Josh declared that he'd been saved.

Back at Ventura High School, Josh's spiritual awakening didn't seem to carry over into all areas of his life. Though he continued to attend Young Life meetings on a regular basis, Josh's behavior was extremely unpredictable.

On the morning of May 31, 2005, Josh and a few of his Ventura High teammates received some disturbing news. According to what Josh and his friends were told, a football player at Buena High School had made derogatory statements about Latinos. Buena High was a cross-town rival of Ventura High, and Josh was enraged by the alleged racist's comments. Many of Josh's teammates and friends were Latino, and Josh wouldn't stand for them to be disrespected. After rounding up a mob of six other students, Josh led his group off the Ventura High School campus, across Main Street, and onto a city bus. The bus was headed east, directly toward Buena High School.

When the Ventura High mob got off the bus, Josh led them across the sidewalk and onto the Buena High campus. It didn't take long before Josh spied the boy who had supposedly made the derogatory comments about Latino students at Ventura High School.

In a strange and confusing irony that lacks any logical foundation, the alleged racist was a boy named Christian Morales*. The fact that Morales was himself a Latino seems to have mattered little to Josh. As he marched swiftly in Morales's direction, Josh's hands balled themselves into tight, rock-hard fists. As soon as Josh reached Morales, he unleashed a vicious right hook to the unsuspecting boy's head. The blow connected below Morales's eye with a sickly, crippling splat. Morales immediately went to the ground.

With Morales bleeding on the concrete, Josh and his group of friends fled the scene. Minutes later, Morales was transported to the emergency room. An x-ray revealed that Josh had fractured the orbital bone below Morales's eye, as well as Morales's nose. Morales's parents were understandably livid about their son's condition. It didn't take long before a call was placed to the Ventura Police Department.

Before the day was over, Josh had been taken into custody for his first serious offense: felony battery on Christian Morales.

Josh was fifteen years old.

As a minor and a first-time offender, there was no way to make the felony charge stick against Josh. After writing a letter of apology to Christian Morales and promising to refrain for violent conduct in the future, Josh was placed on probation. Though the terms of his probation were clear—stay in school and stay out of trouble—the events of the next few months demonstrated that Josh's inner turmoil was far from settled.

In the summer of 2005, Josh joined his Young Life friends for an out-of-town retreat. The retreat was to be held at a rural camp in Northern California. The retreat held the promise of fun activities and spiritual development in the great outdoors. Josh loved such trips.

When the Young Life members arrived at the camp, Josh was assigned to a cabin with Kyle Frawley, Sean Kirkpatrick*, and several other boys. Josh and Kyle attended different high schools, so they were still little more than passing acquaintances. However, Josh was very close friends with Sean Kirkpatrick. Not only did Josh and Kirkpatrick know each other through Young Life, they were also fellow members of the Ventura High School football team.

From all indications, Young Life's summer retreat went off without a hitch. A photograph taken that week captures the mood of the retreat. The forty-plus members of Young Life are gathered in front of a red-brick building. Towering pine trees hover in the background. Dressed in casual summer attire, many of the Young Life members have their arms draped around one another's shoulders. Most of the male

Young Life members are standing along the back row of the picture. Most of the female Young Life members are sitting or kneeling in the picture's foreground. In the middle of it all, Josh is lying on his right side with his body draped across the laps of two female Young Life members. One of the girls Josh is lying atop in the picture is a smiling Elizabeth Frawley. Josh is wearing red basketball shorts, a gray tank top, a yellow "Live Strong" bracelet, and a blue baseball cap that's turned around backwards. An unrestrained smile beams from Josh's face. The smile completely obfuscates the vicious circumstances of Josh's youth.

When the summer retreat drew to a close, the members of Young Life returned to Ventura. The retreat had given Josh a much-needed break from the tense, volatile, and often unsavory world he occupied at home. Back in Ventura, surrounded by unhealthy influences and bad memories, Josh's aggression would continue to flare.

CHAPTER 12

Josh Packer's explosive temper and predilection for violence had a way of getting him in trouble. At certain times, however, these same qualities proved to be Josh's most powerful assets. When Josh stepped onto the football field or the wrestling mat, his pent-up rage transformed him into an indomitable athletic juggernaut. Regardless of their size or experience, opponents never intimidated Josh. Using tremendous speed and strength, Josh had an intuitive sense of how to get underneath his opponents, neutralize their defenses, and destroy them. As a defensive back and wide receiver for the Ventura Cougars football program, Josh was often unstoppable.

The full extent of Josh's athletic prowess can be seen in video footage from the fall of 2006. The footage was captured during a Friday-night football game between Ventura High School and Oxnard High School. In the video, wearing jersey number 4, Josh charges across the field at top speed at the beginning of the play. He immediately zeros in on the Oxnard ball-handler. Fast, nimble, and ferocious, Josh sidesteps several

Oxnard defenders and blasts his way toward the ball-handler like a guided missile. Before the Oxnard ball-handler—number 22—has a chance to take two steps, Josh plows into him with bone-rattling force, hurling his opponent back a good three yards and crushing him into the grass. Once his opponent is grounded, Josh immediately springs to his feet, rejoins his backslapping teammates, and readies himself for the next play. Meanwhile, number 22 has trouble standing up. When number 22 is finally helped to his feet by his cardinal-and-gold-jerseyed teammates, he's forced to hobble off the field, doubled over at the waist.

Realizing that he might be able to parlay his athletic gifts into a football scholarship, Josh was thinking seriously about college by the time he reached the eleventh grade. Football had the potential to open many doors for Josh that academics never could. Although he'd demonstrated a respectable aptitude for mathematics, Josh had never been enthusiastic about his academic classes. As Terri readily acknowledges, an academic scholarship was out of the question for Josh.

"Josh's favorite class was football," Terri explained with a chuckle when asked about Josh's academic interests. "He liked P.E., wrestling, you know, physical types of classes. I know Joshua also took wood shop and metal shop, but he never really talked much about his other classes."

College and football scholarships weren't the only things on Josh's mind during the fall of his junior year. Around that time, Josh became involved with a girl named Jessica Rossi*. Petite, dark-haired, and attractive, Jessica was two years older than Josh and the daughter of a local police sergeant. When she became romantically involved with Josh, Jessica was living with her family in an upscale neighborhood on Ventura's east side. Filled with spacious stucco homes, freshly waxed cars, and leafy streets, Jessica's neighborhood off North Bank Drive was a far cry from the neighborhoods around The Avenue where Josh had grown up.

Once their relationship was established, it didn't take long for Josh to become extremely protective of Jessica. To some people, Josh's protectiveness appeared heartfelt. For example, when Jessica started having problems at home, Josh talked to Terri about Jessica's living situation. Eventually, Josh convinced Terri to allow Jessica to live with them for a while. In the eyes of many people, Josh looked like a concerned boyfriend who only wanted the best for Jessica. To others, however, Josh's watchfulness over Jessica took on obsessive proportions.

When Josh and Jessica attended social functions together, Josh was always the life of the party. Outgoing, uninhibited, and fearless, Josh had a natural gift for charming those around him. However, Josh's mood could turn on a dime.

One night, while they were attending a party with a large group of Ventura High School students, Josh and Jessica drifted away from each other for a few minutes. Once they were separated, Josh yucked it up with his friends while Jessica made the rounds of the party. A few minutes later, Josh spied Jessica talking to a tall male student with a buzz cut. The kid with the buzz cut stood at least 6'2" tall. Without warning, Josh walked away from his friends, balled up his fists, and stormed toward Jessica and the long-boned male student. Josh, who stood barely 5'10", didn't ask any questions or mince any words. As soon as Josh reached the kid with the buzz cut, he unload a volley of punches to the tall kid's head. Before anyone knew what was happening, the tall kid was on the ground, bleeding and dazed. Josh stood over the tall kid and glared down at him, his shoulders heaving and his eyes blazing with an unnerving intensity. The incident helped cement Josh's reputation as volatile, violent, and extremely territorial when it came to Jessica Rossi. [27]

Josh's growing reputation for violence wasn't just based on altercations with strangers at parties. One afternoon, Josh and Shauna were sitting in his bedroom talking about mutual acquaintances. At some point during their conversation, Shauna made a derogatory comment about one of her brother's friends. Angered by Shauna's comment, Josh demanded that she take back what she'd said. Shauna refused. Over the next several minutes, the atmosphere in the bedroom became more and more tense. Josh continued to demand that Shauna take back her comment about his friend. Shauna continued to refuse. Eventually, Shauna stood up to leave the room. Springing to his feet and blocking the doorway, Josh told his sister that she couldn't leave the bedroom until she'd retracted her disparaging comment about his friend. Again, she refused.

Josh's swing was so swift that Shauna didn't have time to flinch.

Josh's closed fist smashed into his sister's head, rattling her brain. Apparently remembering that he was still on probation for the Buena High School incident, Josh darted out of the bedroom and sprinted away from the house. Shauna, still reeling from Josh's punch, picked up the phone and called 911. When officers arrived at the scene, Josh was gone. Soon enough, though, Josh returned to the house. When he arrived, he was promptly arrested for committing misdemeanor battery against his sister. [28]

Josh wasn't the only member of his family who was having trouble with the police around this time. Since she'd quit using drugs in 1998, Terri had worked hard to turn her life around and provide a positive home-life for her children. There was no way Terri could undo the damage that had been done to Shauna and Josh when they were children, but she wanted to make their young-adult years as comfortable as possible. However, despite all of the progress she'd made, Terri once again found herself in trouble with the law in 2006.

It all happened while Terri, her children, her new husband Rudy Cobos, and "Uncle Bob" Miller (who was living with the family at the time) were transitioning between homes. While they were waiting to move into their new home, Terri and her family were forced to stay in a motel for a few days. They chose the Motel 6 on Johnson Drive in Ventura. One afternoon, the family went to the motel's swimming pool to relax. Although the motel did not employ a lifeguard, the owners had posted a list of rules and regulations for guests to follow at the pool. One of the rules strictly forbid diving.

Terri, who was thirty-seven at the time, didn't see the sign that prohibited diving. As a result, she decided to show her kids some diving techniques. Terri's diving display drew the attention of the motel security guard, who'd known Terri when she and the kids lived near The Avenue years earlier.

The security guard ordered Terri to stop diving. Heated words were exchanged between Terri and the security guard and the incident quickly escalated. In an attempt to calm the situation, Rudy Cobos intervened on Terri's behalf. It's not clear exactly what happened next, but somehow the altercation between Cobos and the security guard turned physical. It didn't take long before the security guard produced a can of pepper spray and blasted a cloud of aerosolized cayenne into Cobos's face. With his eyes ablaze and his body convulsing in pain, Cobos dropped to the pool deck. Terri and the security guard charged at one another. The children looked on in horror. The motel manager called 911.

When officers arrived at the motel, Terri was taken into custody for battery. To this day, Terri protests her innocence.

"While Rudy was on the ground, the woman cop arrested me in front of my kids," Terri explained. "I asked why I was being arrested. She lied and said I'd kicked somebody in the head. I turned to that cop and I said 'You're a lying bitch!'"

Although Terri was transported to jail and booked for the poolside melee, no formal charges were filed in the case. According to the Ventura Police Department, Terri was "detained," not arrested, for the Motel 6 incident. Not long after she was booked, the battery case against Terri was dropped and she was released from custody. Meanwhile, the Motel 6 manager evicted Terri from her room and her children went to stay with Bob Miller.

The poolside scuffle was just one more violent incident in Josh's life. Growing up in a psychosocial maelstrom—where violence, arrests, criminality, sexual depravity, mental illness, and exploitation were commonplace—it's not surprising that Josh's moral compass had a tendency to spin away from magnetic north from time to time. When he was feeling good, Josh was funny, charismatic, and likable. Other guys gravitated toward him and there was no shortage of girls who fawned over him. However, when Josh's mood darkened, his personality could shift in an instant. By the spring of his junior year in high school, serious fissures had started to appear in Josh's facade of normalcy. Some of these fissures, such as driving without a license (which Josh was cited for on multiple occasions), were relatively benign. Other fissures revealed a much darker side of the popular, athletic young man.

———————

According to local sources, by the second semester of his junior year, Josh had started lurking around Jessica Rossi's neighborhood at odd hours. Members of the Rossi household would see Josh's car parked down the block from their large, two-story home. [29] Josh's headlights would be turned off and his motor would be silent. From what the Rossi family could tell, Josh would just sit in his car watching their home, his face a mask of focused vacancy.

In the fall of 2006, Josh's presence in the Rossis' neighborhood took a turn for the worse. One evening, Jessica's younger sister Brittany* was returning home with their father. As Brittany and her father drove down their quiet street, they noticed a pick-up truck parked in front of their residence. Moments later, as Sergeant Rossi's headlights swept across the front of his property, he and Brittany saw Josh standing in their driveway. Josh appeared to be staring at their house. Sergeant Rossi rolled down his window and asked Josh what he was doing. In a terse-but-respectful tone, Josh explained that he'd been driving through the Rossis' neighborhood and had seen the strange pick-up parked in front of their house. Josh said that he wanted to make sure that Jessica was alright.

As Sergeant Rossi and Brittany talked with Josh in their driveway, the young football star became more and more agitated about what might be taking place inside the house. Josh had no idea who was in the house with Jessica, but he was determined to find out. Finally, Josh couldn't take it anymore. Spinning away from Sergeant Rossi and Brittany, Josh bolted down the driveway, sprinted to the side of the Rossi home, and let himself into the house. Once inside, Josh bounded up the stairs and dashed toward Jessica's bedroom. When Josh threw open Jessica's door, he saw a sight that made his blood boil: Jessica was in her room talking with a young man named Henry*.

Henry was well aware of Josh's reputation for violence, particularly when it came to Jessica and perceived romantic rivals. Seeing the palsied expression on Josh's face and the fiery look in Josh's eyes, Henry decided that the best thing he could do in that awkward moment was leave the house. Henry immediately stood up, walked past Josh, exited Jessica's bedroom, and started down the stairs.

Josh followed, hot on Henry's heels.

"Why the fuck are you at my girlfriend's house?" Josh demanded to know as Henry made his way down the stairs, out of the house, and onto the driveway.

"Just talking with Jessica," Henry answered.

"You know she's my girlfriend, right?" Josh hissed.

"The last time I checked you weren't together," Henry retorted.

Henry was telling the truth. By all accounts, Josh and Jessica—though still close—were no longer a steady item at that time.

Not knowing how to respond to Henry's rebuke, Josh stopped in his tracks and glared as Henry continued walking toward his truck. When Henry reached the driver's side of his vehicle, he pulled out his keys to unlock the door. That's when Josh broke into a full-on sprint and charged. A couple of seconds later, as Henry stood frozen in place on the street, Josh unloaded a brutal, brain-jarring hook to the side of Henry's head.

The fight or flight response took over and Henry opted for the latter. Henry jumped in his truck and departed the scene.

After Henry was gone, Josh and Jessica argued about the attack. Jessica was concerned, not only about Josh's penchant for unprovoked violence, but also about his habit of watching her house. Jessica told Josh that she wanted to spend some time apart.

Josh could feel Jessica pulling away from him and he couldn't take it. His feelings for Jessica were profound and he didn't want to let her go. The more Jessica excoriated Josh for his attack on Henry, the more confused Josh became. Nothing in Josh's emotional arsenal had prepared him for such a conversation. Finally, in a desperate attempt to maintain his hold on Jessica, Josh threatened to kill himself if she left him. Josh told Jessica that he couldn't bare to live if they were apart. Josh said that he would overdose on pills if Jessica broke off their relationship. [30]

Confused and troubled by Josh's suicide threat, Jessica didn't know what to do. She was stuck in a relationship with a young man whose actions could oscillate between loving and brutal at the drop of a hat. Jessica was trapped.

CHAPTER 13

As Josh's high school years drew to a close, his mood swings became less and less predictable. Josh had never received any counseling for the abuse he'd suffered as a child, and like his mother before him, he lacked effective coping skills. Josh was at his best on the football field, where all challenges could be met with brute force. Unfortunately, Josh's days of gridiron glory were about to come to an end.

Josh had never been a spectacular student, but his lackluster academic record had more to do with apathy than a lack of intelligence. Unlike his presence on the football field, which was powerful and dynamic, Josh did little more than get by in his academic classes. Nonetheless, Josh found other ways to make himself useful around the Ventura High School campus. Specifically, Josh secured a position as a teacher's aide during his senior year. As it turned out, though, spending more time around teachers failed to keep Josh out of trouble.

One day, as Josh was walking to the classroom where he worked as a T.A., he was approached by one of his friends. The friend told Josh that he'd scored a new type of drug called Fentanyl. According to the friend, Fentanyl was a time-release narcotics patch that cancer patients used to control their pain. Intrigued by the highly potent patch, Josh decided to experiment with it right then and there. Josh popped the patch in his mouth, chewed it up thoroughly, sucked down the medication, then proceeded to the classroom where he worked as a T.A.

Within minutes of arriving for his T.A. assignment, Josh could barely stand up. Time slowed, the classroom became a blur, and Josh started to feel woozy. Josh was high—*really* high—and he suddenly felt a powerful need to sleep. Realizing that he was in no condition to work as a T.A., Josh informed the teacher that he wasn't feeling well. Josh added that he wanted—*needed*—to rest for a while. Receptive to Josh's request but not seriously concerned, the teacher told Josh to go to the back of the classroom and put his head down for a few minutes. With the Fentanyl inundating his central nervous system, Josh staggered to the back of the room.

Several minutes later, when the teacher went to check on Josh, the teacher was alarmed to find that Josh had stopped breathing. An urgent 911 call was placed immediately.

When paramedics arrived at the high school, they found Josh in full respiratory arrest. With sirens blaring and red lights flashing, the ambulance team rushed Josh to the emergency room, where it was determined that he'd overdosed on the highly concentrated, opiate-based cancer drug. Using an opiate antagonist to counteract the Fentanyl's effects, a team of emergency physicians managed to revive

Josh and stabilize his breathing. It was a close call, but Josh survived.

Josh spent the next couple of days in the hospital. Terri stayed by his side the entire time. When Josh finally returned to school, he was not welcomed back with open arms. The Ventura Cougars' head football coach immediately kicked Josh off the team. Both Terri and Rudy Cobos pleaded with the coach to accept Josh back on the team, but their efforts were to no avail. Josh was a great football player, but his debauched antics had become a black eye for Ventura High School. Not long after he was kicked off the football team, Josh was asked to leave Ventura High altogether. The school district recommended that Josh complete his graduation requirements at a local adult-education center. In a life filled with disappointment, Josh's ousting from the football team and ejection from high school were just two more blows—albeit self-inflicted blows—to his identity.

A few months after he started classes at the adult-education center, Josh agreed to help his mother with a moving project. At the time, Terri and Rudy Cobos were preparing to move into a new home on Ocean Avenue in Midtown Ventura. Because she was nine-months pregnant at the time, Terri needed Josh's help with the move.

Moving day got off to a bad start. When Josh arrived at his mother's soon-to-be-vacated house on June 10, 2007, he told her that he couldn't help with the move. Josh explained that one of his old friends was in town for the day and that he wanted to spend time with him. Terri reminded Josh that he'd promised to help with the move. Terri pointed out that she and Cobos were relying on him. Josh hemmed and hawed. He was adamant about spending time with his friend and helping with the move later.

Frustrated, out of options, and on the verge of going into labor, Terri insisted that Josh make good on his commitment to help with the move. Josh and Terri began squabbling back and forth. It didn't take long before the situation turned tense, then violent.

According to Terri, she struck the first blow. As she was hitting Josh, he grabbed her arms and slammed her into a wall.

From all indications, Josh had a great relationship with Rudy Cobos. However, when Cobos tried to intervene in the moving-day fight, Josh turned on his stepfather and threatened to kill him. Chilled to the bone by Josh's threat, Terri struggled free from her son's grip and called 911.

Josh fled the scene before officers arrived. In Josh's absence, Terri explained to the responding officers that Josh had been placed in Vista Del Mar, a local mental facility, on three separate occasions for violent conduct. This came as news to the officers, who thought they were responding to a run-of-the-mill domestic situation. Terri also explained to the officers that she wanted Josh to receive additional psychiatric help. [31]

Later that day, Josh was contacted and questioned by Ventura police officers. When the officers asked Josh why he'd grabbed his mother by the arms and slammed her into the wall, Josh explained that he was acting in self-defense. When one of the officers asked Josh why he'd threatened to kill Rudy Cobos, Josh supplied the lawmen with an answer that offered a clear window into his tortured mind.

"I was mad," Josh explained to the officers. "People do stupid things when they're mad."

The officers deemed Josh a danger to himself or others and detained him on a 51-50 hold. [32] As a result, instead of taking Josh to jail, the officers transported him to a local psychiatric facility for a three-day observation. When the officers dropped Josh off at the hospital, they probably realized that they hadn't seen the last of him. By the ripe old age of seventeen, Josh had racked up a lengthy arrest record. In addition, Josh had been involved in a myriad of violent altercations in which he was the aggressor. Now Josh had admitted to making a death threat against his stepfather, a man he not only liked, but one who had treated Josh very well in the past. It was obvious that Josh was on the road to serious trouble.

A few days after the moving-day incident, Josh completed his credits at the adult-education center and was awarded his high-school diploma. For Josh, receiving the diploma was a bittersweet experience. Josh had started ninth grade with tremendous potential, and during his three and a half years at Ventura High School, he'd distinguished himself as a first-rate athlete. Nonetheless, after his Fentanyl overdose, Josh's dreams of attending college on a football scholarship were dead. Unlike most of his peers, Josh's high-school graduation marked the end of a dream, not a fresh start.

After graduation, while his friends and former

teammates were heading off to college, Josh took a job as a security guard at Baxter Pharmaceuticals in the city of Newberry Park. Though he was disappointed about not attending college, Josh was excited about his new job at Baxter.

"Josh was so proud of getting that job," Terri recalled. "Right after he got it, he came home in his new uniform and we took pictures."

Jessica Rossi also stayed in Ventura after graduating from high school. After Josh was hired at Baxter Pharmaceuticals, his relationship with Jessica became more charged than ever. As 2007 ended and 2008 began, Josh was living at Terri's house on Ocean Avenue, working steadily at his security job, and spending time with Jessica and other friends during his off hours.

For a kid who'd endured unspeakable horrors growing up, Josh seemed to be doing well given his unique set of challenges. Not only did Josh have full-time employment in a bad economy, he was also preparing for his future. Specifically, Josh was interested in joining the United States Marine Corps. To this end, Josh had spoken with a Marine recruiter and taken the Armed Services Vocational Aptitude Battery (ASVAB), a standardized intelligence test that's required for all prospective military recruits. By early 2008, Josh was in the process of getting several tattoos removed so he would qualify for induction into the military.

Despite the positive progress Josh was making, not everything in his life was cause for celebration. Every once in a while, Josh's violent side would surface. It was impossible to predict when these episodes would occur, but like a great white rising from the depths to rip off a surfer's leg, Josh's rage could manifest without warning. When it did, the results could be explosive. One such incident occurred on January 10, 2008, as Terri was driving Josh to work in her 1999 Ford Taurus.

That afternoon, Terri and Josh were driving along the busy, multi-lane thoroughfare of Mills Road in Ventura. Terri and Josh were sitting in the front seat of the car. Terri's infant daughter, who had been born the previous year with developmental disabilities, was strapped into her carseat in the rear of the vehicle. As Terri, Josh, and the baby proceeded along Mills Road, another motorist cut Terri off and began weaving through traffic. Angered by the breach of roadway decorum, Terri hit the gas and pursued the weaving driver. A few blocks later, the weaving driver got caught at a red light. Terri pulled alongside the weaving driver and honked the Taurus's horn. When the weaving driver turned toward the Taurus, Terri could see that the offending motorist was a young black woman. The young woman lowered her window and Terri did the same. The back-and-forth shouting started immediately. According to Terri, as the argument escalated, the young woman in the other car coughed up a glob of phlegm and spit it at Terri. At that moment, the traffic light turned green. Repulsed by the young woman's spitting, Terri punched the gas and roared away from the intersection. The young woman in the other car pulled in behind Terri's Taurus and gave chase.

As Terri, Josh, and the baby raced along Mills Road, the young woman followed close on their tail. Josh turned around in the front seat and watched the enraged young woman ride Terri's bumper for several blocks. When the two vehicles reached the intersection of Mills Road and Maple Street, the young spitter came to a screeching stop behind Terri's Taurus. The spitter then threw her car in park and leapt out of her vehicle for a public display of road rage.

With her Taurus pinned in by other cars and the traffic light glowing red, Terri had nowhere to go. As soon as the irate young woman reached Terri's car, she began beating her fists on the Taurus's rear window and shouting. With her seven-month-old daughter in her carseat below the back window, Terri was scared that the glass would shatter under the young woman's pounding fists. Both Terri and Josh began yelling at the young woman to stop beating on the window. The young woman refused to stop. Finally, with the young woman pounding harder and harder on the back window and the situation becoming increasingly tense, Josh opened his door, stepped out of the car, and attempted to move the young woman away from his mother's Taurus.

According to Terri, as soon as Josh stepped near the trunk, the young woman attacked him. Clawing at Josh's face like a grizzly, the young woman ripped off Josh's eyeglasses and knocked them into the street. Moments earlier, the stop light on Maple had turned green and traffic on Mills had started moving again. Josh watched as another vehicle rolled over his prescription glasses, crushing them into dust.

When Josh turned back toward the young woman, something flashed across his face. It's unknown what the girl saw in Josh's eyes at that moment, but in a nanosecond, the dynamics of the situation had shifted dramatically. Before she knew what was happening, the young woman had morphed from the bully into the potential victim.

Backing quickly away from Josh and running for her car, the young woman jumped into the driver's seat of her vehicle, rolled up the windows, and locked her doors. However, with Terri's Taurus blocking her path and both lanes of traffic moving parallel to her vehicle, the young woman was trapped like a rat.

By that point, Josh was quaking with rage. As if reenacting a scene from *The Terminator*, Josh stormed up to the young woman's windshield and swung his clenched his fist as hard as he could. Josh's powerhouse blow crashed into windshield with maximum velocity, producing a crater of glass. Filagreed cracks radiated away from the glass crater like a spider web.

"How do you like it!" Josh bellowed at the now-petrified young woman. "*HOW DO YOU LIKE IT!*"

As Josh raged at the young woman and Terri screamed from the Taurus, curious commuters rubbernecked for a view of the show. At least one of the commuters picked up a cell phone and dialed 911.

It only took police a couple of minutes to arrive on scene. After gathering statements from the various parties and examining the damage to the vehicles, both Josh and the young woman received citations for misdemeanor vandalism. Later, the vandalism charge against Josh was dismissed.

———————————

With the road-rage incident behind him, Josh continued to work his security job at Baxter, spend his off hours with Jessica Rossi, and live at Terri's house on Ocean Avenue. All things considered, Josh had a sweet set-up at the Ocean Avenue property. Not only did Josh have most of the first floor to himself, he also had a private entrance and exit from the home. However, Josh soon received an offer that would move his life in a new direction.

During the closing months of 2008, Robert "Uncle Bob" Miller had been living in Arizona. Upon returning to Ventura in early 2009, Miller began encouraging Josh to rent an apartment with him so they could share expenses. According to Terri, Josh was initially opposed to the idea.

"Josh didn't want to leave," Terri explained. "He basically had his own apartment at our house and he could do whatever he wanted. There was no reason for him to leave."

By that point, Terri had other reservations about Bob Miller. Though she'd known Miller for nearly a decade and was initially encouraged his interest in serving as Josh's mentor, Terri had revised her opinion of the youth worker. According to Terri, when Josh was in high school, Miller wrote notes to get Josh dismissed from class. Terri also noticed that Josh's personality would change when he spent time around Miller. Terri wasn't exactly sure what was going on between Miller and her son, but she didn't like it.

Despite Terri's reservations about Miller and despite the fact that Josh was happy living at home, Miller continued to pressure Josh about the apartment proposal. Josh was worried that if he didn't move in with Miller and help out with the bills, his mentor would be unable to afford an apartment in Ventura's pricy rental market. Plus, after suffering a concussion in a bicycle accident, Josh had been deemed unfit to join the Marines. With few opportunities on the horizon, Josh gave more and more consideration to Miller's apartment proposal. Finally, against Terri's wishes, Josh agreed to move in with Miller. However, Josh added a clause to the agreement: Jessica would live with them in the apartment and they'd split the expenses three ways. Uncle Bob agreed to the terms.

Josh, Jessica, and Miller moved into the Jefferson Apartments in mid-March 2009. Located at 6630 Webster Street in Ventura, the Jefferson Apartments (which were renamed the Capes at Ventura in 2013) were a collection of thirty-three four-plex stucco units clustered around a central swimming pool. In an interesting coincidence, the Jefferson Apartments were located on the same block as the Ventura County Hall of Justice, the Sheriff's Department headquarters, and the county jail.

When they moved into unit 310 at the Jefferson Apartments, Josh was nineteen, Jessica was twenty-one, and Miller was a few weeks shy of his fortieth birthday. As the unlikely roommates settled into their new life together, they had no idea that the good times were about to end forever.

CHAPTER 14

As 2009 drew to a close, Santa Barbara County detectives continued digging into Josh Packer's background. The detectives liked Josh as a suspect in the Thrifty robbery, but they didn't have enough evidence to arrest him for the hold-up. Josh's record contained many blemishes, but in and of themselves, these blemishes didn't prove that Josh was the Thrifty robber. However, when detectives learned that Josh had been positively identified as the prime suspect in a Ventura street robbery, their suspicions about the former football star kicked into high gear. The alleged street robbery had taken place on April 25, 2009, only a few weeks after Josh, Jessica, and Uncle Bob moved into the Jefferson Apartments.

When the three roommates moved into the Jefferson Apartments, they planned to split the rent three ways. However, within a month of moving into unit 310, Jessica was ready to leave. Sources gave conflicting reasons for Jessica's decision to move out of the apartment. Some sources indicated that Jessica would not be allowed to go on her family's annual trip to Hawaii if she was living away from home. Others said that Jessica was tired of Josh and his friends sitting around all day smoking marijuana. Still others speculated that Jessica was frightened by Josh's increasingly possessive and violent behavior. With regard to the third point, Josh had once pushed a knife into Jessica's palm, wrapped her fingers around the knife's handle, clasped his own powerful hands around her closed fist, and forced Jessica to slice into his leg with the blade. While the cutting incident was deeply troubling for Jessica, it wasn't Josh's first foray into self-mutilation. The top of Josh's thigh revealed a grotesque knot of jagged, criss-crossed scar tissue— the result of many previous self-cutting incidents.

When Jessica moved out of unit 310, her relationship with Josh started to cool significantly. Nevertheless, before she vacated the apartment, Jessica presented Josh with two parting gifts: an Enduro motorcycle and a matching helmet.

As an avid motorcycle enthusiast, Josh was elated about his new toy. However, if Jessica meant the motorcycle as a peace offering, her gesture missed the mark. Ripping around Ventura on his new bike, Josh was angry that Jessica had moved out of the apartment. He recognized that their relationship was breaking up, but he didn't know what to do. With no suitors to fend off and no football or wrestling matches to help sublimate his anger, Josh began looking for other ways to blow off steam.

Just before 9 p.m. on April 27, 2009, Ventura police officer Mary Eltz was dispatched on a non-emergency robbery call. The caller was a twenty-one-year-old man named Matt Russell*. Russell told Officer Eltz that he'd been robbed two nights earlier. Russell stated that, at the time of the robbery, he was riding his bicycle westbound on a quiet side street called Aurora Drive, which is located just west of Buena High School. Around 11:30 p.m., as he approached the intersection of Aurora and Wake Forest Avenue, Russell noticed another young man on a bicycle who was also riding westbound. The other cyclist was riding very slowly according to Russell, so Russell passed him and continued pedaling toward his home. Seconds after passing the other cyclist, Russell felt something crash into the rear wheel of his bicycle. Swiveling his head around, Russell noticed that the other cyclist had intentionally rammed his front tire into the back wheel of Russell's bicycle.

"The fuck, dude?" Russell asked incredulously.

"You didn't need to pass me like that," the other cyclist told Russell in a throaty-but-dispassionate tone.

Russell could see that the other cyclist was a young white man about his own age. Russell could also see that, although the other cyclist was of modest stature, he had an athletic build. Nevertheless, Russell wasn't the type to back down from a fight when openly challenged. Within seconds of their initial exchange, both Russell and the other cyclist had jumped off their bicycles, dropped their backpacks, and started slugging it out in the quiet, tree-lined darkness of Aurora Drive.

As the fight progressed, Russell and the other

cyclist moved a short distance away from their bicycles. Without warning, the other cyclist pushed himself away from Russell, ran back toward his bicycle, and retrieved a folding knife from his backpack. Houses along the street provided just enough light to illuminate the knife's long steel blade.

"Gimme your shit now!" the antagonistic cyclist ordered Russell.

Stunned by the sudden turn of events, Russell didn't know how to respond. First the guy had crashed into his bike for no reason, then they'd fought. Now Russell was being robbed? The whole thing made no sense. However, with his assailant now armed with a knife, Russell didn't want to get any closer than necessary.

"I said gimme your shit!" the other cyclist shouted at Russell.

Russell remained frozen in place a short distance from the downed bicycles.

Moving swiftly, the knife-wielding robber rushed to Russell's bicycle, jabbed his blade through its front and rear tires, snatched Russell's backpack, and sped away from the scene on his own bicycle.

As Russell explained to Officer Eltz, the whole incident took only a couple of minutes. When it was over, Russell was unsure of what to do. Finally, Russell picked up his bicycle and began pushing it on flat tires in the direction of Buena High School.

When he reached the Buena High campus, Russell decided to cut through the school's tennis courts so he could access the busy, well-lit thoroughfare of Victoria Avenue. As he moved through the chain-link maze of tennis courts on the south side of Buena High's campus, Russell detected movement in his peripheral vision. Out of the corner of his eye, Russell saw a flash of colour. When he turned his head and looked across the tennis courts, Russell saw the young man who had just robbed him. From what Russell could tell, the robber was rifling through his stolen backpack.

As Russell watched his assailant dig through the backpack, the young robber jerked his head up and glared at Russell. Moments later, the young robber was racing toward Russell, knife in hand.

With two flat tires and tall fences on all sides, Russell had nowhere to go. Things were about to get really strange.

The young robber barreled up to Russell and told him that he'd found marijuana in his stolen backpack. With his knife pointing in Russell's direction, the robber demanded that Russell empty his pockets. The robber threatened to "...stab him in the throat..." if Russell did not comply. [33]

Russell admitted to Officer Eltz that he had about a quarter ounce of marijuana in his backpack when he was robbed. Russell also told Officer Eltz that he was extremely unnerved by the robber's unhinged demeanor.

With the robber brandishing his knife, Russell started to empty his pockets. As it turned out, Russell had been paid that day by his employer. As a result, Russell had over $300 in his pockets at the time of the robbery. Russell handed over the thick wad of bills and expected the robber to flee, but what happened next came as a complete shock.

As soon as the young robber had the wad of cash in hand, he asked Russell how much money he wanted back.

Russell was dumfounded. Why would someone

commit a robbery, then offer to give back a portion of the stolen loot? What sense did that make? Though he was beginning to question the robber's mental stability, Russell wanted to get back as much money as possible. Russell explained to the robber that he'd just cashed his paycheck that afternoon, and he needed to get back at least $200.

At that point, according to Russell's statement, the young robber began making strange comments that were nonsensical and close to incoherent. The robber asked Russell about his birth name and date of birth.

Finally, the robber ripped a crisp $5 bill from the wad of cash and threw it at Russell. The robber then handed Russell two items from his stolen backpack: a small pencil sharpener and a broken cell phone.

With the hold-up complete, the young robber ran back to his bicycle and pedaled away from the scene. The knife-wielding bandit made off with over $300 in cash, several grams of marijuana, and an easily fencible iPod from Russell's backpack. Before leaving the scene, the robber also made a point of taking another curious item: Russell's state-issued identification card.

Officer Eltz asked Matt Russell if he knew the person who'd robbed him. Russell said that he did; he said the robber was one of his former classmates at Ventura High School.

Officer Eltz asked for the robber's name.

"Josh Packer," Russell said.

Later that day, Officer Eltz put together a photographic line-up of young white male suspects and showed it to Russell. She wanted to see if Russell could make a positive photo identification of the person who'd robbed him on April 25, 2009.

Presented with the photo line-up, Russell looked at the pictures for only a few seconds before choosing the photo in position Number One.

Photograph Number One was a picture of Josh Packer.

Officer Eltz thanked Russell for his assistance. She then booked the photo line-up into evidence and wrote her report. Because the suspect had taken Russell's backpack and money by force, he had violated state Penal Code section 211—robbery. Also, because the suspect had punctured both tires on Russell's bicycle, the young robber was also in violation of Penal Code section 594b(2)—vandalism causing less than $400 in damage.

With Russell's statement on the books and a positive photo identification of the suspect, the Ventura Police Department issued a probable-cause declaration for Josh Packer's arrest. As it turned out, though, officers were never able to arrest Josh for the Russell robbery.

After the probable-cause declaration was filed, the Russell robbery case was forwarded to the District Attorney's Office. In evaluating the circumstances and elements of the alleged crimes, prosecutors decided not to pursue the case against Josh Packer. Russell had waited two days before making his report, and prosecutors weren't sure they could make the robbery case stick. [34] Despite the bizarre and aggressive circumstances of the Russell robbery, despite the fact that a weapon was involved, and despite the fact that Josh was accused of threatening to stab Russell in the throat, the case was dropped.

CHAPTER 15

Cunning criminals can utilize the elements of surprise and anonymity to their advantage. For this reason, in the immediate aftermath of a crime, the scales of justice are often tipped in favor of the offender. However, as detectives amass clues, tips, leads, and background information on specific suspects, the scales of justice begin to level. Eventually, if detectives gather enough good evidence against a specific suspect, the scales of justice tip in the state's favor. When this occurs, an arrest can be made.

When Santa Barbara County detectives learned the details of Matt Russell's robbery, their investigation of the Thrifty heist reached a tipping point. Detectives were particularly interested in one detail of the Russell robbery: Like Azael Pinzon, Matt Russell had his identification stolen during the hold-up.

Around the same time, Santa Barbara County detectives also learned that Josh was a frequent visitor to their county. Specifically, detectives learned that Josh enjoyed gambling at the Chumash Casino. Located north of Santa Barbara near the tourist town of Solvang, the Chumash Casino is a gambling mecca in the Santa Ynez Valley. Detectives assigned to the Thrifty case no doubt realized that the 101 Freeway is the shortest route from Ventura to Chumash, and that this route passes within fifty yards of the State Street Thrifty.

After detectives learned about Josh's gambling activity at the Chumash Casino, they began examining his cell-phone records. Detectives noted that, on the night of the Thrifty robbery, signals from Josh's cell phone had bounced off a cellular tower near the Chumash Casino. This bit of evidence placed Josh in Santa Barbara County on the night of the Thrifty robbery. Detectives also turned up more damning details in Josh's cell-phone records. Specifically, detectives discovered that, a few minutes before the Thrifty robbery, a signal from Josh's cell phone bounced off a cellular tower on the west side of Santa Barbara. [35] This cellular tower is located only a few blocks from the State Street Thrifty.

Detectives were intrigued by the cell-phone evidence they were gathering, but they weren't going to jump the gun on making an arrest. As every good detective knows, getting the job done right is more important than getting the job done fast. To this end, Santa Barbara County detectives wanted to gather as much evidence as possible before they made an arrest. The detectives' quest for evidence led them directly to the upper management of the Chumash Casino.

After being contacted by the robbery detectives, Chumash managers checked the information on Josh's Player's Club card. The card-check revealed that, on the night of the Thrifty robbery, Josh suffered a $268 loss while gaming at the Chumash Casino. [36] For a young man who worked a low-paying security job, $268 was not an insubstantial loss.

Next, detectives asked the Chumash managers if the casino had any video footage from the night of the robbery. Because the entire casino complex was outfitted with high-quality surveillance cameras, the Chumash managers were able to provide detectives with some remarkable footage. First, the managers were able to show detectives footage of Josh walking through the casino. From what detectives could tell, the attire Josh wore at the casino on September 23, 2009, was similar to the attire worn by the Thrifty robber. Also, video footage from the Chumash parking structure showed Josh's Chevy Trailblazer snaking through the garage prior to the robbery. When detectives looked at the Trailblazer's bumper, everything clicked. There was no license plate on Josh's SUV.

The noose was tightening.

***

As Santa Barbara County detectives were putting the finishing touches on their Thrifty investigation, Josh was finding plenty of trouble for himself in Ventura.

On October 7, 2009, Josh was involved in a major traffic accident while roaring down Telephone Road on his motorcycle. The high-velocity collision was so powerful that it propelled Josh off his bike and sent him tumbling more than 100 feet down Telephone Road. Every rib on Josh's right side was broken, his right lung collapsed, and he stopped breathing for a short time. After paramedics arrived at the scene, Josh was intubated, rushed to the emergency room at Ventura County Medical Center, and placed in a medically induced coma.

While Josh was being treated in the Intensive Care Unit, Terri went to visit him. Although he was heavily sedated, Josh remained lucid long enough to recognize his mother.

"I'm okay, Mom," Josh whispered in a husky croak before lapsing back into his coma.

The thought of that incident still brings tears to Terri's eyes. However, not all of Josh's visitors shared such tender moments with him while he was in the hospital.

After Josh's motorcycle crash, Bob Miller had written a letter to the local newspaper about the accident. In his letter, Miller referred to Josh as his nephew.

Days later, when Josh emerged from his coma and was transferred out of the Intensive Care Unit, Miller paid him a visit. Terri was sitting at Josh's bedside when Miller walked into the room and handed Josh a copy of the newspaper containing his published letter. As soon as Josh finished reading the syrupy letter, he offered a searing critique.

"That's gay," Josh scoffed before flinging the newspaper across the room.

Upon witnessing this, Terri could tell that something was seriously wrong between her son and Bob Miller. When Josh fell asleep, Terri pulled Miller aside in the hallway.

"What's going on?" Terri asked Miller.

"Nothing," Miller said. "Everything's fine."

Terri wasn't convinced.

Being young and resilient, Josh grew stronger

with each passing day. However, as Josh's strength improved, his behavior became increasingly volatile.

On November 7, 2009, security officers Ryan Deleon and Imelda Kemblowski were working the day shift at Ventura County Medical Center. While manning the security post in the emergency room, Deleon and Kemblowski received an alert that there was a problem in room 206. The security officers were told that nurses needed immediate assistance with an unruly patient.

When Deleon and Kemblowski arrived at the nurses station near room 206, they were briefed on the situation. The security officers were told that the patient in room 206 had become argumentative and combative after his request for a larger dose of pain medication was denied. The officers were also told that the patient's name was Joshua Packer.

Along with two floor nurses, Deleon and Kemblowski made their way to room 206. When they arrived, Deleon and Kemblowski waited outside the door while the nurses entered the room and attempted to calm Josh. It soon became obvious that Josh had no intention of calming down. As the nurses attempted to assuage their recently comatose patient, Josh escalated his level of aggression.

Moving into the room to back up the nurses, Deleon and Kemblowski saw Josh lying on his hospital bed near the door. An IV tube ran into Josh's right arm and tears streamed from his eyes. It was obvious to the security officers that Josh was crying.

As soon as Josh saw the security officers, the situation became even more intense.

"Get the fuck outta my room!" Josh yelled at the officers. "You have no right to be here! I do security and I know what you're allowed to do."

In an effort to protect the nurses and regain control of the situation, Deleon took a position at the front of Josh's bed and Kemblowski stood off to the side. When it became clear that the guards weren't going to leave the room, Josh started to get physical.

Leaping from his bed and ripping the IV tube from his arm, Josh plowed into Deleon with full force. Though he was still injured after his motorcycle accident, Josh's speed and strength were ferocious. Kemblowski attempted to pull Josh away from Deleon, but Josh's feral strength was too much for the female security officer to handle. Within seconds, Josh had placed Deleon in a headlock and the men crashed into the wall.

Not knowing what else to do, Deleon wrapped his flailing arm around Josh's neck. Grappling awkwardly with one another in dual chokeholds, Josh and Deleon smashed around the hospital room until Josh was able to throw Deleon to the floor. With Deleon out of the way, Josh turned his attention to Kemblowski, who was still stunned from his initial assault. In one fluid motion, Josh reached out, grabbed Kemblowski, threw her over his shoulder, and slammed her head into the wall of the room. By that point, Deleon had regained his footing. Deleon attempted to help the now-immobilized Kemblowski, but Josh's strength was too great. With few options available, Deleon plowed into Josh, who still had the struggling Kemblowski pinned over his shoulder like a professional wrestler. All three went to the floor. Kemblowski's head and shoulder smashed into the clean white tile as Josh and Deleon landed on top of her.

Moments later, additional security officers and hospital staff flooded into room 206. Through their combined efforts, they were able to pin Josh to the floor, then four-point him onto a plastic backboard using padded restraints. Josh was then placed on a gurney so he could be removed from room 206. The goal was to transport Josh to the ER for a psychiatric evaluation.

As Josh was being wheeled out of room 206, he managed to wrench one of his arms free from the padded restraints. With all his might, Josh lashed out and smashed Deleon in the face. The security team immediately restrained Josh's arm, but not before Josh spit at Deleon, striking the security officer in his right eye.

"I'm gonna fuckin' kill you!" Josh screamed at Deleon as he was fitted with a spit guard and wheeled away to the emergency room. "I know where you live!"
(37)

While Josh, Deleon, and Kemblowski were being treated in the ER, a call was placed to the Ventura Police Department. The responding officers took a report on the fight in room 206, and in the coming days, Josh found himself facing two new criminal charges: misdemeanor battery and felony assault with force likely to produce great bodily injury.

Once he was out of the hospital, it didn't take long for Josh to find more trouble for himself.

On the afternoon of December 11, 2009, just days after Josh was discharged from Ventura County Medical Center, a young man Damian Perea was sitting in his apartment at 41 Baylor Drive. Perea's apartment was located on a quiet side street near Ventura College. At 4:20 p.m., Perea heard a godless boom come from the street in front of his apartment building. Leaving his apartment and running outside, Perea immediately saw the source of the boom: a Chevy Trailblazer had crashed into his silver Infiniti, which had been parked on the street.

As Perea made his way toward the accident scene, he quickly assessed the aftermath of the collision. Both his Infiniti and the Trailblazer had suffered major body damage, and debris from the crash was scattered across the roadway. Perea could see the Trailblazer's twisted bumper lying haphazardly across the sidewalk.

As Perea took in the extent of the damage, he saw a young white man with brown hair stumble out from behind the wrecked Trailblazer. The young man appeared to be dazed.

"Hey man, I just hit your car," the young man said to Perea. The young man then introduced himself as Josh Packer.

Josh went on to explain that, as he was driving northbound on Baylor, his foot "got stuck" on the accelerator. This caused him to accidentally plow into Perea's Infiniti.

With little else to do, Perea invited Josh into his apartment so they could exchange insurance information. On their walk toward the building, Josh handed his driver's license and insurance card to Perea. When Josh placed the documents in Perea's hand, Perea could tell that Josh's speech was slurred and that he was talking far too slowly. [38]

When they got inside the apartment, Perea detected a strong, unmistakable odor of alcohol coming from Josh. Perea asked Josh if he'd been drinking. Josh immediately became defensive.

"Hey man, I've had a few beers, but what's the big

deal?" Josh said. "I didn't have to stop. I could've just left and the cops couldn't get me for DUI."

This lame rationalization carried little weight with Perea. The Infiniti owner immediately pulled out his cell phone.

"Who are you calling?" Josh demanded to know.

"The police," Perea responded.

Before Perea could dial 911, Josh reached out and slapped the phone from Perea's hand. Josh then attempted to snatch his license and insurance card. When Perea pushed his drunken guest away, Josh began to level threats.

"Don't touch me!" Josh ordered. "My girlfriend's dad is a cop and I'll have you arrested on assault charges!"

By that point, Perea just wanted Josh out of his home. In an instant, Josh snatched his license and insurance card from Perea's hand, bolted for the door, and fled the scene in his badly damaged Trailblazer. As Josh was fleeing the scene, Perea's 911 call was answered by the Ventura Police Department.

In a strange twist of fate, Officer Mary Eltz—the same officer who'd responded to Matt Russell's robbery call in April 2009—was dispatched to the scene of the hit-and-run on Baylor Drive. After obtaining a statement from Perea, Officer Eltz and her partner contacted Josh. When everything was said and done, Josh found himself facing three new charges: leaving the scene of an accident, battery, and dissuading a witness. The first two charges were misdemeanors. The third was a felony.

By early January 2010, Santa Barbara County robbery detectives were ready to make their move. The detectives had accrued a wealth of evidence that pointed, in no uncertain terms, to Josh Packer's involvement in the Thrifty robbery. The direct and circumstantial evidence against Josh included the following:

1. On the night of the Thrifty robbery, detectives could prove that the phone call made to Javier Espinoza from Azael Pinzon's stolen cell phone originated in Josh Packer's Ventura neighborhood;

2. Josh Packer matched the physical description of the Thrifty robber;

3. Josh Packer's Chevy Trailblazer matched the description of the vehicle seen leaving the Thrifty immediately after the robbery;

4. Video footage from the Chumash Casino, as well as casino records, placed Josh Packer in Santa Barbara County on the night of the robbery. Casino records also showed that Josh experienced a significant financial loss on the night of the robbery;

5. The M.O. used by the Thrifty robber matched the M.O. used by the Ventura serial robber, whose hold-ups had come to an abrupt stop after Josh Packer's near-fatal motorcycle accident on October 7, 2009;

6. Josh Packer's personal cell phone was used within blocks of the Thrifty around the time of the robbery.

Armed with this evidence, Santa Barbara County detectives decided that it was time to take Josh into custody. On January 13, 2010, Detective Ray Gamboa authored a search warrant for Josh's apartment on Webster Street, as well as Josh's Trailblazer. Judge George Eskin signed the warrant the same day.

Although the detectives didn't know it at the time, Bob Miller had evicted Josh from their apartment in September 2009. The reason: Josh's failure to pay rent. Since that time, Josh had moved back into Terri's home on Ocean Avenue. As a result, when Santa Barbara County detectives arrived at the Jefferson Apartments to serve their search warrant at 6 a.m. on January 14, 2010, Miller was the only person home.

After banging on the front door and making entry into the residence, the detectives learned that Josh no longer resided in unit 310. However, Miller told detectives that he allowed his "nephew" to store some belongings in the east bedroom of the apartment. Detectives immediately flooded into the east bedroom and started searching.

While the east bedroom was being searched, Detective Gamboa questioned Miller about his relationship with Josh. Miller explained that he, Josh, and Jessica Rossi had moved into the apartment in March 2009, and that Jessica had moved out a few weeks later. Miller also explained that he evicted Josh for non-payment of rent in the fall of 2009.

"When did you last see Josh?" Detective Gamboa asked Miller.

"About two weeks ago," Miller answered. "He came by here to get some of his stuff."

Detective Gamboa then showed Miller surveillance footage from the Chumash Casino.

"Do you recognize the person in this video?" Detective Gamboa asked.

"Yeah," Miller said. "That's Josh."

Meanwhile, in the portion of the east bedroom where Josh stored his possessions, detectives were unearthing valuable evidence. Detectives found a pair of black gloves and a black-on-white bandana among Josh's things. The gloves and bandana appeared to be identical to the ones worn by the Thrifty bandit on the night of the robbery. Detectives also located a black airsoft pistol, which bore a strong likeness to an actual semiautomatic handgun. [39] Following proper procedure, all of the items were collected and booked into evidence.

"We're interested in talking to Josh," Detective Gamboa explained to Miller as searchers continued to comb through Josh's possessions. "Where can we find him?"

Miller told the detective that Josh was living with Terri at 1808 Ocean Avenue in Ventura. With sufficient probable cause to arrest Josh, detectives began making their way toward Terri's house.

As soon as the detectives left the Jefferson Apartments, Miller picked up the phone and called Terri. With unfettered excitement in his voice, Miller explained that the Santa Barbara County Sheriff's Department had just raided his apartment and that detectives were looking for Josh. According to Terri, Josh wasn't home when Miller called that morning. However, Miller's call did forewarn Terri that detectives were on their way to her home.

When detectives Gamboa and Scherbarth arrived at 1808 Ocean Avenue, they were greeted by Terri and Rudy Cobos. Cobos explained to the detectives that Josh had stayed with friends the previous night. The detectives asked to see Josh's bedroom, so Terri showed it to them. Without a warrant, the detectives couldn't search the room. However, the detectives noted various pieces of clothing scattered around the room, indicating that Josh had recently been there.

Without getting into too many details, the detectives explained that they needed to speak with Josh about a very important matter. Terri agreed to contact Josh, pick him up, and bring him home so he could meet with the detectives.

Around 12:30 p.m., the detectives watched as Terri pulled into her driveway with Josh sitting in the passenger seat of her vehicle. This was the first time the detectives were seeing their young robbery suspect up close and personal.

In a calm and professional manner, detectives Gamboa and Scherbarth approached Josh and introduced themselves. Josh shook their hands. Once the introductions were out of the way, Josh, the detectives, Terri, and Rudy sat down in plastic chairs in the yard and began talking.

Detective Gamboa told Josh that his agency was investigating a serious incident from the previous September. Detective Gamboa then read Josh his Miranda rights. Once Josh was Mirandized, Gamboa told him that they wanted to look in his bedroom. Josh did not consent to have his bedroom searched. Undeterred, Detective Gamboa explained that he had a warrant to search Josh's vehicle. When Gamboa inquired about the Trailblazer's whereabouts, Josh explained that he'd parked it behind a nearby big-box store. By that point, another pair of detectives had arrived at Terri's house. Josh handed his car keys to the second pair of detectives while Gamboa and Scherbarth continued the interview.

Gamboa asked Josh a series of questions about his gambling activity at the Chumash Casino. Josh admitted to gaming at the casino from time to time. When asked if he ever went to the casino alone, Josh gave an answer that was so profoundly non-committal, it should've qualified him for induction into the *Guinness Book of World Records.*

"Do you ever go to Chumash alone?" Detective Gamboa asked.

"No, or yeah, or no, yeah," Josh hemmed and hawed. "I don't know." [40]

Terri explained to the detectives that, since his motorcycle accident the previous October, Josh had trouble remembering things. She attributed Josh's memory loss to the medications he was taking.

With their preliminary questions out of the way, the detectives got down to brass tacks.

"Josh, do you recall what you were doing on the night of September 23, 2009?" Detective Gamboa asked.

"Nope," Josh answered. "That's two days after my birthday, but I don't remember what I was doing that night."

"Did you go to the Chumash Casino that night?" Detective Gamboa followed up.

"I don't remember."

"You lost $268 that night," Detective Scherbarth reminded him. "Does that ring a bell?"

"Nope."

With the interview going nowhere, Detective Gamboa moved things along. He told Josh that they were investigating a robbery at the Thrifty gas station on State Street. Gamboa then summarized all of the evidence detectives had collected up to that point.

After listening to the detective's evidence summary, Josh's response was succinct.

"I think I need to speak to an attorney," Josh said.

The interview was over, but Josh's day was just getting started. After invoking his Sixth Amendment right to counsel, Josh was placed under arrest for robbery and two felony counts of intimidating a witness.

According to Terri, the arrest was handled with total professionalism. Years later, Terri explained how impressed she was by detectives Gamboa and Scherbarth, as well as the other Santa Barbara County detectives she met that day.

"The Santa Barbara people, they were great!" Terri said. "They were honest with us, treated Josh right, everything."

Cuffed and secured in the backseat of the sheriff's car, Josh was driven out of Ventura and up the coast. When Josh arrived in Santa Barbara, he was booked into the county jail. In the process of being booked, Josh had his mugshot taken, his fingerprints scanned, his vital information recorded, and a buccal swab taken from the inside of his cheek. The buccal swab was then bagged and sent to the Department of Justice Lab for processing.

It was all part of the standard booking process.

CHAPTER 16

Within hours of being booked into the Santa Barbara County Jail, Josh Packer was bailed out by his mother and Bob Miller. Free again, Josh was driven home to Ventura. Terri was glad to have Josh home, but with three serious felony charges hanging over his head, she was anxious about her son's pending trial and the prison sentence that would surely follow if he was convicted.

Terri wasn't the only one struggling with anxiety around that time. By January 2010, Ventura County detectives were completely stumped by the Faria murder investigation. Ventura County detectives had no suspects, no leads, and no answers for the Husted and DeBoni family members, who were still reeling from the nearly year-old murders.

With Ventura County homicide detectives making zero progress with their investigation, the Husted and DeBoni families had taken matters into their own hands. In November 2009, the families staged a candlelight vigil in front of Faria Beach Colony. Against a backdrop of banners and flickering candles, the assembled family members and their supporters held signs and implored the public to call detectives if they had any information about the murders. Although the local media did an excellent job of covering the vigil and *Dateline NBC* broadcast a special about the Faria murders, Ventura County detectives received no substantive tips regarding the Husted case.

Unbeknownst to Ventura County detectives, an important sequence of events was already playing out in another part of the state. Specifically, Josh Packer's buccal swab—which was obtained after his arrest for the Thrifty robbery—had been scheduled for processing at the California Department of Justice Lab. Once the buccal swab was processed, Josh's DNA profile was entered into the state's genetic database of known, suspected, and unidentified felons. This database was the culmination of years of scientific innovation, legal wrangling, and electoral victories.

The unique biological identifier known as deoxyribonucleic acid, or DNA, was first used to obtain a criminal conviction in the United States in 1987. The case involved a Florida man named Tommy Lee Andrews, who was accused of breaking into an elderly woman's home and raping her at knife-point. Orlando prosecutor Jeff Ashton (who later rose to fame as the lead prosecutor in Casey Anthony's 2011 murder trial) argued that DNA recovered from the old woman's home was identical to Andrews' DNA, and should therefore be admitted as evidence at Andrews' trial. After getting the biological evidence past a Frye hearing (which establishes the scientific validity of a forensic technique or procedure), Ashton presented Andrews' DNA to a jury. On November 6, 1987, the jury convicted Andrews of rape, burglary, and related charges.

After Andrews' verdict was handed down, DNA became a powerful tool for prosecutors and law-enforcement officials across the nation. By 1989, Ventura County prosecutors were using DNA in a landmark case of their own. The case involved a thirty-five-year-old woman named Lynda Patricia Axell.

On February 24, 1988, sixty-three-year-old George White was murdered during an attempted robbery at the Top Hat hamburger stand in Ventura. Evidence left at the crime scene indicated that, as he was being stabbed to death, White ripped a chunk of hair from his assailant's scalp. Using technology that was cutting-edge at the time, scientists at the Ventura County Crime Lab developed a DNA profile from the hair found in White's dead fist. Eventually, this profile was matched to Lynda Axell's DNA. [41] On September 13, 1989, after a six-month trial, Axell was convicted of first-degree murder and attempted robbery. She was sentenced to life in prison. Over the years, thanks in part to the DNA evidence against her, Axell's appeals have been denied consistently. Axell is currently housed at the California Institute for Women in Chowchilla.

Ventura County Superior Court Judge Lawrence Storch presided over Axell's murder trial. When the trial ended, Judge Storch commented on the verdict.

"The DNA evidence in this case was critical to the court's finding of guilt," Judge Storch said. "Without the DNA test results, there's not enough evidence."

Throughout the 1990s, as the O.J. Simpson murder trial seized the public's fascination, DNA's investigative utility became deeply ingrained in the American psyche. In 1999, Louisiana became the first state to enact legislation that allowed law enforcement to collect and catalog DNA from arrestees. [42] Once the arrestee DNA-collection law was on the books in Louisiana, it didn't take long for other states to follow suit.

In 2000, California passed a law that allowed state-prison inmates to request DNA screening as part of the appeals process. Two years later, on September 17, 2002, then-Governor Gray Davis signed into law Senate Bill 1242, which passed both houses of the California State Legislature without a single dissenting vote. SB 1242 allowed state-prison officials to use reasonable force to collect DNA samples from inmates. Lawmakers hoped that DNA collected from state prisoners could be used to identify suspects in unsolved crimes.

"I guarantee you that when we have those DNA samples, a host of crimes will be solved," Governor Davis said upon signing the bill into law. The governor added that the DNA collected under SB 1242 would "... bring peace of mind and closure to the victims of that crime who are not getting that closure they deserve." [43]

Two years later, California voters were asked to decide whether the state's DNA-collection program should be expanded to include all felony arrestees, as well as select misdemeanor arrestees. The state ballot initiative, known as Proposition 69, was put to a vote in November 2004. When the votes were tallied, Proposition 69 was approved by more than sixty-two percent of California voters. [44] Although the specific provisions of Proposition 69 would not go into effect until January 1, 2009, the popularity of the measure presaged sweeping changes in the American legal landscape.

A year after Proposition 69 was approved by California voters, Congress passed the DNA Fingerprint Act of 2005. This piece of legislation allowed the U.S. Justice Department to collect DNA from anyone arrested for a federal felony. Codified formally as 42 U.S.C. § 14135a(a)(5), the DNA Fingerprint Act made it a federal crime *not* to provide DNA after bring arrested for a federal felony.

With new DNA-collection laws sweeping the nation, DNA proved itself to be a valuable tool in the fight against crime. However, despite DNA's populist appeal and its proven efficacy in solving crimes, the growing number of DNA-collection laws were not without controversy.

In March 2009, an Oakland woman named Elizabeth "Lily" Haskell was arrested in San Francisco while protesting the Iraq War. San Francisco police officers alleged that Haskell had attempted to free another protester who was already in police custody. Per the state Penal Code, attempting to free an arrestee from official custody is a felony.

When Haskell was booked into the county jail, she was ordered to provide a DNA sample under the provisions of Proposition 69. Haskell was informed that refusing to provide a buccal swab would result in an additional misdemeanor charge. Haskell provided the DNA sample, but as soon as she was released from custody, she contacted an attorney. Eventually, Haskell's case was taken up by the American Civil Liberties Union of Northern California, which argued that forcing Haskell to provide a buccal swab was unconstitutional. The court disagreed. In December

2009, the United States District Court for the Northern District of California held that collecting arrestee DNA under the provisions of Proposition 69 was constitutional. [45] It was under the shadow of this ruling that Josh Packer's buccal swab was received by the Department of Justice Lab, processed by technicians, and entered into CODIS.

———————————

On April 1, 2010, Sergeant William Schierman of the Ventura County Sheriff's Department's Gang Unit received a mysterious phone call from another member of his department. The call, which was serious in tone, requested Schierman's presence the Camarillo Police Department that afternoon. When he arrived at the Camarillo police station, Schierman had no idea what to expect. Along with several other detectives and deputies, Schierman was ushered into a conference room where a meeting was about to begin. Once the meeting started, it didn't take long for the assembled lawmen to understand the momentous importance of that day.

With Ventura County detectives and deputies filling the Camarillo conference room, Sergeant Billy Hester stood up to address the audience.

"We have a break in the Faria murder case," Sergeant Hester told the assembled lawmen.

The excitement in the air was palpable.

For almost a year, Ventura County homicide detectives had been completely flummoxed by the Faria murders. The grieving family members had received no justice and the community remained on edge. Some people believed that the Faria murders would never be solved. The stakes in the Faria case couldn't have been higher.

Sergeant Hester explained that CODIS had matched the Faria murderer's DNA to a local man named Joshua Graham Packer. Hester explained that Josh's DNA had been obtained after he was arrested for a Santa Barbara robbery in January 2010. Hester added that Josh was living at his mother's home on Ocean Avenue in Ventura.

With the preliminaries out of the way, Sergeant Hester began laying out the game plan. While detectives with the Sheriff's Major Crimes Unit worked to build a murder case against Josh, Sergeant Schierman and the Gang Unit would conduct round-the-clock surveillance of the Faria suspect. It didn't take long to get the game plan up and running.

Within hours of the meeting in Camarillo, the Gang Unit had Josh in its crosshairs. From what the Gang Unit could tell, Josh had no idea that he was being tailed. Members of the Gang Unit watched as Josh picked up a friend in his Chevy Trailblazer and the young men cruised into the night. Eventually, the Trailblazer ended up on Pacific Coast Highway.

Suspecting that Josh's Trailblazer might contain narcotics, members of the Gang Unit decided to execute a traffic stop. Hitting their blue lights, the surveillance team pulled Josh over on an isolated stretch of PCH. Once the vehicle was stopped, it didn't take long to establish probable cause for an arrest. The arresting deputies alleged that cocaine was found in the car and Josh was taken into custody.

For his part, Josh vehemently denied the drug charge.

Over the next five days, as Josh sat in jail on

the cocaine charge, detectives were dotting their i's, crossing their t's, and building an air-tight murder case against him.

For many Ventura County law-enforcement officials, having the prime suspect in the Faria murders off the streets was comforting in and of itself. However, because they lacked evidence in the cocaine case, the Sheriff's Department was forced to drop the narcotics charge against Josh. As a result, Josh was released from jail on the evening of April 5, 2010. He returned to Terri's house.

Sergeant Schierman and his Gang Unit colleagues immediately resumed their surveillance.

On the evening of April 11, 2010, just before 7:30 p.m., Terri was in the upstairs bathroom of her home bathing her two youngest children. Through the splashing and babbling of her babies, Terri became aware of an unusual sound rising in the distance. At first the sound was faint. As the second ticked by, though, the sound became louder. Within a couple of minutes, there was a deafening roar above Terri's house. Terri realized that it was the sound of a helicopter.

About that time, Terri heard loud, determined banging on her front door. Before she had time to react, Terri heard the sound of wood cracking, her front door crashing open, and heavy footsteps running through her home.

Terri walked out of her upstairs bathroom and was immediately confronted by armed Ventura County deputies pointing guns at her.

"Get down!" the deputies shouted.

Terri tried to explain that she had two small children in the bathtub and that she couldn't leave them.

The deputies didn't care. They wanted all of the home's occupants immobilized.

Being assertive, Terri again refused to leave her two small children in the bathtub unattended. Rudy Cobos was out bowling at the time and Terri feared that her babies would drown if she didn't watch them.

As deputies attempted to subdue Terri, Josh walked out of his back bedroom near the garage.

"Freeze Packer!" the deputies shouted as they caught sight of their long-sought Faria murder suspect.

Josh was ordered to the floor at gunpoint and cuffed.

Terri was finally allowed to attend to her children in the bathtub. As a procession of Sheriff's Department officials stormed into Terri's house to search for evidence, she removed her youngest children from the bathtub and quickly dressed them. She then rushed to the front door to see what was happening to Josh.

According to Terri, Josh was dragged out of the house in handcuffs, dropped on the ground in their front yard, and punched in the face by a member of the Sheriff's Department. Josh's booking photo from that night shows him with a fresh, purplish black eye.

For his part, Sergeant Schierman remembered arrest differently. According to Schierman's report, Josh attempted to stand up and resist arrest after being ordered to the floor. It was at that point that sheriff's officials became physical.

"Detective Whittaker and I pulled (Josh) outside away from the doorway and pushed him to the ground," Schierman wrote in his report. "Once on the ground, Packer had his hands to his sides. As I grabbed his right arm and attempted to put it behind his back, he resisted my efforts to bring it behind his back. I quickly punched him in the upper right side of his back with light to moderate force and at the same time told him to put his hands behind his back. Packer went limp and allowed me to put his right hand behind his back. I kept my right knee on packers [sic] upper body and Deputy Whittaker and I handcuffed him." [46]

With the air-ship still roaring overhead and detectives tearing her house apart, Terri watched as Josh was placed in the backseat of an unmarked car and driven to jail. It was the last time Terri would ever see her first-born son in the free world.

CHAPTER 17

Known formally and euphemistically as the Pretrial Detention Facility, the Ventura County jail sits on a wide, flat piece of land between the Hall of Justice and the Jefferson Apartments. After Josh was booked into the Pretrial Detention Facility on April 11, 2010, he was held in near-total isolation. According to Terri, the conditions of Josh's confinement were extreme. Not only was Josh denied regular contact with other inmates, he was also barred from using utensils when he ate.

"They treated my son like an animal!" Terri raged. She added that, in lieu of eating utensils, Josh was given a small piece of styrofoam, which he used to scoop the gooey jailhouse victuals into his mouth.

Because he was outgoing and naturally gregarious, the solitary conditions of the Pretrial Detention Facility were particularly hard on Josh. He'd been to jail in the past, but he'd never been booked on such serious charges and he'd never faced indefinite confinement. This time, however, there would be no quick resolutions. As Josh sat alone in his cell, isolated from the world and facing the most serious charges imaginable, he was blasted by a never-ending stream of arctic air from the vent on his cell wall. Josh's experience in the Pretrial Detention Facility was chilling, both literally and figuratively.

While Josh sat shivering in his jail cell, his case was forwarded to the District Attorney's Office and handed off to Mike Frawley, the father of Josh's former Young Life acquaintances Kyle and Elizabeth Frawley. As Chief Deputy District Attorney, Mike Frawley is in charge of prosecuting high-level felony cases in Ventura County.

Reading through the case file on the Faria crimes, Frawley was evaluating the elements of each charged offense. Based on what he read, Frawley concluded that Josh had committed numerous felonies against the Husteds on May 20, 2009. These felonies included two counts of residential robbery with use of a deadly weapon, one count of first-degree burglary, and three counts of first-degree murder. The former charges carried a potential penalty of decades in prison. The latter charges carried the possibility of execution by lethal injection.

As Frawley was preparing to bring formal charges in the Faria case, Deputy Public Defender Benjamin Maserang was appointed as Josh's lead defense counsel. Maserang did not respond to an interview request for this book, but based on his dogged defense work in Josh's case, it's clear that Maserang is a committed attorney and a zealous advocate for the accused. After being appointed to defend Josh, Maserang fought valiantly to ensure that his client's rights were protected. To this end, Maserang and the other members of the defense team became some of the strongest advocates Josh ever had.

After Josh was formally charged with the Faria crimes in April 2010, the District Attorney's Office wasted no time in announcing that it would seek the death penalty. Considering that Josh's DNA had been found throughout the Husteds' bedroom, his defense position was perilous at best. As a result, Maserang had only one move: stall, stall, stall.

In the meantime, Josh's behavior at the Pretrial Detention Facility took a turn for the worse. Although he was kept in an isolated section of the jail, Josh was able to communicate with other inmates from time to time. According to an official report by the Sheriff's Department, Josh made an extremely damaging admission to one of his fellow inmates. The inmate asked Josh about the Faria case, which was a major news story at the time. According to the Sheriff's Department's report, Josh obliged his fellow inmate by describing—in graphic detail—how he'd stabbed the Husteds to death. Josh even told his jailhouse neighbor that, as he was plunging the butcher knife into Brock and Davina Husted, he couldn't stop himself. Josh compared stabbing his victims to the addictive rhythm of pushing buttons on the video slot machines at the Chumash Casino. [47]

True to jailhouse form, Josh's new acquaintance immediately snitched him out to sheriff's officials. According to the Sheriff's Department's report, the acquaintance relayed all of Josh's statements to staff and was transferred off the unit. After that, Josh's jailhouse outbursts became a regular occurrence.

As the spring of 2010 turned into summer, Maserang and the defense team poured untold hours into Josh's case. As he dug deeper and deeper into the high-stakes defense, Maserang no doubt realized that a direct fight against the D.A.'s Office was unwinnable. Mike Frawley and his team were holding all the cards; they had large quantities of powerful evidence that unequivocally linked Josh to the Faria crime scene. In addition to the DNA evidence that had already been processed in the case, detectives had continued collecting evidence after Josh was arrested for the Faria murders. Some of the newly collected evidence was extremely inculpatory for Josh. For example, after learning that Jessica Rossi had purchased Josh's motorcycle, detectives served a search warrant at the Rossi home. In the course of their search, detectives found Josh's black motorcycle helmet in the Rossis' garage. When detectives examined the helmet, they noticed that its plastic visor was in place. However, when the helmet was examined more carefully at the county crime lab, it was determined that the visor did not come stock from the helmet's manufacturer. Instead, the visor was a replacement part that had been purchased from a different manufacturer. [48]

After assessing the evidence that tied his client to the Faria murders, Maserang undoubtedly realized that the proverbial writing was on the wall. And, as it turned out, the writing on the wall happened to be a syllogism:

> **If Josh's case proceeds to trial,**
> **then Josh will be convicted.**
> **And if Josh is convicted, then Josh**
> **will receive the death penalty.**

Ergo, Josh's case could not go to trial. Period.

Since a direct fight wouldn't work to save Josh's life, Maserang shifted tactics and opted for an oblique approach. If he couldn't achieve a not guilty verdict in the case, Maserang could achieve two other crucial goals: He could save Josh's life and help Josh take responsibility for his atrocious crimes in Faria. However, Josh wasn't making Maserang's job any easier.

Back at the Pretrial Detention Facility, Josh was quickly gaining a reputation as a problem inmate. During the first four months of his confinement, Josh received major write-ups for attempting to manipulate staff members, acting verbally aggressive and confrontational, and generally thumbing his nose at the institution's rules. [49] On several occasions, Josh had become physical with staff members. Josh had also started to engage in acts of self-harm.

On August 15, 2010, Josh began banging his head into the solid steel door of his cell. Fearing for Josh's safety, deputies arranged to have their Faria murder suspect transferred to Ventura County Medical Center's emergency room. When he arrived at the emergency room, Josh made it known that he wanted to be housed in the Medical Center's psychiatric facility, which is known as Hillmont. Josh told deputies and hospital staff that if he was returned to the Pretrial Detention Facility, he would continue to injure himself. Worried that Josh would make good on his threats of self-harm and deeming him a danger to himself, Josh was admitted to Hillmont.

Because Josh's charges were extremely serious, two deputies were assigned to guard him at all times during his stay at Hillmont. During his first night at Hillmont, deputies Jauregui and Tao were assigned to guard Josh. Not long after they started their shift at 6 p.m., Jauregui and Tao went into Josh's room to check on him. After seeing that Josh was lying in bed with his right leg shackled to the bed frame, the deputies were convinced that everything was under control. Josh had other plans.

From his supine position on the bed, Josh asked the deputies if he could make a phone call. Deputy Tao told Josh that, for safety reasons, he was not allowed to use the phone. Josh immediately became indignant and called Deputy Tao a "butthead." [50]

Remaining calm, Tao explained that disrespect would not be tolerated, and that Josh was going to receive a write-up.

Josh muttered that the deputy must have misheard him. Deputy Jauregui promptly stepped up and told Josh that he was going to receive another write-up for dishonesty.

With that, Josh exploded.

Leaping to his feet and shouting at the top of his lungs, Josh unleashed a torrent of verbal abuse on the deputies. Jauregui and Tao ordered Josh to lie down and be quiet. Josh refused.

Before the deputies had time to react, Josh picked up a plastic hospital urinal and hurled it at them. Although neither deputy was struck by the flying urinal, the aggressive act was cause for concern.

Both deputies unholstered their tasers, pointed them at Josh, and ordered him to lie down on the bed. Josh responded by snatching a cup of water from his hospital table and flinging it across the room, drenching Deputy Jauregui.

Soaked with water, Jauregui attempted to deploy his taser. It failed to function properly. As a result, both Jauregui and Tao rushed Josh, tackled him onto the bed, and began calling for help from hospital staff.

As Josh struggled with the deputies, nurses and orderlies flooded into the room. Eventually, through their combined efforts, the deputies and hospital staff were able to get Josh under control. Using padded restraints, the staff members four-pointed Josh to the bed and used sedatives to calm him.

Though Josh's outburst at Hillmont was intense, it was not an isolated incident. After Josh was discharged from Hillmont and transferred back to the Pretrial Detention Facility, he continued to clash with deputies and other jail personnel on a regular basis.

By the fall of 2010, Maserang had formulated an initial plan to save Josh's life. No doubt realizing that a trial would be disastrous for Josh, Maserang prepared an offer and presented it to the District Attorney's Office on October 14, 2010. The terms of the plea offer were simple: In exchange for taking the death penalty off the table, Josh would plead guilty to the murders of Brock, Davina, and Grant Husted and accept a sentence of life in prison without the possibility of parole.

The Ventura County D.A.'s Office was having none of it. Knowing full well that they had enough evidence to convict Josh at trial, prosecutors rejected Maserang's plea offer. The calculus behind the prosecution's decision was easy to follow: Given the extreme nature of the Faria murders, there was no way the prosecution could acquiesce to a life sentence. After all, if prosecutors didn't push for the death penalty against Josh Packer, when could they push for the death penalty? By caving in to Maserang's plea offer, prosecutors undoubtedly realized that they'd be painting themselves into a corner.

With the plea offer rejected, Maserang and the defense team went into full-scale mitigation mode. The purpose of mitigation is to ensure that, if a murder defendant convicted in a death-penalty case, jurors will learn the full context of the defendant's actions during the penalty phase of the trial. At its core, mitigation is designed to help jurors recognize a defendant's humanity. In turn, jurors will be less inclined to recommend a death sentence, or so the thinking goes. Defense attorneys don't wait for a guilty verdict to begin assembling their mitigation packages. Instead, because mitigation can be such a valuable tool, defense attorneys begin assembling their mitigation packages in the earliest stages of capital cases.

Considering the sensational and brutal circumstances of the Faria murders, Maserang undoubtedly knew that the mitigation package would play an integral role in saving Josh's life if the case made it to trial. And with the D.A.'s Office adamantly refusing to plea bargain, the possibility of a trial was looking more and more likely.

To gather information for the mitigation package, Maserang and the defense team interviewed a wide range of people from Josh's past. They talked to teachers and friends and social-service employees. They spoke with Shauna and Terri's former husbands and neighbors. Members of the defense team even traveled to Ohio to interview Randy Packer. After divorcing Terri, Randy had converted to Mormonism and was raising dogs near Cincinnati. Randy hadn't seen Josh since he was a baby, but to his credit,

BLACK NIGHT, GOLD COAST

Randy did his best to cooperate with the mitigation investigators and help save the life of the son he'd never known.

The most important person in the mitigation process was Terri, who went to extraordinary lengths to put Josh's dreadful childhood into perspective for the defense team. Terri's conversations with the mitigation investigators brought to the surface all of the difficult truths from her past. Terri told the mitigation investigators about her history of arrests, her former drug problem, and the constant domestic violence that Josh had witnessed as a child. She told the investigators about Josh being dragged into detention facilities and impound offices when she was put in jail or their cars were towed. She told the investigators about the multiple instances of parental abandonment Josh had experienced as a child, as well as the serious injuries he'd experienced as a result of adult negligence. She even told the mitigation investigators about the horrific sexual assaults Josh had suffered as a boy. With capital-murder charges hanging over Josh's head and the prospect of an unwinnable trial looming large on the horizon, Terri's candor played a vital role in the defense's mitigation effort.

As the ignominious circumstances of Josh's youth came into full focus, the defense felt that it had a foothold for asking the court for leniency if a conviction was obtained against Josh. When it was all said and done, Josh's mitigation package ran to more than 10,000 pages.

<hr/>

For their part, the prosecution team wasn't leaving anything to chance. A prosecutor's job is to seek justice for crime victims, their loved ones, and the state, while simultaneously protecting the community from further harm. Prosecutors use hard evidence to guide their decision making, and the evidence in the Faria murders pointed to one inescapable conclusion: Josh Packer was a dangerous predator who had callously murdered three human beings in their own home. In the eyes of the law, neither Josh's childhood abuse nor the dysfunctional circumstances of his youth justified his criminal behavior. As a result, the Ventura County District Attorney's Office deemed the death penalty the only appropriate sanction for Josh's conduct.

Although the D.A.'s Office was adamant about convicting Josh and securing a death sentence against him, Ventura County prosecutors wanted to hedge their bets. Because jurors can be unpredictable when it comes to verdicts and sentencing recommendations, Ventura County prosecutors wanted to increase the quantity of ammunition in their already bulging war chest. Specifically, prosecutors wanted to bolster the perception that Josh was a lawless thug with a lengthy criminal history and a proclivity for violence. To this end, in the spring of 2011, the Ventura County D.A.'s Office put Josh on trial for two incidents that were unrelated to the Faria murders: the hospital brawl that took place after his motorcycle accident in October 2009 and the hit-and-run incident involving Damian Perea that happened in December 2009.

Although it occurred second chronologically, the Perea case went to trial first. The hit-and-run trial began on April 4, 2011. The state was represented by Deputy District Attorney Anthony Sabo. Attorney Gay Zide was appointed to represent Josh.

On the opening day of the hit-and-run trial, a local

reporter asked Sabo why the prime suspect in a high-profile murder case was being tried for a relatively picayune traffic incident.

"There's a victim in this case too, and we think that's important," Sabo told the reporter. [51]

While Sabo's answer was technically accurate, it omitted an important consideration for the prosecution: Any convictions obtained against Josh before his murder trial would be extremely valuable to prosecutors when it came time to argue for the death penalty. In other words, if the prosecution could demonstrate to the murder-trial jurors that Josh had a long history of felony convictions and violent behavior, it would enhance the probability that jurors would return a death sentence.

Sabo called several witnesses during the hit-and-run trial. One of the most effective witnesses was Mary Eltz, the Ventura police officer who responded to Perea's 911 call on December 11, 2009. Officer Eltz told the hit-and-run jurors about Josh's demeanor that day. According to Officer Eltz's testimony, Josh said the accident was caused when a water bottle became wedged under the Trailblazer's gas pedal.

For her part, Gay Zide argued that Josh left the scene of the accident because he was afraid. According to Zide, Josh became frightened by Damian Perea's aggressive behavior in the apartment. Zide left out that Josh had precipitated Perea's behavior by attempting to slap the phone out of Perea's hand.

Jurors didn't buy Josh's defense in the Perea case. Nine days after the trial started, the jury returned its verdict: Josh was guilty of misdemeanor hit-and-run driving, misdemeanor battery, and one felony count of dissuading a witness.

On April 17, 2011, four days after the Perea trial wrapped up, Josh went berserk at the Pretrial Detention Facility and tried to destroy his bed. He was forcibly removed from his normal housing at the jail, stripped naked, and placed in a safety cell for his own protection.

While Josh sat in the safety call and awaited sentencing in the Perea case, the D.A.'s Office was busy preparing additional charges against him. Emboldened by their success in the Perea case, prosecutors were eager to try Josh for his attack on hospital security officers Ryan Deleon and Imelda Kemblowski in November 2009.

The hospital-assault trial got underway in mid-June 2011. However, going on trial for serious violent-crime charges didn't diminish Josh's volatility. If anything, the pressure of the hospital-assault trial seemed to exacerbate Josh's instability.

Just as the hospital-assault trial was getting under way, Josh became involved in an extremely violent altercation at the Pretrial Detention Facility. The incident started over a phone call.

On June 19, 2011, Josh asked to call Rudy Cobos and wish him a happy Father's Day. When jail staff refused the request, Josh exploded. According to the Sheriff's Department, after he was told that he couldn't use the phone, Josh started destroying property in his cell. When deputies ordered Josh to stop damaging his cell, he refused to comply with their orders. Josh then began to "board up"—or barricade himself—inside his cell.

Calling for reinforcements—including a deputy to serve as videographer— members of the Ventura County Sheriff's Department prepared to enter Josh's cell and subdue him. This was easier said than done. By June 2011, Josh had been in jail for more than a year and he was wise to the ways of the jailhouse. Knowing that deputies could deploy pepper spray or tasers to bring him under control, Josh utilized all of the tools at his disposal to frustrate his jailers. Snatching an orange jail-issued t-shirt from his bed, Josh quickly wrapped the article of clothing around his head to guard against any pepper spray the deputies might deploy. Next, Josh grabbed the wool blanket off his bed and held it up in front of him to stop any taser probes that might be fired in his direction. Josh stood rigid and defiant in the middle of his cell, ready for battle.

As video footage of the incident makes clear, deputies didn't want to use force against Josh.

"If we have to go in there, we can cause you harm, we can hurt you. We don't want to do that," a firm-voiced deputy tells Josh in the video. "But if you don't cuff up, we're gonna hurt you. We're gonna use force on you and it's gonna hurt. We don't want to do that. Get on the ground and comply."

As Josh continued to disobey the orders, a small army of deputies gathered outside his cell. Josh attempted to say something to the assembled lawmen, but with the orange t-shirt over his head, the video wasn't able to pick up his words. However, based on Josh's defiant posture and the fact that he didn't drop the blanket, it's clear that Josh had no intention of complying with the deputy's instructions.

"Packer, get on the ground and put your hands behind your back or force will be used against you," another deputy tells Josh in a clear, firm tone. "Do you understand? This is your last opportunity."

Josh refused to comply. With his head wrapped in the orange t-shirt and the blanket dangling in front of him like a matador, Josh had the appearance of an insane jailhouse bullfighter. It was clear that deputies were going to use force to restore order.

The entry team made its move. The ensuing brawl inside the cell was one of fury and frustration and frenzy.

After the cell door is yanked open, the video shows the first two deputies run into the cell, push past the blanket, plow into Josh, and shove him toward the left side of the screen. More deputies flood into the cell behind the first two. Undeterred by the superior power of his opposition, Josh drops his blanket and begins swinging his fists wildly. Two of Josh's right hooks connect solidly with a young deputy's face. The young deputy grimaces in pain as Josh's blows hammer into his jaw. Thrashing and grappling ensues for several seconds until the six-man scrum of deputies drags Josh to the cell floor. Once Josh is down and his arms are immobilized with cuffs, a rip-hobble is used to secure his legs. Toward the end of the video, a nurse appears in the corner of the screen and holds up a syringe containing some type of liquid. Order had been restored.

Eight days later, his face still bruised from the brawl in his cell, Josh heard the verdict in the hospital-assault case. On a positive note, jurors had deadlocked on the felony assault charge. However, the jury convicted Josh of misdemeanor battery for his attack on Deleon and Kemblowski.

Undeterred by the deadlocked jury, prosecutors prepared to retry Josh on the felony assault charge. When the case was presented to another jury in the fall of 2011, Josh was found guilty. At the age of twenty-two, Josh was a twice-convicted felon with a potential death sentence hanging over his head.

Weeks turned into months and 2011 dragged on. The murder-trial extensions, the isolation, and the helplessness of his situation were taking a toll on Josh. As he spent more and more time in isolation at the Pretrial Detention Facility, Josh's flesh blanched to a sickly pallor, he lost weight, and his hair started to thin prematurely.

While Josh languished in jail, Terri struggled with problems of her own. Since Josh's arrest for the Faria murders in April 2010, Terri had suffered from a profound sense of helplessness and guilt and sadness. One of the most frustrating aspects of the situation was Terri's lack of access to information about Josh's case. Because Josh was over the age of eighteen when the Faria murders were committed, Benjamin Maserang was not able to share privileged information about the case with Terri. At the same time, because she was concerned that the jailhouse phones might be bugged, Terri couldn't ask Josh about his murder case during their biweekly visits at the Pretrial Detention Facility. Instead, Terri and Josh spent their visits making small talk and listening to music.

"Whenever I'd visit him in jail, Josh would have me play *Demons* for him. He'd listen to it over and over again," Terri said, referring to the popular song by the rock band Imagine Dragons. "He'd just look over at me while the song played, and you know, I think maybe it was his way of trying to tell me something."

Between its morbidly suggestive lyrics and its melancholy harmony, *Demons* is a song that emanates a powerful sense of pain and regret and eternal purgatory. The song speaks in generalities about sins committed, temptations succumbed to, avarice indulged, and the inevitability of consequences. *Demons* served as a chilling soundtrack for Terri's visits with Josh.

Josh and Terri weren't the only ones experiencing heartache and emotional pain in 2011. On June 18, 2011, Davina Husted's father, David DeBoni, passed away. He was four days shy of his seventy-second birthday. Family members claimed that Davina's murder hastened her father's demise. Regardless of whether this was factually true or not, David DeBoni's passing was a grim reminder that, in the two years since the Faria slayings, no one had been brought to justice for the murders of Brock, Davina, and Grant Husted.

Then, in early 2012, it was announced that Josh Packer was facing a new charge related to the Faria murder case. It had taken two years, but prosecutors had finally amassed enough evidence to charge Josh with the crime of oral copulation by force against Davina Husted. If the charge stuck and a guilty verdict was rendered, it meant that Josh would become the lowest specimen in the state's correctional menagerie: a convicted sex offender.

CHAPTER 18

Before a criminal case can proceed to trial in the United States, the factual basis for bringing charges against the defendant—otherwise known as probable cause—must be evaluated. There are two ways to evaluate probable cause: a preliminary hearing or a grand jury. In a preliminary hearing, the prosecution summarizes its evidence against the defendant in front of a judge. The judge then decides whether there's sufficient probable cause to warrant a trial. A grand jury works in much the same way, only instead of a judge, a group of eighteen community members evaluates the probable cause. Neither a preliminary hearing nor a grand jury is used to assess a defendant's guilt. Instead, both legal proceedings are designed to test the probable cause against the defendant and determine whether the state has sufficient evidence to justify a trial.

When it came time to charge Josh Packer with oral copulation by force, the Ventura County District Attorney's Office opted to take the case before a grand jury. In early May 2012, nearly three years after the Faria murders, members of the grand jury were brought to the Hall of Justice to hear the evidence against Josh. According to the prosecution, the case against Josh went something like this:

In March 2009, Josh Packer, Jessica Rossi, and Bob Miller moved into unit 310 at the Jefferson Apartments. Their living arrangement seemed fun at first, but by mid-April 2009, Jessica was ready to move out.

Not long after Jessica vacated the apartment, Josh was accused of slashing the tires on Matt Russell's bicycle, then robbing him at knifepoint. Although Josh was never arrested for the Russell incident, it foreshadowed an escalation in Josh's violent tendencies.

Over the coming weeks, Josh continued his downward spiral. Josh seemed obsessed with Jessica and continued to prowl around her parents' neighborhood off North Bank Drive. With Josh watching Jessica's home for any signs of male rivals, it didn't take long for another violent incident to occur.

On May 19, 2009—the eve of the Faria murders—a nineteen-year-old man named Travis Marshall* was driving his pick-up truck along North Bank Drive. Marshall worked as the manager of a local coffee shop, and on the evening of May 19, he was returning home after visiting one of his co-workers. That co-worker was Jessica Rossi.

As Marshall drove through the quiet, upscale, lightly traveled neighborhoods along North Bank Drive, he noticed a motorcycle approaching quickly in his rearview mirror. The motorcycle started to follow Marshall's truck at a disturbingly close distance. As he continued to travel west on North Bank Drive, Marshall attempted to maneuver away from the motorcycle, but its black-helmeted rider stayed right on his tail. After following Marshall's truck for several blocks, the agile motorcycle roared around Marshall, cut him off, and forced his pick-up to the curb.

Trapped in his truck at the corner of North Bank Drive and Petit Avenue, Marshall had nowhere to go. From the driver seat, Marshall watched as the motorcycle rider leapt off his machine, wrenched the black helmet from his head, and started marching in Marshall's direction. Marshall recognized the motorcycle rider as a young man who had visited Jessica at the coffee shop in the past. [52] The young man's name, Marshall recalled, was Josh Packer. Marshall knew that Josh had a reputation for violence.

When Josh reached the driver-side window of Marshall's truck (which was broken at the time and couldn't be rolled up), he immediately began throwing punches. Marshall's head bounced around the tiny cab of his pick-up like a basketball.

"What the fuck were you doing at Jessica's house?" Josh demanded to know.

"Nothing! Nothing!" Marshall attempted to explain between blows.

"Don't lie to me motherfucker!" Josh shouted. "I wanna know what you were doin' over there."

"We're just friends, man! We're just friends!" Marshall managed to choke out.

With that, the punches stopped. Josh stepped back from Marshall's truck, his shoulders heaving from the volley of blows he'd just delivered. Josh glared at the battered coffee-shop manager for several seconds. Then, pivoting on his heel and storming away from the truck, Josh climbed on his motorcycle, yanked his black helmet over his head, and roared away into the night.

Marshall immediately dialed 911 and reported the attack.

The Ventura Police Department filed a report on the incident, but Josh was not arrested.

The next day, May 20, 2009, Josh awoke to some very bad news. That morning, Uncle Bob sat down with Josh and told him that they needed to talk about the living situation at the apartment. Miller explained that when he'd signed the lease on unit 310, he'd been counting on Jessica to pay a third of the rent. Because she'd moved out, Miller said that he now expected Josh to cover Jessica's portion of the expenses. According to Miller's logic, Josh had encouraged Jessica to move in with them, so Josh was on the hook for her share of the rent.

For better or worse, Uncle Bob was the longest-lasting male influence in Josh's life and Josh didn't want to let him down. At the same time, Josh realized that his meager earnings as a security guard were inadequate to cover two-thirds of the rent. Nevertheless, Josh decided to check his bank account to see what he could do to help Uncle Bob.

After calling Wells Fargo and tapping his account number into the phone, a mechanized voice informed Josh that he had $35.37 in his checking account. It was barely enough money to buy Uncle Bob lunch, much less pay two thirds of the rent.

Later that morning, Josh used his cell phone to call the utility company and check the balance for unit 310. The utility bill was high. Josh couldn't cover it.

Josh began to sweat.

The walls began to close in on Josh. He had no

money and he didn't want to disappoint Uncle Bob. Josh was desperate, and the more he thought about his financial situation, the more desperate he became.

Finally, by the time night fell on May 20, 2009, Josh had made a fateful decision. It was a decision that would irreparably change both his life and the lives of many other people. Josh decided to obtain his rent money by force.

The boy who had gone on retreats with Young Life donned a black jumpsuit. The boy who had proven himself to be a remarkable athlete in high school pushed his hands into black gloves. The boy who had worked diligently for multiple employers put a replica firearm in his pocket. And the boy who knew first-hand what it meant to be a helpless victim pulled a black, faceless helmet over his head.

Then he went outside, walked down the stairs, and mounted his motorcycle.

During the short drive from his apartment to the freeway, Josh passed the Ventura County Hall of Justice, the Sheriff's Department headquarters, and the Pretrial Detention Facility. The symbolic significance of these buildings didn't register with Josh as he raced through the mild night air and roared onto the northbound 101.

Explaining these events to the grand jury, Mike Frawley tied the overarching narrative of May 20, 2009, to the physical evidence found at the Husteds' home after the slaughter. The grand jurors heard about the semen in Davina Husted's mouth, the fingernail scrapings recovered from Brock Husted, the spittle-laden plastic visor found beneath Brock Husted's head, and the green towel that contained traces of Davina Husted's blood, Josh's blood, and Josh's semen.

On May 7, 2012, the grand jury rendered its decision: There was sufficient probable cause to try Josh for the crime of oral copulation by force. The fact that Davina Husted had been murdered during the commission of a sexual assault stood as another special circumstance (or death-penalty qualifying factor) in the case.

Josh went back to his cell at the Pretrial Detention Facility.

His defense team went back to work.

CHAPTER 19

The grand jury handed down its decision on the forced oral copulation charge in May 2012. The following month, Ventura County Superior Court Judge Patricia Murphy, who was presiding over the Faria case, joined the sexual-assault charge to the murder, robbery, and burglary charges Josh Packer was already facing. From a logistical standpoint, Josh's defense position had just gone from really bad to extremely awful.

Contrary to public opinion, criminal-defense attorneys don't help bad guys get away with crimes. Instead, criminal-defense attorneys ensure that their clients' rights are protected, that witnesses for the state are cross-examined thoroughly, that testimony favorable to the defendant is heard, and that exculpatory evidence is presented. In short, criminal-defense attorneys force governments to prove their cases. Just as American prosecutors protect the public from criminals, American defense attorneys protect the accused from persecutors, lynch mobs, and rushes to judgment.

Considering the quantity and quality of evidence in the state's war chest, Benjamin Maserang doubtlessly understood that mounting an effective defense in the Faria case would be nearly impossible. The state's stockpile of evidence included:

1. Josh's blood at the Faria crime scene;

2. A blood-soaked towel, found at the Faria crime scene, that contained Josh's blood, Davina Husted's blood, and Josh's semen;

3. A plastic visor, found beneath Brock Husted's head, that contained Josh's DNA;

4. Josh's DNA under Brock Husted's fingernails;

5. A replica firearm, seized during the search of Josh's former apartment, that bore a strong similarity to the weapon seen by Brockie Husted on the night of the murders.

In addition to these extremely incriminating pieces of evidence, the prosecution also had a star witness waiting in the wings. That witness was Robert "Uncle Bob" Miller.

After Josh was arrested for the Faria murders in April 2010, Ventura County detectives contacted Bob Miller and pulled him in for an interview. The detectives wanted to find out if Josh's former mentor and roommate had any information about the Faria crimes. Initially, Miller claimed to know nothing about the murders. It took several interviews and some firm pressure, but eventually, Uncle Bob started singing like a canary.

Miller explained to detectives that he'd been out

with friends on the night of May 20, 2009. At 11:10 p.m., Miller said that he'd received a phone call from Josh. Josh told Miller that he was at their apartment and that they needed to talk right away. According to Miller, Josh's voice sounded very serious. Miller explained to Josh that he would be home in a little while.

Arriving back at the Jefferson Apartments at a few minutes before midnight, Miller found Josh in the kitchen of their apartment. As Miller drew closer to his roommate, he could see that Josh was scrubbing off his motorcycle helmet in the kitchen sink.

Miller asked Josh what was wrong. Without missing a beat, Josh told Miller that he'd invaded an occupied home, robbed the residents, then stabbed them to death with a large knife. Josh added that he was very worried because he'd cut himself during the stabbings and bled all over the crime scene. In his statement to detectives, Miller made it clear that Josh was aware of the investigatory value of his DNA.

Miller told detectives that he encouraged Josh to turn himself in to law enforcement. Miller also told detectives that Josh immediately nixed the idea.

"If I turn myself in, they'll put me away for life," Josh told Miller. [53]

At this point, Miller's actions become almost incomprehensible to any reasonable person. Instead of leaving the apartment and calling the police (or at least calling an attorney to negotiate Josh's surrender), Miller sat down with Josh in their living room and began watching television. Around 2 a.m., after Josh fell asleep on the living-room sofa, Miller retired to his room and went to bed.

Four hours later, as detectives were combing the

crime scene in Faria and the Husted children were being comforted by thunderstruck relatives, Miller awoke to Josh shaking his shoulder. Josh informed Miller that he needed a ride to work. Despite having murdered three human beings just hours earlier, Josh didn't want to miss his scheduled shift at Baxter. Miller agreed to give Josh a ride.

As they made their way toward the Baxter facility in Newberry Park, Josh made a significant request.

"I need you to get rid of some stuff for me," Josh told Miller.

Josh went on to explain that he'd bagged the bloody jumpsuit, gloves, and other evidence from the previous night. Miller told detectives that he agreed to dispose of the evidence. [54] It's not clear whether Miller expressed any shame or remorse over this decision, but one fact is glaringly obvious: Miller completely missed the perverse irony of his relationship with Josh. When they'd met at the Ventura Boys and Girls Club in 1999, Miller had volunteered to serve as Josh's mentor. To any reasonable person, a child's mentor instills morals, integrity, compassion, and a sense of personal responsibility. Ten years after becoming Josh's mentor, Uncle Bob was disposing of evidence and helping Josh cover up his involvement in a brutal triple murder.

At 8:15 a.m. on May 21, 2009—around the time Miller was chucking Josh's bloody jumpsuit and gloves into the dumpster behind the Jefferson Apartments— Josh paid a visit to Baxter's in-house nurse. Although he wasn't specific about where he'd received his injuries, Josh explained to the nurse that he'd hurt his hand and sprained his ankle the previous night. Josh was known as an affable, hard-working employee at Baxter. His co-worker acknowledged that, although he was young, Josh was always polite, kept his work boots spit-shined, and said hello to everyone on the job. [55] Because Josh was so well liked at Baxter, the nurse thought little of his request for medical aid.

After fitting Josh with an Ace bandage for his sprained ankle, the nurse examined the injury to Josh's right hand. From what the nurse could tell, Josh had suffered some sort of laceration from a sharp object. The nurse asked Josh how he'd received the injury. Josh told her that he'd cut himself while he was "messing around." [56] Not inquiring further, the nurse cleaned and sterilized Josh's wound, wrapped it in a butterfly bandage, and sent him on his way.

Once his injuries had been treated at Baxter's infirmary, Josh finished his shift without incident. None of his co-workers remembered anything out of the ordinary about that day.

At 3 p.m., Miller picked Josh up and drove him back to their apartment in Ventura. Less than twenty-four hours had elapsed since the Faria murders, but Josh and Miller were feeling anything but down. As Brockie and Isabella Husted sat in shock at a relative's home and the entire community struggled to comprehend the unspeakable tragedy in Faria, Josh made plans to go out partying with his friends.

A few days before the Husted murders, as he was cruising around Ventura on his motorcycle, Josh had run into Sean Kirkpatrick, his old friend from Young Life. When they saw each other in mid-May 2009, Josh proposed that he and Kirkpatrick hang out and "catch up" at some point in the near future. Kirkpatrick agreed that it would be good to catch up with his old friend, so they made plans for May 21, 2009.

On the evening of May 21, 2009, with his lacerated hand still wrapped in the butterfly bandage from Baxter, Josh descended the stairs from his second floor apartment to meet Kirkpatrick in the Jefferson's parking lot. That night, Josh and Kirkpatrick were joined by two of their other friends from Young Life, Eddie Reyes* and Timothy Gonzalez*. Since they weren't old enough to drink at a regular night club, the foursome was planning to spend the evening at an under-twenty-one club called Chapter 8. Located across the Los Angeles County line in the upscale community of Agoura Hills, Chapter 8 was a place where minors could congregate, socialize, and sip soda pop.

Ever the dutiful friend to young boys in need, Bob Miller agreed to drive Josh, Kirkpatrick, Reyes, and Gonzales to Chapter 8. However, as the four teens stood in the Jefferson parking lot and waited for Miller to descend the stairs, there was a discernible level of tension in the air. As Reyes would later recall, Josh just wasn't himself that night. He seemed tense and on edge, like he could explode at any second. Over the years, Reyes had spent a lot of time with Josh. Not only had the boys played football together at Ventura High School and prayed together in Young Life, they had also spent time gambling at the Chumash Casino and hanging out at the beach. However, before the night of May 21, 2009, Reyes had never seen Josh behave in such an unusually aggressive manner.

As Reyes watched his old friend and tried to understand why he was behaving so oddly, the lighthearted situation in the Jefferson parking lot turned violent. As Reyes would later explain to detectives, Josh and Sean Kirkpatrick had been joking about who was going to ride shotgun in Miller's car that night. Josh said that he was riding shotgun because it was his roommate's vehicle. Kirkpatrick claimed that he'd called shotgun first and was therefore entitled to the front seat. At first, the back-and-forth over who would ride shotgun seemed to be jovial and fun. Then, without warning, Josh lashed out and punched Kirkpatrick across the face. It was a hard, unexpected blow.

Reyes and Gonzalez were stunned. They hadn't seen the punch coming and they had no idea what would happen next.

As it turned out, the punch was a one-off. Instead of launching a counterattack on Josh, Kirkpatrick passively laughed off the incident. Kirkpatrick seemed willing to let the punch go, and not knowing quite how to respond to the sudden awkwardness, Reyes and Gonzalez decided to let it go as well. Before long, Miller came down from the apartment and the group took off for Chapter 8.

Years later, while Josh was awaiting trial for the Faria murders, Eddie Reyes was interviewed about the night of May 21, 2009. The interview was conducted by detectives from the Ventura County Sheriff's Department, as well as investigators from the District Attorney's Office.

Reyes was extremely candid during his interview. He admitted that he was one of the students who had ditched class and traveled to Buena High School with Josh on May 31, 2005. He also admitted that his group of Ventura High classmates was looking for trouble that day, but he added that they weren't necessarily looking to put someone in the hospital. To this end, Reyes explained to detectives that Josh was the instigator at Buena High School. Reyes said that he and the other students followed Josh to the school and wanted to leave as soon as Christian Morales was punched.

After hearing about the Buena High School incident and establishing Reyes's credibility, the detectives and D.A. investigators steered him back to the night of May 21, 2009. Reyes told the lawmen that after Josh broke up with Jessica Rossi in the spring of 2009, he started "...acting really weird." When a detective asked Reyes to clarify what he meant, Reyes said that Josh was restless, hyperactive, and quick to anger after Jessica left him. Reyes added that Josh was less social and spent more time by himself after his break-up with Jessica. [57]

Detectives asked Reyes about the nature of Josh's relationship with Bob Miller. Reyes told the detectives that Miller would do anything for Josh. He added that, on several occasions, Miller had purchased alcohol for Josh and his underage friends. [58] Reyes went on to say that, on the night of the Chapter 8 sojourn, things seemed very strained between Josh and Miller. It was obvious to Reyes that Josh and Miller weren't getting along. As Reyes explained to detectives, he asked Josh what was going on between him and Miller. Josh told Reyes that he wanted to leave the Jefferson Apartments and move back to his mother's house.

When asked by detectives if he'd ever seen Josh act violently, Reyes reiterated that Josh had punched Sean Kirkpatrick on the night of the Chapter 8 outing.

"Was (Sean) afraid of Packer?" Sergeant Billy Hester asked Reyes.

"All of us are a little," Reyes answered.

"Is that because he likes to fight and has a reputation for fighting?" Hester asked.

"Yes," Reyes said. "He's known for that."

For his part, Kirkpatrick told the detectives and investigators the same thing when he was interviewed. Kirkpatrick verified that Josh seemed disturbed and violent after his break-up with Jessica Rossi. [59] Kirkpatrick also explained that he was stunned by Josh's punch on the night of May 21, 2009. In the moments before Josh threw the punch, Kirkpatrick thought they were just joking about who would ride shotgun in Miller's car. In a split second, however, Josh's temper had flared and the situation had turned violent.

Reyes filled in more details about the trip to Chapter 8.

After Miller dropped the boys off that night, Josh and his friends headed inside the club. Over the next several hours, they socialized and had a good time. However, when it came time to leave, no one could find Josh.

Reyes, Gonzalez, and Kirkpatrick searched Chapter 8's parking lot and the businesses around the club. Josh was nowhere to be found.

They tried calling Josh's cell phone, but there was no answer.

They asked other people if they'd seen Josh, but no one had.

Finally, with Chapter 8 shutting down for the night, the parking lot emptying out, and the early morning hours creeping in, Miller arrived to shuttle Josh and his friends back to Ventura.

After learning from Reyes that Josh was missing, Miller joined in the search. Hunting high and low,

Reyes, Gonzalez, Kirkpatrick, and Miller scoured the area around Chapter 8. Josh could not be located. Eventually, with no sign of Josh, the four decided to return to Ventura without him.

The next day, Josh's whereabouts were finally discovered. It turned out that, after stepping outside Chapter 8 to get some air, Josh had been spotted by a deputy with the Los Angeles County Sheriff's Department. Suspecting that Josh might be intoxicated, the deputy moved in to investigate. Josh offered no resistance to the deputy. After determining that Josh was inebriated, the deputy placed Josh in handcuffs and transported him to the local drunk tank on a charge of public intoxication.

It's not clear whether Josh obtained the alcohol from Miller or someone else on the night of his Chapter 8 arrest, but it's clear that after being released from the L.A. County drunk tank, Josh went on with his life as if nothing had happened.

On May 25, 2009, less than a week after the Faria murders, Jessica paid Josh a visit at the Jefferson Apartments. She found him in good spirits. The next day was Jessica's twenty-second birthday and Josh stopped by to see her. From what Jessica could tell, Josh was still upbeat and in good spirits. She noticed that Josh had a bandage on his right hand, but this was far from unusual. Because he was aggressive and accident prone, Jessica frequently found Josh wearing casts, sporting bruises, and picking at scabs. As far as Jessica was concerned, Josh's hand wound was nothing out the ordinary.

Despite his outward facade of normalcy, things weren't going so well in other areas of Josh's life. The rift between Josh and Miller was continuing to grow, and the delicate balance of their relationship was becoming increasingly strained. Even as the Faria murders were making international headlines, Josh and Miller continued to live together at the Jefferson Apartments. However, the power dynamic in their relationship had shifted. Throughout the time they'd known each other, Miller had been the strong adult who had called the shots. After the murders, however, Josh was clearly the one in charge. In July 2009, Josh stopped paying rent to Miller. Then, in September 2009—around the time the Ventura robbery series began—Josh moved out of the apartment altogether.

Miller told detectives that Josh moved out of the apartment because he didn't want to pay rent anymore. Miller added that he had remained Josh's friend.

"After you got rid of the bloody jumpsuit and all the other evidence, what did Josh tell you about the murders?" a detective asked Miller.

"Nothing," Miller answered. "We never talked about it again."

Disgusted by Miller and his role in covering up the Faria murders, the state explored the possibility of filing charges against him. At the end of the day, though, there were no crimes for which Miller could be charged. It was true that Miller had disposed of evidence and failed to notify authorities about Josh's involvement in the murders. However, Miller had also spilled his guts to detectives and given them valuable information against his former roommate. For the time being, Miller was off the hook.

Miller's statements to detectives were absolutely devastating to Josh's defense. Reading through Miller's admissions, Maserang no doubt realized that the youth worker's testimony would help put Josh on the fast-track to Death Row if the case went to trial.

Coupled with all the other evidence in the case, Miller's statements made the prospect of a trial more unfathomable than ever from a defense standpoint. There was no way that a group of jurors in Ventura County—or any other county for that matter—would vote for acquittal in light of the prosecution's evidence. States pass capital-punishment legislation precisely for cases like Josh's, and no amount of mitigation was going to change that.

The defense also had to consider its opposition, which was formidable. Mike Frawley was a highly skilled veteran prosecutor with an amazing wealth of evidence at his disposal. If Frawley had been given ten hours, a legal pad, and a couple of Bic pens, he could've convicted Josh Packer of the Faria murders—not just beyond a reasonable doubt—but beyond all possible doubt. And the defense unquestionably knew it.

With all of this in mind, there was only one good option left for the defense: Keep the case from going to trial at all costs.

Knowing that the Faria murder trial could never see the inside of a courtroom, Maserang and his team were about to pull out all the stops on Josh's defense. They weren't trying to delay the administration of justice; they were trying to save their client's life.

CHAPTER 20

Benjamin Maserang had been practicing law for sixteen years when he was appointed as Josh Packer's lead defense attorney. To fully comprehend the enormity of Maserang's job, one only has to look at the brutality captured in the Faria crime-scene photos. The blood-splattered bedroom, the look of anguish on Brock Husted's dead face, and the multiplicity of vicious stab wounds to Davina Husted's pregnant body are just some of the images captured in the prosecution's powerful visual montage. Perhaps worst of all are the pictures of little Grant Husted. In the pictures, Grant's umbilical cord is still attached, his tiny fists are clenched, his mouth is arced down in a painful frown, and his lashless eyes are squeezed tightly shut. These are the types of jarring, incendiary images that would inflame the passions and rankle the ire of even the kindliest jurors. Maserang undoubtedly knew that if a group of capital-qualified jurors ever caught sight of these images, they wouldn't just convict Josh Packer and condemn him to death, they'd be ready to drive to San Quentin and drop the potassium chloride themselves.

Maserang needed a toehold to stop Josh's case from going to trial, and soon enough, he found one. As it turned out, the toehold was supplied by none other than Mike Frawley himself.

After Josh was arrested for the Faria murders in April 2010, Mike Frawley became the lead prosecutor on the case. As Ventura County's chief deputy district attorney and the most experienced capital-case prosecutor in the D.A.'s Office, Frawley's role as lead prosecutor in the Faria case made perfect sense. However, as Frawley explained in an e-mail to Maserang and the defense team shortly after Josh's arrest, he had a very tenuous personal connection to their client.

In his e-mail to the defense, Frawley explained that his son Kyle and his daughter Elizabeth had known Josh when they participated in Young Life. Frawley also explained to the defense that his current wife had been a group leader for Young Life and that his ex-wife was personally acquainted with Davina Husted through her charity work for the National Charity Junior League of Ventura. However, Frawley also pointed out that he'd never had any significant personal contact with Josh Packer.

It's not surprising that Frawley voluntarily supplied this information to the defense. Mike Frawley is a man with a firm handshake, unwavering eye contact, and a demeanor that screams untrammeled honesty. When he's asked a direct question, Frawley doesn't hesitate before answering. When he's asked for his opinion, Frawley doesn't equivocate. In fact, after graduating from law school in 1987 (the same year DNA was first used to obtain a criminal conviction in the U.S.), Frawley decided to become a prosecutor because it would allow him to practice law while always acting in an honest, forthright manner.

"In law, to make a living, you have to take one person's position and you're not always going to be in the right. As a prosecutor, it's absolutely against the ethical code to file a case if you don't believe the person is guilty," Frawley explained. "There are no ethical dilemmas in prosecution, and that's what attracts me to it."

Throughout his career, Frawley has brought a wide variety of hardcore predators to justice. However, Frawley doesn't consider murders the most difficult cases he's handled.

"Murders are tough to do, but I always thought that rapes and child molests were even tougher," Frawley said. "When you have a live rape victim sitting across from you hoping that you can get them some justice, there's a lot more pressure and a lot more emotional entanglement so that justice can be served."

Frawley says that speaking for victims and keeping citizens safe are the most rewarding aspects of his job.

"You can never make someone whole and you can never undo what was done to them," Frawley continued. "But if you can get a court—through a jury or a judge—to say you were wronged, it means a lot to victims. And you're helping to protect the community."

When Frawley sent his e-mail to the defense team in April 2010, he was doing his part to protect the community. After all, protecting the community isn't limited to sending criminals to prison. From the ethical prosecutor's standpoint, protecting the community also means being candid and forthright in all matters pertaining to a case. Such honesty fosters trust in the community and allows juries to render guilty verdicts with a high degree of confidence.

Despite the good intentions behind Frawley's e-mail, the defense team seized on the electronic missive. With the prosecution unwilling to plea bargain and no viable defense strategies available, Maserang wasn't going to pass up the opportunity to leverage Frawley's personal connection to Josh. The Perea trial was finished, the hospital-assault trial was finished, and if the Faria murder case made it in front of a jury, Josh was finished. As a result, in September 2012, almost three and a half years after the Husteds were murdered, Maserang filed a motion to have Mike Frawley removed from the case.

Maserang filed his motion in accordance with section 1424 of the California Penal Code. This statute allows a defendant to request a prosecutor's removal from a case. However, before a prosecutor can be removed from a case, certain criteria must be satisfied. First, the defendant must file a notice with the court that explains the prosecutor's conflict of interest in the case and why the prosecutor should be disqualified. Then, if the court finds that a conflict of interest exists, an evidentiary hearing should be held to determine whether "...the conflict is so grave as to make a fair trial unlikely..." for the defendant. [60] The central issue in a 1424 motion is not whether a conflict of interest exists. In and of itself, a conflict of interest does not disqualify a prosecutor from trying a case. Instead, under the provisions of Penal Code section 1424, a prosecutor should only be disqualified if his conflict of interest will imperil the defendant's right to a fair trial.

Once the defense team filed its 1424 motion, it didn't take long before more details came to light about Frawley's connection to the Husteds and Josh Packer. For example, it was discovered that Frawley's ex-wife was on Davina Husted's Christmas card list. It also came out that, on at least two occasions, Josh Packer had visited the Frawley home. On one occasion, Josh had attended a Young Life Bible study meeting at the Frawley home. On another occasion, Josh had crashed a party that was being thrown by Elizabeth Frawley in her family's backyard. However, at no time during these events did Mike Frawley have any direct contact with Josh. According to paperwork filed with the court, Mike Frawley was "...mostly in the background..." while these events were taking place. [61]

There was no doubt that Mike Frawley had a conflict of interest in the Faria case. His ex-wife exchanged Christmas cards with one of the victims, his son had roomed with the defendant on a snowboarding trip almost a decade earlier, and the defendant had crashed his daughter's party. However, there was absolutely no indication that Josh's right to a fair trial would be jeopardized if Frawley prosecuted the case. And, as Penal Code section 1424 makes clear, it is the critical issue of fairness that should determine whether a prosecutor is removed from a case. [62]

Although there was no evidence that Frawley could not be fair in prosecuting Josh, Maserang soldiered on with his 1424 motion. Maserang made it clear that if Josh was convicted, the defense would call Kyle and Elizabeth Frawley as character witnesses during the sentencing phase. The defense argued that, because Kyle and Elizabeth Frawley were the children of a prosecutor, their statements as character witnesses would be given greater weight by the jury. Maserang also pointed out that Mike Frawley could not remain fair and objective if his children were acting as character witnesses for the defense.

The defense team's decision to use the Frawley children as character witnesses was purely strategic. Kyle and Elizabeth Frawley had never been close friends with Josh. Furthermore, as the prosecution pointed out, Josh had many other close friends who would've made much more compelling character witnesses. Nonetheless, because Maserang was steadfastly committed to saving Josh's life, he dug in his heels and pushed the character-witness angle as hard as possible. With the 1424 motion in play, Josh's case was stalled. Considering the pitfalls of going to trial, this was a small-but-critical victory for the defense.

For his part, Mike Frawley wanted to get the trial underway so he could deliver justice to the victims, their family members, and the people of the State of California. In an attempt to break up the 1424 logjam, Frawley agreed to have another prosecutor handle the questioning of his children if a conviction was obtained and Kyle and Elizabeth were called as character witnesses during the sentencing phase. [63]

Frawley's offer failed to placate the defense team and the 1424 motion remained in play.

Finally, in November 2012, Judge Patricia Murphy ruled on the 1424 motion. Finding no reason why *State v. Packer* should not proceed to trial, Judge Murphy denied the defense's 1424 motion and a trial date was set.

Refusing to give up their fight to save Josh's life, Maserang and the defense team appealed Judge

Murphy's ruling. The defense contended that, because Frawley's conflict of interest had been established in the case, Josh was entitled to an evidentiary hearing on the 1424 motion. To deny Josh an evidentiary hearing on the motion, the defense argued, was to deny Josh a fair trial.

Over the next two years, the defense team's 1424 motion wound its way through various appellate courts. Eventually, the motion ended up in the California Supreme Court. As it turned out, a critical dimension of Josh Packer's defense was about to be decided by the state's highest court.

In the meantime, as the seasons changed and the years continued to pass, Brock, Davina, and Grant Husted lay dead in their graves. Some in the community wondered if Josh Packer would ever face justice for the Faria murders.

CHAPTER 21

The gears of California's justice machine turn slowly, but they never stop turning. With Josh Packer's 1424 appeal waiting to be heard by the California Supreme Court, both the defense and the prosecution remained on edge. The defense wanted a plea bargain that would spare Josh's life. The prosecution wanted the death penalty. The two sides were at cross-purposes. No one was willing to flinch.

There was an interesting aspect to this controversy: Although the Ventura County D.A.'s Office pushed aggressively for the death penalty in the Faria case, there was a very real chance that Josh would never face an executioner if he was convicted and sentenced to die. California's recent history of capital punishment proves as much.

On July 2, 1976, two days before the nation's bicentennial, the U.S. Supreme Court handed down a landmark ruling in the case of *Gregg v. Georgia*. In a 7-2 decision, the court held that capital punishment does not automatically violate the Eighth and Fourteenth amendments of the U.S. Constitution. The

Gregg ruling paved the way for the reinstatement of the death penalty in the United States, which had effectively ended in 1972.

While the *Gregg* ruling allowed states to begin implementing the death penalty in 1976, not every state rushed to put capital-punishment laws on its books. It wasn't until 1978 that California made capital punishment a potential sanction for the crime of murder. Since that time, California's Death Row population has ballooned to the largest in the nation. While Josh Packer's 1424 motion was winding its way through the state appellate system, California had more than 700 inmates on Death Row. These inmates constituted almost a quarter of the nation's condemned population. However, while California's Death Row population is inordinately large, the Golden State executes only a minuscule fraction of its condemned prisoners. Since California reinstated the death penalty in 1978, only a handful of inmates have been put to death. These inmates, all of whom were male, represent less than one percent of American executions since 1976.

The first California inmate to be executed after the reinstatement of the death penalty was a double murderer from San Diego County named Robert Alton Harris. On the day he was executed in August 1992, Harris chose a darkly poetic statement for his last words.

"You can be a king or a street sweeper, but everyone dances with the Grim Reaper," Harris intoned.

Moments later, Harris was strapped into San Quentin's gas chamber and silenced for eternity.

Two years later, the state changed its primary means of execution to lethal injection. The first condemned prisoner to get the needle was William Bonin, a serial killer from Los Angeles who spent more than thirteen years on Death Row before his execution. After Bonin was dispatched on February 23, 1996, the amount of time inmates spent on California's Death Row before execution grew significantly longer.

At the time of Josh Packer's appeal on the 1424 motion, the last inmate to be executed in California was a seventy-six-year-old murderer named Clarence Ray Allen. Convicted of organizing three Fresno murders in 1980, Allen spent more than twenty-three years on the Row before he was snuffed on January 17, 2006.

All totaled, only thirteen inmates have been executed in California since 1978. [64] Consequently, a condemned prisoner in California is much more likely to die from natural causes than from lethal injection. This is true even for notorious, high-profile killers.

Beginning in the spring of 1985, the Los Angeles area was plagued by a brutal series of home-invasion murders. Though the victims in these murders were demographically dissimilar, the M.O. used by the offender and the clues left at each crime scene made one fact abundantly clear: Authorities were looking for a serial killer. Over the next several months, the mysterious slayer claimed more than a dozen victims. Eventually, the Southern California slayings were linked to a string of murders in San Francisco. The media dubbed the offender the Night Stalker (not to be confused with the Original Night Stalker).

Because the Night Stalker struck at random and selected victims from a broad cross-section of society, the Los Angeles region was gripped with fear during the first half of 1985. At first, detectives were unable to solve the case. Then, in August 1985, authorities got the break they needed.

While prowling in an upscale Orange County suburb, the Night Stalker's stolen getaway car was spotted by a victim's neighbor. The neighbor reported the suspicious vehicle and its plate number to police. When the vehicle was found abandoned in Los Angeles days later, a print was recovered from its rearview mirror. Using an electronic fingerprint database (which was a cutting-edge tool at the time), LAPD detectives matched the print from the stolen vehicle to a Skid Row cocaine addict and car thief named Richard Ramirez.

After being spotted on a city bus, chased through the streets of East Los Angeles, and nearly beaten to death by an angry mob, Ramirez was taken into custody on August 31, 1985. It took more than four years for Ramirez's case to be resolved, but on September 20, 1989, Ramirez was convicted on thirteen counts of first-degree murder, fourteen counts of burglary, eleven counts of rape, and five counts of attempted murder. Two months later, Ramirez was sentenced to death.

For more than twenty years, Ramirez sat on San Quentin's Death Row awaiting execution. Despite the severity of his crimes and the overwhelming evidence of his guilt, Ramirez never came close to facing an executioner. Ramirez's conviction went through round after round after round after round of appeals. Finally, on June 7, 2013, Ramirez died of cancer at a Marin County hospital. At the time of his death, Ramirez still had many rounds of appeals pending.

If Richard Ramirez was the poster boy for the lumbering inefficiency of California's appellate system, then Josh Packer was the poster boy for the impractical nature of California's capital-punishment system. Simply put, even if the Ventura County D.A.'s Office had convicted Josh of the Faria murders and scored a death sentence against him, there was no guarantee that Josh would ever be put to death. In this sense, a death sentence for Josh Packer would've amounted to little more than a Pyrrhic victory. Or, more precisely, a Pyrrhic victory with a multi-million-dollar appellate price-tag attached to it.

———————

On January 17, 2013, Josh's defense team submitted a brief to the California Supreme Court. The brief was frank about the mitigation in Josh's case, including the horrific abuse he'd suffered as a child.

"Joshua Packer's upbringing was unimaginably horrible," the brief stated. "Direct damage was done to Packer from being molested as a child on multiple occasions by separate men who were given access to him by negligent caretakers; from being abandoned by caretakers; from receiving a head injury at age 6 and a disfigurement at age 8 due to parental neglect; from being attacked in his home by a drug addict at age 6; from being attacked in his bed by a wanted sex offender at age 11; and from being exposed in his home to drug use, drug trafficking, and domestic violence." [65]

The brief went on to say that Josh's cumulative history of abuse and neglect, coupled with character-witness testimony from Mike Frawley's children, could sway a jury to impose a sentence of life without parole if a guilty verdict was reached at trial.

"Although the prosecution may get this case to a penalty phase, the defense has powerful evidence in mitigation and has an excellent chance of an LWOP (life without parole) verdict if given a fair trial after full and fair discovery and unimpeded pretrial investigation," the brief continued.

Considering that California executes almost none of its condemned prisoners and that the state's death penalty is little more than judicial window dressing, the defense team's brief made a powerful case for granting an evidentiary hearing under Penal Code section 1424.

The Supreme Court heard oral arguments on the defense's 1424 appeal in December 2013 and the gears of California's judicial machinery continued to grind forward. Finally, by the autumn of 2014, it was widely understood that the Supreme Court would rule on Josh's 1424 appeal in the near future. It was also widely understood that the Supreme Court's decision would have enormous consequences. If the Supreme Court denied Josh's appeal, he was headed to trial and an almost-certain death sentence. On the other hand, if the Supreme Court ruled in favor of the defense, Josh would be able to challenge Mike Frawley's role as prosecutor with an evidentiary hearing, thereby allowing for further delays in the trial.

By the fall of 2014, as both sides awaited the Supreme Court's ruling on the 1424 appeal, the wrangling between the prosecution and Josh's defense team had turned personal. Because he subscribed to an unshakable code of ethics, Mike Frawley had volunteered personal information about his family to the defense. When the defense's plea offer was rejected in October 2010, Frawley's children became a wedge issue in the Faria case. Both sides fought hard for what they thought was right, and at the end of the day, it had all come down to a decision by the state's highest court.

The California Supreme Court announced its decision on December 11, 2014.

In explaining the Supreme Court's unanimous ruling in *Joshua Packer v. Ventura County Superior Court*, Chief Justice Tani Cantil-Sakauye wrote, "It is not difficult to understand and to sympathize with a parent's strong inclination to protect his or her children from being drawn into the role of witness in a death penalty case, and a prosecutor who is a parent is, of course, not immune from such feelings. At the same time, however, a criminal defendant's right to present potentially favorable witnesses on his behalf is a fundamental right—a right that takes on added significance in the capital setting. In light of the affidavits submitted in support of and in opposition to petitioner's motion to recuse the prosecutor under section 1424, and the conflicts and contradictions reflected in those affidavits, we conclude that the trial court abused its discretion in declining to hold an evidentiary hearing."

Josh's defense team had prevailed.

The 1424 motion was headed back to Ventura County for an evidentiary hearing before Judge Murphy.

By the time the Supreme Court issued its ruling on the 1424 appeal, almost six years had passed since the Faria murders. During that time, Isabella and Brockie Husted had grown from small children into teenagers on the cusp of adulthood. The Faria case was old, there'd been lots of waiting, and the evidentiary hearing on the 1424 motion was sure to turn into a knock-down-drag-out affair. With all of this in mind, a practical decision was reached. It was a decision that combined a solid commitment to justice with a pragmatic understanding of reality.

The prosecution agreed to a plea deal.

News of the plea deal brought enormous relief to Josh, Terri, and the entire defense team. Since his arrest in April 2010, Josh had been under enormous duress.

"(Josh) felt totally helpless with what was going on," Terri said of Josh's long confinement in the Pretrial Detention Facility. "At one point, he even considered pleading guilty in exchange for the death penalty just so he could get out of there."

Everyone was ready for the Faria murder saga to be finished.

The terms of the state's plea offer were straightforward: Josh would plead guilty to three counts of first-degree murder, two counts of residential robbery, one count of armed residential burglary, and one count of oral copulation by force. The latter charge guaranteed that Josh would be branded a sex offender for the rest of his life. In exchange for pleading guilty to these charges, Josh would be given a sentence of life in prison without the possibility of parole. As an extra-added bonus for California's taxpayers, Josh's plea agreement prevented him from appealing his sentence. This stipulation ensured that Josh would spend the balance of his life in the California Department of Corrections and Rehabilitation at a minimal financial cost to society.

On December 18, 2014, just one week after the Supreme Court ruled on the 1424 appeal, Josh was shuttled from the Pretrial Detention Facility to Judge Murphy's courtroom in the Hall of Justice. Josh arrived in court to acknowledge, formally and forever, that he was the Faria murderer.

Wearing blue jailhouse scrubs and sporting a cast on his right arm, Josh looked haggard and significantly older than his twenty-five years. It was obvious that five years in jail—with a possible death sentence hanging over his head—had taken its toll on Josh. During his time in the Pretrial Detention Facility, Josh had fought with deputies, destroyed property, engaged in self-injurious behavior, and eaten parts of his own eyeglasses so he could get transferred to the psychiatric facility at Hillmont. Because of Josh's propensity for self-harm, large doses of medication had been used to control him at various times. This medication often left Josh woozy and unable to function normally.

"He'd stumble when he was in the courtroom," Mike Frawley recalled. "One time I even saw him drooling on himself at the defense table."

On the day of his guilty plea, it did not appear that Josh had been drugged in any way. His eyes looked focused and lucid behind thick, black-rimmed glasses. As he sat behind the defense table and prepared to plead guilty to the most serious charges imaginable, Josh maintained his composure.

With Benjamin Maserang sitting at his side and Mike Frawley reading the charges from a lectern in the center of Judge Murphy's courtroom, Josh took responsibility for the Faria murders. As Frawley read off the litany of charges, it was clear that one of the guilty pleas hit Josh particularly hard.

"Is it your intention today to admit to the first-degree murder of Grant Husted, a fetus, on May 20, 2009?" Frawley asked Josh.

Josh hesitated. He looked down and rubbed his lips together for several second. Finally, his head began to bob up and down.

"Ye-es," Josh said in a strained, almost trembling voice. It sounded as if Josh was fighting hard to hold back tears and just barely succeeding.

When it was all over and Josh's guilty pleas had been entered, he was escorted from the courtroom and taken back to his cell. Josh had been through this process many times in the past, but this time was different. Now he was a convicted triple murderer and sex offender.

On several occasions in the past, Josh had been involved in violent encounters with deputies once he was placed back in his cell after court appearances. On December 18, 2014, things were different. There were no problems once Josh was returned to the Pretrial Detention Facility. After his long, pitched battle to avoid execution, it almost seemed as if Josh was resigned to his fate.

His sentencing was scheduled for Friday, February 6, 2015.

PART II

CHAPTER 22

There was no way I was going to miss Josh Packer's sentencing. His case had languished in the courts for five and a half years, and during that time, the Faria saga had morphed into something much weightier than a regional homicide matter. As far as I was concerned, Josh's case symbolized the changing face of American justice. While detectives had failed to identify Josh as a suspect in the Faria murders, DNA had succeeded. While long-standing government institutions had been unable to protect the public from Josh's wrath, emerging science had triumphed. And while traditional law enforcement had proven itself incapable of delivering justice to grieving family members and a traumatized community, a computer database in Richmond had blown the lid off the Faria case.

Over the years, as I followed the twists and turns in Josh's case, one truth became inescapable: Without the DNA database, there was an extremely high likelihood that the Faria murders would've gone unsolved. Moreover, if Josh's DNA had not been collected after his robbery arrest in Santa Barbara County, he would not have been identified as quickly as the Faria murderer. In turn, this delayed identification might've given Josh a chance to claim more victims. Although I remained confident that Santa Barbara County would've nabbed Josh for the Thrifty robbery, this collar would've meant little if Josh had murdered more victims while he was awaiting trial on the robbery charge. Thanks to CODIS and Proposition 69, however, Josh's criminal career had been brought to an expedited halt. In this sense, Josh's case was a metaphor for a safer and better world.

Human ingenuity and technological innovation had delivered justice in the Faria case, but this was just the tip of the iceberg. When I looked at pictures of Josh Packer, I thought of all the violent offenders who would be identified through comprehensive DNA databases in the coming years and locked away before they could maximize their body counts. When I looked at pictures of Brock and Davina Husted, I thought of all the victims DNA databases would protect preemptively in the future. It was true that DNA had been used to solve other difficult cases before the Faria murders. However, like no other case in history, the Faria murders underscored the vital necessity of arrestee DNA collection. In this sense, Josh Packer's sentencing represented the dawn of a new and better era. The sentencing was akin to Edward Jenner injecting his first patient with smallpox vaccine; it was Neil Armstrong's giant leap for mankind.

The sun wasn't up yet when I left for the sentencing on Friday, February 6, 2015. Making my way through the city, across the San Fernando Valley, and up the 101, traffic was minimal and a soft marine layer diffused the glow of the sodium lamps along the freeway. The sentencing wasn't scheduled to start until 9 a.m., but considering the unpredictability of traffic, I didn't want to take any chances on being late. There was too much at stake.

As I crested the Conejo Pass and descended the steep grade into Camarillo, the sun came blazing out from behind the clouds. The darkness of night was gone and brilliant sunlight flooded the sylvan landscape below me. The fields of Ventura County shimmered with a rich, verdant splendor. There was no doubt that it was going to be a great day.

Traffic flowed smoothly and I arrived at the Hall of Justice almost an hour and a half before the sentencing was scheduled to begin. Since I had a meeting scheduled with Mike Frawley later that afternoon, I was able to put my pre-sentencing time to good use. Triple checking my notes, rereading some of the legal filings I'd brought, and going over my list of interview questions, I bided my time until 8:15 a.m., then made my way into the Hall of Justice.

After passing through the security checkpoint, I ascended the stairs to the second floor and located Judge Murphy's courtroom. The courtroom was not yet open, so I took a seat on a bench in the hallway. There were already several people gathered in the hallway for Josh's sentencing. As I sat on the hallway bench, making notes and thinking through the momentous implications of what I was about to witness, the courthouse came alive around me. Before long, the hour of sentencing was at hand.

The victims' family members arrived en masse around 8:40 a.m. and were immediately ushered into the courtroom. A few minutes later, a deputy sheriff emerged from the courtroom and announced that, once the family members were seated, members of the media would be allowed into the courtroom. By that point, the hallway in front of Judge Murphy's courtroom had started to fill up with reporters and cameramen. My anticipation was reaching a zenith.

Eight minutes before Josh's sentencing was scheduled to start, the deputy reappeared in the hallway and stated that the courtroom was now open to members of the media. Along with cameramen, still photographers, and other media representatives, I prepared to enter the courtroom. Following the procession, I passed through a set of wooden doors, entered a small vestibule, and saw the courtroom just a few feet in front of me. Justice was about to be delivered. Science was about to prove itself a partial panacea to man's shortcomings. The future had arrived.

Stepping out of the vestibule and entering the courtroom proper, I was immediately shocked by the minuscule size of the sentencing room. In Los Angeles County, where I'd once served as an alternate juror in the late 1990s, courtrooms are huge, cavernous chambers with seating for days. Even in tiny Calaveras County, where I had covered court cases for the local newspaper, the courthouse was a giant, modern affair with seating for at least a hundred people in each courtroom. Considering that Ventura County's population is nearly twenty times the size of Calaveras County's, I was astonished that Judge Murphy's courtroom contained only sixty or so seats. I was even more astonished to see that, at the moment I stepped into the packed courtroom, the last seat was being taken.

"You've gotta be freaking kidding me!" I thought to myself. The sentencing was the culmination of much work and thought and anticipation on my part. A crueler anticlimax was hardly imaginable.

About that time, a young deputy turned to me and spoke.

"I'm sorry, sir, but we're out of seats," the deputy said. "You're going to have to wait outside."

Stunned by the turn of events, I hardly processed the deputy's words. I looked toward the front of the courtroom and saw Mike Frawley and Benjamin Maserang sitting at their respective tables. Josh had not yet been led into the chamber.

"Um, sir," the deputy said.

This was a monumental event and there was no way I was going to miss it. I wasn't giving up without a fight.

Straining to find just the right tone of equanimity and firmness, I turned to the deputy and explained that I'd traveled a considerable distance to attend the sentencing. I emphasized that the sentencing was extremely important to me.

"I'm really sorry, sir, but I can't help that," the deputy said.

I asked if I could stand with the deputy in the back of the courtroom and observe.

The deputy was immovable.

"Sorry, sir," he repeated. "It's a safety issue. You're going to have to wait in the hall."

It took a few beats to force my body into motion, but before I knew it, I'd walked out of the courtroom, back through the vestibule, and into the hallway.

Jenner's syringe had just been smashed.

Apollo 11 had just crashed into the dark side of the moon.

Fuming silently, I passed through a crowd of other people who'd been unable to find seating at Josh's public sentencing. I walked to a nearby window and glared out at the tranquil Ventura morning. The sunlight blazed, the weather was perfect, and nicely dressed professionals moved across the sidewalk with determined efficiency. The beautifully manicured grounds of the Hall of Justice mocked me with their perfection.

"How could they not realize that a bigger courtroom was needed for this sentencing?" I raged internally. "This is probably the biggest criminal case in the county's history! Wasn't it patently obvious that there would be significant media interest in the case? Didn't anyone have the foresight to understand that traumatized community members would want to attend the sentencing to gain some modicum of closure? Wouldn't that suggest that a larger courtroom was needed for this hearing!"

Continuing to fume over the regrettable turn of events, my ire wasn't restricted to court personnel. Other members of the media were safely ensconced in the courtroom while I was stuck in the hall. This added nothing but insult to my injury.

"What does it say about our society that someone who's looking for deeper implications in this case is relegated to the hallway while members of the sound-bite media are sitting pretty?" I ranted to myself. "The sound-bite media serves one purpose: to feed the morbid, prurient, momentary interests of its audience. Those reporters in the courtroom are going to file their stories and broadcast their reports and five minutes later the audience won't even remember that the Faria murders occurred! They'll just move on to the next tragedy and the next tragedy and the next tragedy without extrapolating anything of substance. Where's the existential equity in that? Where's the cosmic proportionality!"

As I continued to glare out the courthouse window, thoughts like these coursed through my mind for a good five minutes. By the time those five minutes had passed, I'd worked myself up into a seething fit of petty indignation.

Eventually, I turned my attention away from the window and looked back at the closed wooden doors of Judge Murphy's courtroom. That's when the epiphany hit me.

In an instant, my mind flooded with thoughts of the family members sitting inside that courtroom. I thought about what they must've been feeling at that moment. Isabella Husted had seen her parents ripped to shreds on their bedroom floor. Brockie Husted was forced to step over his mother's blood-soaked body. The other family members had been subjected to years of unimaginable pain and unanswerable questions and insufferable waiting. Compared to the pain of those family members, my disappointment over the lack of courtroom seating was beyond shallow.

It was time to get back to work.

After exiting the courthouse, returning to my car, and driving back to the freeway, I began making my way north toward Faria.

Recognizing the pain of the victims' family members had put things in perspective for me. Lots of thoughts were tugging at the fringes of my consciousness and I needed time to think.

Exiting the freeway and making my way up Pacific Coast Highway, I wheeled into Faria Beach Park. I wanted to find some solitude and a good place to ruminate. What I found instead was a parking lot filled with rumbling RVs, gaggles of diaper-clad children splashing in dirty puddles of water, and beer-bellied men staring at me with looks of utter bemusement. I needed a place of quiet contemplation. It was quite clear that Faria Beach Park was not that place.

After making a quick left out of the park, I accelerated north toward La Conchita. Cars ripped past me going southbound, RVs lined the highway, and the winter sun blazed above us all. A couple miles north of Faria, I found just what I was looking for: a quiet, secluded parking space. As it turned out, the parking space offered a clear, sweeping view of the Pacific.

The sun sparkled on the waves and a jasmine-scented breeze filled the morning air. I rolled down the windows and inhaled deeply. My thoughts quickly returned to the family members in Judge Murphy's courtroom and what they were experiencing at that moment.

Death is hard to deal with under the best of circumstances, but to lose loved ones so suddenly, so senselessly, and so violently was almost beyond comprehension. Those were wounds that would last a lifetime and no amount of human justice could heal them. Brock, Davina, and Grant Husted were deceased. And their murderer was alive.

My thoughts turned to Josh Packer. Having researched his background thoroughly, I had learned a lot about the terrible circumstances of Josh's childhood. Until that moment, though, sitting along the coastline and looking out at the water, I'd never given a lot of thought to *why* the Faria murders took place.

"Why did Josh commit these crime?" I wondered to myself. "Why Faria? Why the Husteds?"

Perhaps most importantly, why did Josh escalate to murder on May 20, 2009?

Presumably, Josh had gone to Faria to commit a home-invasion robbery so he could pay his rent. However, if robbery was Josh's motive, then why did he murder the Husteds? Once he'd taken their money and valuables, Josh could've tied the Husteds up, locked them in a closet, cut the phone lines, hurled their cell phones into the ocean, and simply sprinted away into the darkness. Not only would such a crime have been easier to execute, it would've carried a much lesser penalty if he was caught.

With the sun sparkling on the waves in front of me, a possible explanation for Josh's actions began to flicker across my consciousness. Synthesizing what I knew about Josh's background with what I knew about the dynamics of the Faria murders, a potential rationale for the carnage started to come into focus.

From what I'd learned about Josh, it was clear that he was a damaged young man who tried to hide his poor coping skills behind an external image of friendliness, athleticism, and machismo. Josh had never been taught to handle his frustration with logic or introspection or effective communication. Instead, since he was a young child, Josh had been surrounded by people who used violence, threats, drugs, and other dysfunctional strategies to deal with their angst. Coupled with the head injuries he'd suffered, the molestation he'd experienced, and the criminality he'd been exposed to from an early age, it was easy to see how Josh had grown into an aggressive, impulsive adult. Over the years, Josh had become adept at camouflaging his inner turmoil, but it was there. It was always there.

It occurred to me that, as he grew older and stronger, Josh looked for socially acceptable outlets to channel his aggression. He'd played football, wrestled, and ridden motorcycles. Even Josh's choice of work as a security guard was significant. By the time he graduated from high school, Josh probably could've landed a higher-paying job than security work. However, as a security guard, Josh was given a certain amount of power and there was always a possibility of confrontation. I believed that both aspects of security work would've appealed to him.

As I thought about the aggression and inner turmoil that were so central to Josh's psyche, I looked away from the ocean and took in the landscape around Faria. Big, beautiful, ocean-view homes climbed the hillsides above the 101. Shiny sports cars roared down Pacific Coast Highway. Tall, regal palms swayed in the salty ocean breeze.

"What would it have been like for Josh Packer to grow up in this environment?" I wondered. "Did he ever think about all this beauty and all this luxury? Or did it simply exist for him on a subconscious level?"

Ventura isn't the wealthiest town on the coast. Nevertheless, it's a town where the accouterments of wealth, status, and privilege are omnipresent. In addition, Ventura's gorgeous scenery, perfect weather, and laid-back lifestyle seem to offer the possibility of limitless success and infinite happiness. Since he was born, though, Josh had never experienced the good life that was all around him. There were no beautiful homes, there were no fancy cars, there were no high expectations in Josh's life. Instead, there was welfare, chaos, chronic abuse, and misery heaped on top of misery. Growing up in Ventura, Josh had been surrounded by society's goodies, but he wasn't allowed to have any. Considering the circumstances, how could Josh—or any reasonable person—have felt anything but bitter?

What must Josh have thought when he visited the homes of his upscale friends from Young Life? What must the Frawley home have looked like to Josh when he dropped by for Bible study meetings? More importantly, how must Josh have felt when he crashed Elizabeth Frawley's party? Even if Josh's feelings existed on a purely subconscious level, how could he have felt like anything but an outsider, an eternal party crasher?

When I tried to put myself in Josh's position and see the world through the lens of his depraved childhood experiences, it was easy to understand how his upbringing was an incubator for rage and pathological frustration. While many of his friends came from loving, supportive, and nurturing backgrounds, Josh's childhood was punctuated with neglect, out-of-school suspensions, and sexual exploitation. Considering the dramatic aberrance of his childhood, how could Josh have felt anything but shortchanged when he looked at the luxurious milieu that surrounded him in Ventura?

Sunlight glinted off the waves as I gave more thought to Josh's coming-of-age experience. The more I thought about it, the more his high-school graduation seemed like a turning point. However, it wasn't a turning point for the better.

After completing his high-school graduation requirements in 2007, Josh's situation only got worse. His glory days on the football field were behind him and many of his friends were headed off to college. Meanwhile, Josh stayed in Ventura where he worked as a security guard, smoked pot, and lived in an apartment he couldn't afford with a guy twice his age. More importantly, when Josh was asked to leave Ventura High School, he lost two of the socially acceptable outlets he'd used to check his aggression: football and wrestling.

By the spring of 2009, one of the few positive things Josh had going for him was his attractive girlfriend, Jessica Rossi. However, when Jessica started to distance herself from Josh, the stage was set for an apocalypse. Josh had already lost so much in life. Although Josh had other girls on his radar at the time, losing Jessica must've seemed like a crushing blow. On top of that, when Bob Miller told Josh that the rent was due and he had no money to pay it, Josh hit rock bottom. The rent, in and of itself, wasn't a big deal. Instead, the rent was simply the straw that broke the camel's back.

"So how did the Faria murders factor into all of this?" I wondered.

Desperate to pay the rent and lacking any legitimate skills to make money quickly, Josh must've realized that crime was his only option. It's not clear why he chose to strike in Faria Beach Colony, but based on Eddie Reyes's statements to detectives, it's clear that Josh was familiar with the area around the Colony. Josh knew that the coast was lined with expensive homes filled with wealthy residents. On May 20, 2009,

Josh needed fast cash. It stood to reason that a house in Faria would be able to supply that kind of cash.

Looking out at the rushing surf, I wondered if murder was even in Josh's mind as he drove to Faria on May 20, 2009. Although I suspected that Josh never intended to commit murder—much less triple murder—on the night of the Faria home invasion, I ultimately concluded that the question of premeditation was a moot point. It wasn't what Josh was thinking on his way to Faria that was important. Instead, it was what Josh started to think once he arrived at the Husteds' home that offered real insight into the Faria crimes.

After breaching the Colony's perimeter wall and noticing that the Husted home was brightly lit, Josh would've moved in for a closer look. When he peered through the Husteds' window, the tenor of the entire evening changed.

Looking through the window and into the Husteds' spacious living room, Josh saw a happy family sitting inside a beautiful, luxurious home. There was a mother, a father, and a son. They were together. They were watching television in a safe, comfortable environment. In other words, the tableau in the Husteds' living room represented everything that Josh had wanted—and been denied—throughout his life.

The more I thought about it, the more I became convinced that Josh harbored no specific animosity toward the Husteds. To him, they existed as nothing more than living, breathing symbols of his own losses and life's unfairness. Brock Husted symbolized the father who had abandoned Josh as an infant, provided him with no financial support, and failed to protect him from life's many dangers. Davina represented the mother who'd exposed Josh to sexual predators, taught him to steal, and forced him to grow up far too quickly. As for Brockie, I began to think that on some deep, sub-limbic level, Josh saw himself in the boy.

Dealing with difficult feelings in a calm, constructive, introspective manner had never been Josh's forte. As he looked through the Husteds' window, complex emotions must've roiled inside Josh's mind. Everything he saw in the Husteds' home was a glaring reminder of all the ways he'd been slighted and shortchanged by life. Unsure of how to deal with his anger, Josh decided to act on the one coping strategy he'd been conditioned to use since birth: violence.

Once he barged into the Husteds' home, I believed that Josh was no longer dealing with his victims as human beings. Instead, the Husteds were just actors on a stage and Josh was the director. Josh wanted to strike back at his own parents—parents who had dragged him into a lifetime of pain, abuse, and raging pathological anger. Josh couldn't strike back at his real father because Randy had abandoned him nearly two decades earlier. Josh couldn't strike back at Terri because she was the only person who had ever really loved him and cared for him on a consistent basis. Josh couldn't redress his grievances with Randy and Terri; he needed surrogate victims to act out his revenge.

Everything went fine at first. Josh took control of the scene, collected the Husteds' money, forced Davina to remove her shirts, and herded the adults into the master bedroom. However, when Brock Husted went for the cordless phone to call 911, he deviated from Josh's script. That was the moment, I believed, when everything went south. Josh wouldn't allow his surrogate father to betray him. The knife rose and fell and rose and fell more than sixty times that night. The stabbings weren't impulsive acts to neutralize potential witnesses. Instead, the stabbings were deeply personal acts. The more I thought through the psychological dynamics of the murders, the more I was convinced that personal catharsis—not witness neutralization—was Josh's end goal.

Grant it, none of this would've existed for Josh on a conscious level. As he was stabbing Brock and Davina Husted to death, Josh probably had no insight into why he was doing what he was doing. However, as I sat on the shoulder of PCH and watched the rolling surf, I felt certain that the real motivation behind the Faria murders lay in the deeper recesses of Josh's primitive, reptilian brain. Josh was angry about his upbringing and he harbored tremendous (if tacit) resentment toward both of his biological parents. To this end, Josh's actions after the murders were extremely revealing. Instead of murdering Brockie— the only living eyewitness to his crimes—Josh just walked out of the Husted home.

As I looked out at the waves and contemplated the underlying causes of the Faria murders, I wondered if my emerging theory was just a bunch of empty psychobabble. Did Josh Packer really murder Brock and Davina Husted to get back at his own parents in some strange, pseudo-cathartic way? On one level my theory seemed too pat, too simple, and too Freudian. On another level, my theory seemed disturbingly cogent. The fact that Brockie had survived the home invasion was especially significant, I thought. It also occurred to me that, at the time of her murder, Davina Husted was about five months pregnant. I noted that on May 20, 2009, Terri was about five months pregnant as well.

Scribbling these ideas into my notebook with furious intensity, I realized that I needed to bounce them off someone who was intimately familiar with the Faria case. Fortunately, I had a 2 p.m. meeting scheduled with Mike Frawley.

Twisting the key, punching the gas, and veering south, I made my way back to the Hall of Justice.

By 2 p.m., I was sitting in Mike Frawley's office on the third floor of the Hall of Justice. Since I'd missed the sentencing that morning, I started by asking him what had happened in the courtroom in my absence.

"It was emotional," Frawley told me, his eyebrows raised as he recalled the sentencing. "You should've seen all the people in there crying today. Even five years after, their lives have never returned to normal, never will be normal. I mean, you have kids stepping over their bloody parents' bodies, all the stab wounds. You don't get over that."

As it turned out, most of the courtroom emotion came from the victim-impact statements. The statements, which were read aloud in court by the victims' family members, had been typed up and presented to Judge Murphy before she pronounced sentence on Josh. The victim-impact statements captured the unmitigated pain, outrage, frustration, and anger of the Husteds and the DeBonis.

"Joshua Packer you are evil!" wrote Allane DeBoni, Davina's mother. "You are a murderer, a rapist, and a baby killer."

Continuing with her statement, Allane DeBoni

pointed out that Josh hadn't just robbed her of her daughter.

"You took away any precious moments I would have had with baby Grant. I never even got to hold him," Allane DeBoni lamented. "It is also my belief that my loving husband David died of a broken heart as he was never able to recover from Davina's untimely death. It is just not natural to outlive your children, and one of the worst words a parent can hear is that one of your children has been murdered."

In her closing remarks to the court, Allane DeBoni described the long-term impact the Faria murders had on her.

"After all of this, I cannot seem to find the joy in my life that I formerly have had. The day after my daughter died, a big piece of me died with her."

In offering his statement to the court, Vincent DeBoni, Davina's brother, also addressed the toll the murders had taken on his parents.

"After hearing the details of my sister's murder I watched my father struggle with his pain every day and I truly believe my father died of a broken heart as he passed away less than two years later," Vincent DeBoni wrote. "My mother has never been the same either…Nothing will ever bring my sister, her unborn child, or her husband back no matter what happens today but I strongly believe in the end you will have to answer for what you have done."

Focusing on the penalty Josh deserved for his crimes, Brock Husted's brother John wrote about Josh's pending prison sentence.

"The coward who stole the future of these three innocent people and who so callously destroyed the normal sense of safety enjoyed by most Americans should be given no more consideration than minimally required by law," John Husted wrote. "To give him any less of a sentence is to say it is ok to be a monster, it is ok to kill and maim with a blatant disregard for life, it is ok to cause unending terror and pain to the families of the victims."

Each victim-impact statement was powerful in its own right, but the most powerful statement came from Isabella Husted, who'd slept through the murders of her parents.

"Joshua Packer has stolen so much from me and my family. He has caused me tremendous pain but my mother taught me well," Isabella wrote. "She taught me that though there is evil in the world, there is also love. She taught me to use my painful experiences to help others and become stronger, not take my torment out on others."

As Frawley described the victim-impact statements and the emotional responses they generated in the courtroom, I couldn't help wondering about Josh's reaction to the proceeding.

"What did Packer say in court today?" I asked.

"Nothing," Frawley replied. "In fact, that's something I addressed with the court. I explained that in this courtroom and in courtrooms across the nation, you've got petty criminals—people who do things that are barely crimes—and they express sincere remorse for what they've done. They're ashamed of themselves. It's an aberration. Then you've got someone who commits a triple murder and never says a word of remorse to anybody. Not to his roommate, nobody."

This allowed us to segue into the subject of the roommate. Bob Miller's role in Josh's life generally and the Faria cover-up specifically was a subject of great interest for me. I was eager to get Frawley's take on it.

"Wasn't there some way to charge the roommate?" I asked. "After all, he jeopardized public safety for months by not reporting Josh."

"He did," Frawley said, "but oddly it's not a crime to not turn someone in after they've admitted a triple murder to you."

Frawley continued.

"We got the information (about the murders) little by little out of him over time and we ultimately had to promise not to prosecute him if he told us the truth. But at the end of the day, there really wasn't anything to charge him with anyway."

I told Frawley that, under the circumstances, I was shocked that Bob Miller or anyone with a basic sense of decency would refrain from contacting the authorities.

"He continued to live with (Josh) for months," Frawley replied. "They continued to share an apartment together and (Miller) told us that they never spoke about the murders again. Packer did the murders between 10 and 10:30, he's asleep within three and a half hours, then he's up at 6 a.m. to go to work. Then, the night following the murders, he went out with his friends, got drunk, and went on with his life as if nothing happened."

"What do you make of that?" I asked.

"Well, there are two labels that fit him," Frawley answered. "One, he's a sadist. He derives sexual satisfaction from causing someone else pain or injury. He's also a sociopath. He doesn't have a conscience."

After waiting a few moments to let that sink in, Frawley and I moved into my theory of the crimes.

Since I'd started piecing it together, I was eager to see if Frawley found any merit in my ideas.

I described how Josh, a kid from an underprivileged and abusive background, harbored tremendous resentment. He resented his parental abandonment, he resented the abject emotional and financial poverty in which he was raised, and he resented that most of his peers had far more than he ever had— both economically and emotionally. Growing up in a beautiful, affluent place like Ventura just exacerbated Josh's bitterness. Over time, having few constructive outlets for his angst, Josh's resentment morphed into pathological anger against his parents who—at least subconsciously—he felt had wronged him.

"Look at the people he killed," I explained. "It was the mother figure and the father figure. And who did he let go? It was the boy. I think that maybe he identified with the son in some way."

Frawley listened to my ideas carefully. When I was done, he shook his head briefly, then responded.

"No, I think that's too complex," Frawley said. "First of all, Ventura isn't all that affluent. Less than half the kids here go to college, far less."

"He just needed money to pay the rent," Frawley continued. "He and his girlfriend and his 'uncle' got this apartment and the girlfriend bailed after six weeks. They were boyfriend-girlfriend for several years, but she realized that living with him was a different story. She leaves, she buys him a motorcycle and helmet, he has a job, but he's using all his money for drugs. So he's got to cover what she was going to cover, plus his share, and he's not good with money. He needed money that night. He went out to get it."

Frawley's point was well taken. After all, as Occam's

razor holds, the most straightforward explanation is often the correct one. I decided to continue ruminating on the reasons behind the Husted slayings.

Meanwhile, I decided to ask Frawley about the sexual element of the Faria murders. Looking at the Faria murders in purview, Davina Husted's assault seemed completely incongruous with the rest of the crime. From a financial standpoint, the home-invasion robbery made sense (or at least as much "sense" as that sort of thing can make). And from a witness-neutralization standpoint, the murders of Brock and Davina Husted made sense. However, Josh's decision to assault Davina Husted made no sense to me. I wanted to get Frawley's take on this.

"The sexual component of this was an opportunity," Frawley said. "He needed money. We know he had $35.37 in his bank account that afternoon and he had to pay rent and bills. He needed cash, so he purposefully broke into the home because it was all lit up. Once he killed the man, he sees the woman there and figures that he might as well sexually assault her. I think it was just a matter of opportunity for him."

"What do you make of the children being allowed to live?" I asked.

"He didn't need to kill them," Frawley said. "He was in full motorcycle regalia, covered from head to toe in black. The daughter slept through the whole thing and the nine-year-old boy only witnessed the initial burglary. Actually, the boy initially reported that hc thought it was a black guy who'd committed the crimes."

Next, Frawley showed me one of the most compelling legal exhibits I had ever seen. There's little doubt that the exhibit would've played a major role in sending

Josh to Death Row if his case had gone to trial. The exhibit was a large, blown-up poster of a green hand towel. It was the same green hand towel that Josh had tossed onto Davina Husted's back like a piece of trash after the murders. The blown-up picture of the towel showed the traces of blood and semen in stunning clarity. At the bottom of the poster were several sequences of numbers. The numbers were arranged as probabilities. According to the exhibit, the probability that someone besides Josh had contributed the semen to the hand towel was more than one in a trillion.

It occurred to me that, on the strength of this one exhibit alone, Frawley could've convicted Josh beyond a reasonable doubt. With this in mind, I decided to inquire about what would happen to Josh now that he'd been sentenced.

"They don't want him around anymore (at the Pretrial Detention Facility)," Frawley said. "He's a burden to them, so they're going to be looking to transfer him to state prison as soon as possible."

Before our meeting ended, Frawley and I discussed some of the contradictory aspects of Josh's persona.

"Another interesting aspect to him is that he's charismatic," Frawley explained. "Girls thought he was cute, paid him a lot of attention, he always had a girlfriend. He was just the life of any party."

Building on a comment Frawley had made earlier in our meeting, I pointed out that superficial charm is one of the hallmarks of the psychopath.

"Oh yeah," Frawley said. "We'd find all these girls who'd say, 'Oh, he's so cute.' But he's also getting in fights at a lot of parties. People told me personally— when we were conducting interviews for this case—

that when Packer got in a fight, it was like watching six people fight."

A tsunami of thoughts flooded my mind on the drive home. In an attempt to beat Friday afternoon traffic in the Valley, I decided to take the 126 East to the 5 South, then sneak into town the back way.

As I drove through the golden hills that line the Santa Clara River, I thought hard about my interview with Frawley. He knew the evidence in the Faria case as well as or better than anyone on the planet. He also understood why DNA was such a critical tool in the administration of true justice. As a DNA expert, Frawley had made several outstanding points during our interview. However, as I went over and over our interview during the drive home, a couple of questions continued to gnaw at me.

If Josh was so concerned about witnesses that he'd murdered Brock and Davina Husted, then why didn't he murder Brockie as well and why did he use such a horrific level of overkill in dispatching his victims? Furthermore, Josh was the prime suspect in no less than five small-business robberies in Santa Barbara and Ventura counties. However, none of the robbery victims had been physically injured in any way. Assuming that Josh committed the small-business robberies in September 2009, why had he allowed those victims to live? After all, the September 2009 robbery victims got much clearer views of their assailant than the Husteds did. If Josh really was the small-business serial robber, then why didn't he murder his victims in September 2009?

The answer, I felt, was relatively straightforward: Brock and Davina Husted, as well as their wealthy lifestyle, symbolized the pain and deprivation Josh had experienced since he was a kid. In murdering the Husteds, Josh was murdering the most painful parts of his own existence. On the other hand, the clerks and cashiers who were targeted during Josh's alleged robberies were the types of low-level service workers with whom he could readily identify. Simply put, the gas-station attendants, Dairy Queen cashiers, and liquor-store clerks would've served no symbolic function in Josh's fevered mind.

There was little traffic on the eastbound 126 and I was able to get a lot of thinking done on the drive. When I reached Santa Clarita, I merged onto the 5 South and continued making my way home. As it turned out, I wasn't the only one traveling east on the 126 that afternoon.

After listening to the victim-impact statements and being sentenced to life without the possibility of parole, Josh was hustled out of Judge Murphy's courtroom. With his wrists cuffed, his legs shackled, and his prematurely thinning hair slicked back in an unctuous coif, Josh was placed in an office beside the courtroom. Moments after he was placed in the office, Ventura County detectives flooded the room and began bombarding Josh with questions. Through it all, Josh kept his mouth shut. As a result, the detectives rounded out their participation in the Faria case the same way they'd started it: by producing absolutely nothing.

With nothing left to offer Ventura County except his absence, Josh was whisked out of the Hall of Justice, loaded into a specially chartered van, and driven out the 126 East. When the vehicle reached the 5 Freeway, it didn't turn south like I had. Instead, the van veered north toward Bakersfield and its ultimate destination: Wasco State Prison.

CHAPTER 23

California's correctional pipeline doesn't flush inmates directly from county jails into the prisons where they'll serve their time. After sentencing, most Golden State felons are bussed to one of ten regional reception centers operated by the Department of Corrections and Rehabilitation. Reception center personnel are responsible for assessing incoming convicts and assigning them to the permanent prisons that are best equipped to meet their needs. For example, a low-level inmate with no history of violence, sexual offenses, or gang affiliations might be sent to a minimum-security conservation camp, where he'll be trained as a wildland firefighter. Conversely, a hardcore felon with a long history of violent gang activity might be sent to the Pelican Bay supermax, where prisoners in the Special Housing Unit are only allowed out of their claustrophobic cells for a couple of hours each week.

When a prisoner arrives at one of the state's reception centers, he's given a pair of bright red prison scrubs, an inmate identification number, basic personal-care items, and a bunk assignment. Over the next 120 days, prison staff gather information about the inmate's criminal record, education and employment background, family life, substance-abuse history, gang affiliations, and psychological issues. Before an inmate is processed out of the reception center and assigned to a permanent prison, he's given a full physical check-up, a comprehensive dental examination, and psychological screening.

On February 6, 2015, just a few hours after he was sentenced to spend the rest of his life behind bars, Josh Packer arrived at the Wasco State Prison Reception Center.

Two weeks later, on February 20, 2015, I mailed Josh a letter. Deciding on the precise tone of the letter was a challenge. After all, what does one say to a twenty-five-year-old triple murderer who will never experience freedom again? Since I'd never written such a letter, I was unsure of how to proceed. Ultimately, I decided that—as with most things in life—the direct approach would work best.

Striving for a tone that balanced firmness with compassion, I wrote to Josh about the book I was planning. In no uncertain terms, I told Josh that I didn't like his crimes and thought that he belonged behind bars. At the same time, I also explained that I didn't think Josh was an inherently bad person. Instead, I wrote that Josh's abysmal childhood experiences, awful crimes, and journey through the justice system provided insight into the some of the most critical issues of our time. In closing, I asked for Josh's help in ensuring the accuracy and completeness of my work.

After mailing the letter, I returned home and waited.

A week passed, then two.

If life has taught me anything, it's that interview requests are either followed up on immediately or they aren't followed up on at all. As the weeks passed, it became clear that Josh wasn't going to write back. While I was initially disappointed by this turn of events, Josh's reluctance to write back was understandable. Adjusting to prison life is a difficult process. The more I thought about Josh's situation at Wasco, the more it made sense that he wasn't in a letter-writing mood.

Convinced that Josh wasn't going to write me back and eager to keep the ball rolling on my project, I decided to explore my next-best avenue for information: Josh's family.

After Josh was arrested for the Faria murders in April 2010, his family was deluged with interview requests from the media. All of the interview requests had been denied. In fact, Josh's family had been almost totally silent in the years after he was taken into custody. While I understood their reluctance to speak with the media, in the back of my mind, I had a feeling that at least one of Josh's family members must want to talk. How could they not? Just as the Faria crimes had turned the lives of the victims' families upside down, the murders also had a profound impact on Josh's family. Keeping emotions bottled up under those circumstances would be profoundly difficult. As a result, I was convinced that if I approached Josh's family in just the right way, someone might agree to speak with me.

In the course of my digging, I'd obtained a phone number for Josh's sister Shauna. On the morning of March 16, 2015, I punched the number into my cell phone and hit send. The phone rang no more than three times before someone picked up.

"Hello?" two female voices said almost simultaneously.

After quickly identifying myself, I asked to speak with Shauna.

"Who are you again?" one of the female voices asked brusquely.

Before I could enunciate the Gr- in my first name, the woman's voice broke in again.

"Is this about Josh Packer!" the woman demanded to know in a voice bordering on rage.

"Yes," I said. "My name's Gray George. I'm doing research on his case."

Realizing that I had about five seconds to establish my credibility before the woman on the other end of the line hung up, I synopsized my project with what I hoped was laconic perfection.

"Well this is his mother, Terri," the voice said. "Shauna's on the line too. What are you going to write about Josh? Are you just going to tell more lies about him like the others?"

"No," I told her. "I want the full truth to finally come out about Josh and his case. I want people to understand Josh's whole story and all the facts surrounding it. I also want people to know what Josh's case says about some of the issues we're confronting as a nation."

Terri was silent for a moment and Shauna got off the phone. Then Terri posited another question.

"Who does this book benefit?" Terri asked in a voice that fused hostility with a creeping sadness.

"Society," I responded automatically.

This seemed to calm Terri down. She was quiet for a few seconds and I waited silently on the other end of the line. When Terri spoke again, the tone of her voice had changed. The anger was gone and in its place was unfettered sorrow. As we began speaking with each other, I realized that my initial instinct was correct: Terri had a willingness to talk. In fact, after years of fearing for Josh's life, it seemed like Terri was almost eager to talk.

Terri and I spent the next twenty minutes discussing my background, my project, and some of the peripheral issues surrounding Josh's case. Unlike some of the people I've interviewed in the past, Terri asked excellent questions. She wanted to know how she and Josh and everyone they knew were going to be portrayed in the book.

"You know, I have small children, kids in school," Terri said. "I still have to live around here. I just want to know what you're going to do with all this."

"I won't kid you," I said. "This book isn't going to make Josh look like some kind of choir boy. We both know that's not the truth. At the same time, I already know that Josh isn't a monster. I'm just going to report honestly on the complexities of Josh's case, as well as the issues surrounding it. Nothing more, nothing less."

"You know everything that's come out about his case is a lie, right?" Terri countered. "If I talk to you, how do I know you're not just going to lie and write more bad things about Josh?"

It was a good question.

"Look," I said. "If all I wanted to do was write bad things about Josh, I wouldn't have called you in the first place. I could just drive up to Ventura, stand on a corner downtown, and ask people on the street what they think of Josh. In fact, if I just wanted to paint

Josh in a bad light, that would be a much, *much* easier book to write. But that's not why I'm in this thing."

My answer seemed to resonate with Terri. We talked a little more about the project and about Josh. Then, without warning, Terri dropped a bombshell.

"Well, you know he didn't do it, right?" Terri asked me. A trace of indignation was creeping into her voice.

"What do you mean?" I asked.

"He just plead guilty because they were going to kill him and he didn't want to make the (Husted) kids testify," Terri responded.

The implausibility of Terri's comment was profound. The Husted home was replete with evidence implicating Josh in the murders. Not only had Josh's DNA been found throughout the Husteds' bedroom, it had actually been found on the murder weapon. Moreover, in his self-serving effort to avoid prosecution, Bob Miller had confessed to abetting Josh in the Faria cover-up. During the short time I'd spoken with Terri, she'd struck me as a highly rational person. It was hard to believe that she actually thought Josh was innocent. However, in an effort to keep our conversation moving, I decided not to push the issue at that point.

After describing Josh's decision not to go to trial, Terri said that she wanted to read some of the pieces I'd published in the past. Terri gave me her e-mail address and I agreed to send her links to some of my work.

I had no idea what to expect when I'd placed my call that morning, but after speaking with Terri for twenty minutes or so, it was clear that she was an extremely intelligent, articulate, and quick-witted person. It was also clear that Terri loved Josh deeply and unconditionally, and that she was beating herself up over the mistakes she'd made as a parent.

Just before we hung up, Terri made a very touching confession.

"I'm sorry I was so angry when you first called," she said. "This is just a really hard time for me...for all of us. Josh is my kid and I love him. I just love him so much."

Tears started to creep into Terri's voice as we said goodbye.

About two hours after my first conversation with Terri, she called me back. She'd read the pieces I'd e-mailed her and was ready to talk in more depth. Getting right down to business, Terri broached a subject we were both itching to discuss: Bob Miller. Since I'd first learned about Uncle Bob and his unorthodox presence in Josh's life, I'd wanted to know more about their relationship. Terri didn't mince words as she began telling me about Miller.

"I think he was obsessed with my son," Terri told me.

"Obsessed how?" I asked.

"Sexually obsessed!" Terri responded.

She went on to describe the circumstances of how Miller had met Josh at the Ventura Boys and Girls Club. She explained how friendly Miller had seemed at first and how thrilled she was when he volunteered to serve as Josh's mentor.

"I trusted him completely," Terri told me. "He became very close with our family. You have to understand though, Gray, men like him prey on women like me. I just didn't know any better back then."

Terri suspected that Miller might have molested Josh. I asked Terri if she had any proof to support her suspicions. Terri mentioned a story that someone had told her about witnessing Josh and Miller at the beach together. According to the witness, Miller had rubbed suntan lotion on Josh's back in a highly suggestive manner.

By statute, the beach incident didn't qualify as a criminal act. I asked Terri if she knew anything else about Josh's relationship with Miller.

"I don't know what they did together, I just don't know," Terri told me. "I have so many questions. For all I know, he wanted to fuck Josh in the ass!"

Although there was no proof that Miller had abused Josh, Terri was steadfast in her belief that Miller had been a negative influence in her son's life. Eventually, our discussion turned to Miller's role in covering up the Faria murders. Terri was flabbergasted that Miller had participated in the cover-up. The more we talked, the more Terri's implications seemed clear: Whatever their relationship, Josh and Miller must've been involved—deeply involved—in criminal activity together prior to the Faria tragedy. Why else would Josh have felt comfortable telling Miller about the murders? And why else would Miller have felt comfortable disposing of evidence in a triple-murder case?

"You know (Miller) still works with kids, don't you?" Terri asked me.

When I told her that I did not, she gave me the name of Miller's employer. As it turned out, Miller worked for a company that provided services to needy children. A few days later, I called Miller at his office. He had a chipper tone in his voice when he answered the phone. After I introduced myself and explained that I was doing research on Josh Packer's case, Miller's tone quickly changed. Stuttering and clearly anxious, Miller said he had to attend a meeting and that he didn't have time to speak with me. I gave Miller my phone number. He said he'd call me back. He never did.

Bob Miller wasn't the only topic Terri and I discussed during our second conversation on March 16. She also told me about the April 2010 raid on her house, Josh's loving relationship with his siblings, and some of the details of her own life. Through it all, Terri always circled back to the mistakes she'd made when Josh was a boy.

"Look, I know I'm not going to win mother of the year," Terri told me with resigned sadness in her voice. "But I love all my kids. I really do. I love them with all my heart. When I look back to when Josh was a kid, it's...it's like another lifetime."

"I did a lot of bad things," Terri continued. "I got mixed up in the wrong things, but I have a good life now, a great husband. But the past five years have been rough. They really have been."

When I asked Terri how she'd managed to pull her life together, she didn't miss a beat.

"When my youngest daughter was born, I think that's what did it," Terri said. "She has disabilities, she's had open-heart surgery and I knew I needed to be there for her because she was totally helpless without me. I just...unfortunately, I wasn't always there for Josh and Shauna."

The more I talked with Terri, the more I liked her. She was completely open, she didn't shy away from the brutal truth, and she never attempted to spin the less-flattering aspects of her past. Like all parents,

Terri had made mistakes. Some of Terri's mistakes, by her own admission, were profound. However, after speaking with Terri, I realized that, in some ways, Josh had been quite fortunate. Despite all her personal shortcomings and all the mistakes she'd made in her twenties, it was clear that Terri loved Josh with every fiber of her being.

Before our second conversation ended on March 16, Terri and I spoke briefly about the Faria murders. When I asked Terri what she would've done if she suspected that Josh might've been involved with the murders, she was as candid as always.

"I don't know what I would've done," she said with a heavy-hearted sigh. "Would I have turned him in? Would I have taken him down to Mexico? I don't know. You know, a mother's love is very strong. I like to think I would've encouraged Josh to turn himself in, but I just don't know how I would've reacted."

We ended that day's talk with a discussion of the death penalty. Terri told me that she was opposed to the death penalty. I told her that I oppose the death penalty as well. I asked Terri if she was opposed to the death penalty because of Josh's situation.

"I've always been against the death penalty. It doesn't get us anywhere," Terri told me. "Josh offered to plead guilty and (Ventura County District Attorney Gregory) Totten was very close to taking the deal. The only reason he didn't is because of the seriousness of the crimes."

I asked Terri how she felt when she learned that the state was going to plea bargain in Josh's case and take the death penalty off the table.

"I was so relieved. I was *so* relieved!" she said. "I can't tell you how...I love Josh. He's my kid. And you know what, for the majority of people who know Josh, this hasn't changed their opinion of him. He's a real likable kind of guy. I mean, his little brother adores him. It's just...it's just I dropped the ball when Josh was young. I dropped the ball and nobody ever picked it up."

———————————

Over the next eleven days, Terri and I exchanged a few text messages. During that time, I gave significant thought to our first conversations. Despite the admittedly poor decisions she'd made when Josh was a boy, it was clear that Terri had matured into a loving parent for her youngest children. Also, Terri's thinking was very clear and she obviously cared about the truth. In light of this, it was hard to understand how Terri could continue to believe that Josh was innocent in the Faria case. The mountain of law-enforcement reports, legal filings, scientific data, crime-scene photos, and other documentation that I'd collected—not to mention Josh's own guilty pleas—pointed directly to Josh's involvement in the murders. I decided that, at some point in the near future, Terri and I needed to delve deeper into the issue of Josh's culpability.

As it happened, Terri and I spoke again on Friday, March 27, 2015. She called around 12:40 p.m. Terri's first question was whether my first name was really Gray. I admitted that it was. I then asked Terri if she'd had a chance to speak with Josh since our last conversation. She said that she had not. Evidently, making phone calls from prison can be a complicated ordeal, especially for new inmates. The fact that Terri couldn't speak with Josh was obviously causing her great distress.

We talked for a while about Josh's status at Wasco's Reception Center. Terri told me that, although she had not spoken with Josh, he had sent her a couple of letters since his arrival at the prison. This led us into a discussion about Josh's specific needs within the state prison system. I asked Terri if she had any idea where Josh would be permanently placed once he was processed through the reception center. Terri said she didn't know precisely where he'd be housed, but that it would probably be somewhere within a reasonable driving distance of her home in Ventura.

"Wherever he goes, Josh is going to be housed in SNY," Terri told me.

"What's SNY?" I asked.

Terri explained that SNY was an acronym for Sensitive Needs Yard. As I found out later, the California Department of Corrections and Rehabilitation maintains SNYs at several prisons across the state. These yards are designed to hold gang dropouts, snitches, pedophiles, convicted sex offenders, and other vulnerable inmates who would be targeted for violence or extortion within the larger prison community.

Our conversation shifted back to Josh's confinement in the Ventura County Pretrial Detention Facility. I asked Terri if she'd seen the video of Josh fighting with deputies on June 19, 2011. She informed me that she had not, but that Josh had described the incident to her during a visit. She added that Josh's entire face was bruised and swollen for days after the fight. Terri also told me that she hadn't seen any evidence in the case because Josh's lawyers hadn't shared anything with her and she couldn't talk with Josh about his charges when she visited him in the county jail. Not knowing anything about the Faria crimes or the evidence against Josh was something that frustrated Terri greatly.

Terri and I talked for more than an hour. Before we ended our call, she asked if I could send her a copy of the jailhouse brawl video. After we hung up, I sent Terri the video. Within minutes, she called me back.

"They didn't need to beat him like that!" Terri raged. "Why didn't they just leave him alone in the cell? They didn't need to hurt him like that!"

Terri pointed out that, in the video, several green and yellow stickers can be seen on the door of Josh's cell. According to Terri, these stickers designated Josh as an inmate with special psychiatric needs. Terri was particularly upset that the jail staff didn't have better protocols for dealing with mentally ill inmates.

It was clear that the brawl video was very upsetting to Terri, but one aspect of the footage was encouraging to her.

"You know what though, the video showed exactly what Joshua told me," Terri said. "You know, Josh is a lot of things, but I'll tell you one thing: My son is honest. He told me he hit that cop during the fight and they slammed him to the floor. He told me exactly what happened and that video proved it."

As Terri continued to talk about Josh's honesty and positive virtues, her close, emotionally charged relationship with her son came into full focus. Terri loved Josh deeply. She also trusted him completely. As a result, it was easy to understand how Terri could continue to believe in Josh's innocence.

A couple hours after Terri and I wrapped up our second conversation on March 27, she sent me a text. Earlier that day, I'd mentioned to Terri that I had obtained a large quantity of materials related to Josh's case. Terri's text message was direct: She asked if I would send her some of the documents in my collection. It seemed that the jailhouse brawl video had shaken Terri up. She'd been haunted by her son's case for the past five years and now she was ready to get some answers to her many questions.

That evening, I converted some of my Faria-related documents and photographs into digital files and e-mailed them to Terri. Once the files were sent, I didn't hear anything back from Terri immediately. Then, at a few minutes before midnight, my phone started ringing. It was Terri. She was crying. We ended up talking until just before dawn.

One of the pictures I'd sent Terri was an autopsy photograph of little Grant Husted. The photo had disturbed Terri greatly. It was the first thing she mentioned after I answered the phone.

"The picture of the baby was awful," Terri wept. "It was just awful."

I agreed with her.

Once Terri regained her composure, we started talking about the documents I'd sent her. With a tone of great relief in her voice, Terri explained that the documents answered some of her long-standing questions about Josh's case. She again described how she had never been able to talk to Josh about the case after his arrest in April 2010.

"Not knowing anything has been one of the hardest

parts of this whole thing," Terri said. "Every time I visited Josh in jail, I wanted...I wanted more than anything to ask him about the case. We couldn't really talk though."

One of the documents I'd e-mailed Terri was an evidence summary that laid out the prosecution's case against Josh. I asked Terri what she thought of the evidence. Sighing deeply, Terri inched closer to the horrifying reality of her first-born son's actions. She told me that she thought Josh *probably* did the murders. This was a significant disclosure for Terri. In the same breath, however, she shifted back to the defense's mitigation package.

"I'm still not exactly sure what happened, though," Terri said. "I mean, if you look at what the defense did...they talked to Randy, people in Ohio. They did an amazing job!"

Terri told me that one of the people who'd spoken to the mitigation investigators was a pedophile from Oxnard. Evidently, the pedophile admitted to the defense team that he'd had sexual contact with Josh when he was ten years old.

"(Pedophile's name) told them what he did," Terri said. "He admitted that he was the one who showed Josh how to jack off in the shower."

As the hours passed, Terri told me about her upbringing in Ohio, her experiences in Straight, and her brief, painful marriage to Randy Packer. She told me about her troubled twenties, her mistakes with Shauna and Josh, and her desperate attempt to pull her life together starting in 1998. At no point did Terri attempt to shirk responsibility for her poor decisions or turn her life into a melodramatic sob story. Throughout the early morning hours of March

28, 2015, Terri came across as heartrendingly honest. At one point, as Terri talked about her many mistakes as a mother, I told her that she shouldn't be too hard on herself. After all, she was just a kid when Shauna and Josh were born and she had no help from their father. Terri's response to me was curt.

"No, no. I chose all that, Gray," she said crisply. "Don't feel sorry for me. They were my mistakes."

Our conversation didn't follow one thematic track. We shifted back and forth between the biographic details of Terri's life, Josh's status in prison, and Josh's childhood. Some of the stories Terri told me were startling in their irony. For example, when he was a teenager, Josh had gotten one of his girlfriends pregnant. However, instead of keeping the baby, the girlfriend had opted to get an abortion.

"Joshua was really upset about that," Terri explained. "He loves kids and, you know, he's also really against abortion."

Apparently, as a staunch pro-lifer, Josh considered abortion to be murder.

Eventually, our conversation shifted back to Josh's confinement in state prison. Terri broke down when she began talking about how much she missed Josh and how much she wanted him home.

"I've kept all his things," Terri choked out between tears. "His clothes are still in his hamper just like they were back then. They still have his scent on them! The only thing I gave away was his snowboard, and I gave that to his brother."

Terri added that she still has Josh's car. Today, when Terri drives Josh's car around Ventura to pick up her younger children from school or run other errands, she often listens to *Demons* by Imagine Dragons on the car's CD player. It's the song that she and Josh listened to so many times when she visited him at the Pretrial Detention Facility.

"You know, I think he might've been trying to tell me something with that song," Terri told me with tears rising in her voice. "He'd just look at me and ask me to play it over and over again. I think he was trying to tell me something he couldn't say in the visiting room."

She took a deep breath. When she spoke again, her words rocked me.

"I'm not stupid, okay," Terri said. "I know he did it. Alright, I know he did. I don't know exactly what happened. I wasn't there, but...But you have to understand that...look, no parent wants to admit that about their child. I love Josh. I really love Josh. He's my son."

It was a stark, powerful moment. Terri breathed heavily into the night on her end of the phone. I sat in silence on my end, unsure of what to say.

Terri broke the silence.

"When I think about Josh, oh God, I get to the point where I can't even breathe sometimes," she said. "And when that happens, I also think about the Husted children. I think about them every day. I pray for them, I pray for their family. I feel so..."

Terri trailed off, crying and breathing heavily.

When she began to talk again, Terri spoke of the profound grief she felt for the Husteds and the DeBonis. Again and again, Terri expressed her sorrow for what had happened and for their losses. Listening to her words, it was clear that this was not a performance. Terri's words of contrition for the victims' families were heartfelt and deeply poignant.

"I pray for their families," Terri said. "If there was anything I could…"

Terri's emotions were profound. It sounded as if words alone were incapable of capturing the depth of her feelings and the wrenching knowledge that she could never do anything to make the victims' families whole.

At the end of our long, painful, revealing conversation, Terri recounted an incident that was as uplifting, tender, and suggestive of human goodness as anything I'd heard in conjunction with the Faria murders.

The incident occurred on April 14, 2011, the day Josh was convicted in the Perea hit-and-run case. To make Josh look presentable in front of the hit-and-run jury, Terri had purchased some new clothes for him and taken them to the Pretrial Detention Facility. Josh was wearing one of his new outfits when he heard the guilty verdicts announced in the hit-and-run trial.

After Josh was convicted in the Perea case, he was led into a cell behind the courtroom and ordered to take off his civilian clothing. Once Josh had changed into his jailhouse scrubs, his courtroom attire was placed in boxes and returned to Terri, who had remained in the courtroom after the trial concluded.

With the stack of boxes piled high in her arms, Terri was ready to go home. To avoid the scrum of reporters and cameras in front of the courthouse, Terri hustled to a bank of elevators at the back of the building. The boxes of khakis, shirts, belts, shoes, and other clothing items were balanced precariously in Terri's arms as she made her way down the hall. Nearing the back elevators, Terri saw several members of the Husted family standing in the hallway. Apparently, they had traveled to the Hall of Justice to watch Josh's hit-and-run trial.

Still reeling from Josh's hit-and-run convictions, Terri wanted nothing more than to board the elevator, leave the Hall of Justice, and go home. When she was a few feet from the elevator, Terri reached out her arm to press the call button. It was at that moment that Terri tripped and fell to the floor. The boxes in Terri's arms went flying and Josh's recently worn clothes were scattered across the hallway.

Rising to her feet and attempting to compose herself as best she could, Terri began gathering up Josh's clothing. As Terri was putting the clothes back in the boxes, she glanced toward the Husted brothers, who were standing a few feet away. The brothers just looked down on Terri. Then, out of nowhere, a woman walked away from the Husted brothers. The woman approached Terri, knelt down, and began helping Terri pick up Josh's things. Although Terri didn't know the woman's name, Terri did know that the woman was Brock Husted's niece.

"I couldn't believe it!" Terri exclaimed with tears in her voice. "She actually helped me. She picked up Josh's shoes—she actually touched his socks!"

Overcome by her memory of the niece's kindness, Terri broke down completely. The fact that a Husted family member had possessed the benevolence to help Terri at such a moment was extraordinary. It was this level of human grace that the Bard captured so timelessly in *Titus Andronicus* when he wrote that "Sweet mercy is nobility's truest badge."

The niece's act of mercy in the Hall of Justice that day was, without a doubt, one of the most noble acts I had ever heard described.

Terri and I continued talking over the next few months. One of the topics we spoke about at length was Terri's relationship with her family. Despite her traumatic experiences in Straight, Terri always spoke in positive terms about her biological parents. Terri wished that her parents had played a larger role in the lives of her children. After Terri moved to California in the late 1980s, she said that it was very difficult having no real support system in place.

"When Josh and Shauna were little, we were all we had," Terri said. "It was just me and them. It was just like...nothing much lasted for us."

Terri was honest about the impact this had on Josh's life.

"I'm trying to teach my (youngest) kids the importance of patience and compassion," Terri told me. "I didn't teach those things to Josh and Shauna and I know it had a bad effect on their lives."

To her credit, Terri's younger children have turned out very well. Terri told me that her middle son, who was eleven when Josh was arrested for the Faria murders, is even thinking about becoming a police officer.

During a conversation on August 27, 2015, I finally asked Terri about my tentative theory on the Faria case.

"I've given a lot of thought to why everything in Faria might've happened the way it did," I said. "Do you think it's possible that Josh might've been angry with you or Randy, and that his anger spilled over onto the Husteds—the parental figures in that house?"

As mentioned previously, Terri is highly intelligent and immediately saw where I was going. Once my question had been asked, Terri waited a couple of beats before answering.

"I don't know," Terri responded in a hesitant voice. "I just don't know. I've never even been able to talk with Joshua about all of this. I guess...I just don't know."

During the same conversation, I also asked Terri if she'd heard anything about the Faria murders before her house was raided in April 2010.

"Oh yeah," Terri told me. "My (youngest) daughter's physical therapist at the time, her husband was a Ventura police officer and she told me that (the police) were really worried about all the knife murders back then. (The physical therapist) told me the police called the guy the 'Beach Butcher' or something like that because all the murders (Husteds and Di Rodio) were happening down by the beach.

"And it's funny because one day while (the physical therapist) and I were talking, Josh came by the house— he just happened to drop by. We were talking and Josh was kind of walking around and doing some stuff and he must've heard us talking because he comes up to me and says something like 'Mom, you really need to keep the doors locked. Bad things can happen when people don't keep their doors locked.' I don't remember exactly what he said, but it was something like that."

"What did you make of that?" I asked.

"Well, I thought Josh was right," Terri responded. "We lived on Ocean (Avenue) back then and that's right across the railroad tracks from the beach—only about a five-minute walk from the beach. So, you know, with all the murders and everything, I started keeping our doors locked all the time."

———————•••——————

During another conversation, I asked about Josh's decision not to offer a statement at his sentencing.

"Josh thought about writing a statement for the sentencing, but he decided not to because there was nothing he could say," Terri explained. "He told me, 'What can I say, Mom?' There was nothing he could say to make things better for the families. He actually sat down and started writing a statement, but he decided not to read it in court."

I asked Terri if she agreed with Josh's decision not to express contrition at his sentencing.

"Yes," she said. "If Josh had said anything, that's what they would've shown on TV and the statements by the family members never would've been heard."

Terri informed me that Josh had been moved from Wasco's Reception Center to the psychiatric unit of the California Medical Facility. Located in Vacaville, the Medical Facility is a secure treatment center for state prisoners with serious health needs.

Knowing that Terri had spoken to Josh on the phone before his transfer, I asked why he'd been sent to Vacaville.

"He told me he was having a lot of trouble with the victim-impact statements," Terri said without elaborating.

Growing emotional again, Terri talked about how much she loved Josh, how much she missed him, and how much she wanted him home. Before long, Terri was once again running through the litany of mistakes she'd made as a parent. It seemed as if, more than anything in the world, Terri wanted to go back in time and repair the damage that had been done when Josh was a kid.

"I didn't want all of this," Terri said in a pitifully strained voice. "I just always thought I could fix things later. But now it's too late."

CHAPTER 24

So what does it all mean?

Are the Faria murders just the story of a brutal kid from a brutal background who became a brutal murderer? Is this just another case about devastated families, a community's loss of innocence, and the rotting moral core of modern society? Or is the Faria case a macabre allegory about the dark-side of the American Dream? Ultimately, the Faria murders are all of these things, and much more.

As much as anything else, the Faria murders highlight the critical, life-saving importance of arrestee DNA collection and comprehensive DNA databases. If serological evidence from the Faria crime scene had not been matched with Josh Packer's DNA, it's very possible that the Faria murders would've gone unsolved. After all, when CODIS linked Josh to the Husted murders in April 2010, Ventura County detectives hadn't even identified Josh as a person of interest in the Faria case. By collecting Josh's DNA as part of the standard booking process and entering it into CODIS, the state was able to take a dangerous criminal off the streets in a (relatively) timely manner, offer a semblance of closure to the Faria victims' families, and protect the public from further harm.

While CODIS and the provisions of Proposition 69 produced outstanding results in the Faria case, Josh Packer's comeuppance is not an isolated example of forensic crime fighting at its finest. Since the late 1980s, DNA has been used to solve tens of thousands of violent crimes, both domestically and abroad. Without DNA, many of these cases would've been difficult—if not impossible—to solve. One such case began in the Pacific Northwest in the early 1980s.

In the summer of 1982, the bodies of five young prostitutes were found in or near the Green River south of Seattle, Washington. Autopsies revealed that each of the victims had been murdered by strangulation. Over the next two years, young prostitutes continued to vanish from stroll areas around Seattle. Eventually, the strangled corpses of more than fifty young prostitutes were dredged from the damp evergreen forests of western Washington. Because the victims disappeared from known prostitution zones, met their fates through strangulation, and were often dumped in clusters, detectives with the King County Sheriff's Office knew that a serial killer was preying in their jurisdiction. It didn't take long before the media gave the unidentified predator a nickname: the Green River Killer.

Between 1982 and 1994, multiple task forces were formed and millions of dollars were poured into the Green River investigation. Law-enforcement officials were desperate to identify their unknown prostitute killer, but despite their best efforts and despite the exorbitant sums that were spent on the Green River investigation, King County detectives were unable to make an arrest in the case.

Although the King County Sheriff's Office kept at least one full-time detective assigned to the Green River investigation between 1995 and the dawn of the twenty-first century, the case remained unsolved. Occasionally, a hiker or a mushroom picker would stumble across the aging skeleton of a young woman in some deep, primeval forest near Seattle. When one of these gruesome discoveries was made, the King County Sheriff's Office would dutifully process the scene and collect evidence. However, detectives got no closer to identifying the elusive Green River Killer.

Then, in an instant, everything changed.

In November 2001, the Washington State Crime Lab used semen found in three of the Green River victims to develop a DNA profile of their killer. The profile was developed using technology that hadn't existed when the victims were murdered in 1982. With the killer's unique DNA sequence in hand, crime-lab personnel began comparing it to the genetic profiles of Green River suspects. It didn't take long before a perfect match was made.

As it turned out, the Green River Killer was a fifty-two-year-old truck painter from the south Seattle area named Gary Leon Ridgway. Ridgway's home had been searched by the Green River Task Force in 1987. When no evidence was uncovered in the search, detectives asked Ridgway if he was willing to chew on a piece of gauze (so that his blood type could be determined) and take a polygraph test regarding his possible involvement in the Green River murders. Ever the accommodating citizen, Ridgway readily agreed to gnaw on the gauze and take the polygraph, which he passed with flying colours. [66] After Ridgway passed the polygraph (which is a notoriously unreliable and unscientific "test"), the Green River Task Force dropped him as a suspect and began focusing on other persons of interest in the case.

When Ridgway was arrested for the Green River murders in November 2001, a team of first-rate defense attorneys was appointed to represent him. With powerful DNA evidence linking their client to the Green River slayings, Ridgway's attorneys quickly realized that traditional defense strategies would not be effective if the case went to trial. Eventually, in a frantic attempt to save their client from the death penalty, Ridgway's attorneys worked with prosecutors to structure a plea agreement. According to the terms of the plea agreement, King County prosecutors would take the death penalty off the table if Ridgway would lead detectives to the bodies of several missing victims, provide detectives with detailed information about his crimes, and plead guilty to forty-nine counts of murder. Eager to save his own skin, Ridgway took the deal. During a marathon interrogation session in the summer of 2003, Ridgway confessed to murdering more than seventy young women, making him the most prolific serial killer in American history.

In the spirit of full transparency, it should be stated that Gary Ridgway's DNA was linked to the Green River victims through the gauze he chewed in 1987, not a post-arrest buccal swab. However, it's worth noting that Ridgway was arrested for solicitation of prostitution on May 11, 1982, just a few weeks before the first Green River victim disappeared. [67] As a result, if modern DNA technology had existed in May 1982, and if Ridgway had been forced to provide a buccal swab at the time of his solicitation arrest, then his involvement in the Green River murders could've been established in days, not decades. In turn, this identification would've spared the lives of at least sixty women.

In December 2003, Gary Ridgway was sentenced to life in prison without the possibility of parole. Thanks to the unassailable science of properly handled DNA evidence, Ridgway is now safely incarcerated at the Washington State Penitentiary in Walla Walla.

———————•••———————

Not every predator who's identified through DNA is a prolific serial slayer like Gary Ridgway. Although their crimes are no less debauched than Ridgway's, many violent offenders claim far fewer victims. An example of this phenomenon is Angelo Speziale, a native of Bergen County, New Jersey, who committed only one known murder. Speziale's case exemplifies, not only the public-safety potential of arrestee DNA collection, but the superiority of DNA screening to other crime-fighting strategies.

In 1977, documentary filmmaker Arnold Shapiro began organizing a cinematic project that would explore a purported breakthrough in crime suppression. This breakthrough, which was touted as a panacea to the youth-crime epidemic of the late 1970s, was designed to give young offenders an up-close-and-personal look at the stark realities of prison life. As part of the program, at-risk teens were taken into prisons and verbally berated by seasoned convicts. Proponents of this model believed that the convicts' verbal abuse, coupled with exposure to the debased milieu of prison, would deter wayward teens from committing future crimes. Shapiro entitled his documentary *Scared Straight!*

To bring his project to life, Shapiro recruited a group of juvenile delinquents from northern New Jersey and New York City. All of the teens featured in *Scared Straight!* had been arrested for crimes ranging from drug dealing to shoplifting to mugging. Angelo Speziale, who was a scrawny sixteen-year-old robber and burglar at the time, was one of the delinquents recruited for Shapiro's film.

On the day of production, Shapiro transported his coterie of teenage hoodlums to Rahway State Prison, a notorious lock-up south of Newark. Cameras rolled as the teens were led across Rahway's parking lot, through the sally port, and into the cell blocks. Over the next several hours, Shapiro captured the astonishment of his young offenders as they were screamed at, humiliated, and terrorized by a group of hardened Rahway inmates who called themselves the Lifers. At the end of the day, after the Lifers were led back to their cells and the teens were escorted from the prison, Shapiro conducted follow-up interviews with his young offenders. Like other members of his cohort, Speziale looked into Shapiro's camera with total earnestness and proclaimed that the Rahway experience had changed his life. Speziale vowed that, as a result of *Scared Straight!*, his criminal lifestyle was a thing of the past.

After *Scared Straight!* was broadcast to a nationwide audience in late 1978, the "scared-straight" model was immediately heralded as a breakthrough in crime prevention. Despite a dearth of longitudinal data on the efficacy of the scared-straight model, adjectives like remarkable, amazing, and miraculous were used to extol Shapiro's work. At the 1978 Academy Awards, *Scared Straight!* won the Oscar for Best Documentary Film. As Shapiro rode high atop a wave of cinematic success, states across the nation rushed to implement scared-straight programs of their own. The conventional "wisdom" of the era held that defiant, long-haired, dope-smoking kids were ruining the country. To this end, *Scared Straight!* offered an easy, feel-good, low-cost solution to Middle America's moral panic *du jour*.

In time, flaws started to emerge in the scared-straight model of reform. Despite its superficial patina of deterrence, studies showed that the scared-straight model was not effective at curbing or preventing crime. Pundits pointed out that many of the teens involved with the 1978 documentary had gone on to reoffend after filming wrapped. Statistical research revealed a more ominous trend: Teens involved with scared-straight programs were *more likely* to commit future crimes than teens who had not participated in such programs. [68]

Meanwhile, after parting ways with Shapiro and his film crew, Angelo Speziale returned to his New Jersey neighborhood. In the years following *Scared Straight!*, Speziale married, worked a steady job, and purchased a home of his own. Aside from a couple of minor brushes with the law, it appeared that Speziale's participation in *Scared Straight!* had done him some good.

That illusion was shattered in the mid-2000s.

One afternoon in 2005, the Hackensack Police Department received a phone call from a local business. According to the business owner, his loss-prevention team had detained a shoplifter who was attempting to steal $354 worth of razor blades. When

Hackensack police officers arrived at the business, they learned that the shoplifting suspect was Angelo Speziale. Under the provisions of a 2003 New Jersey law, a buccal swab was obtained from Speziale when he was booked into the county jail on theft charges. The swab was then sent to the state crime lab. It took more than two years for Garden State lab personnel to process and screen Speziale's buccal swab, but on March 7, 2007, Bergen County police were notified that Speziale's DNA had been matched to an unsolved rape/murder from the early 1980s. The murder was committed less than four years after filming wrapped on *Scared Straight!*

The murder victim was a nineteen-year-old woman named Michele Mika. On January 31, 1982, Mika's mother found her lying facedown in bed with an eight-inch kitchen knife protruding from her back. Detectives later determined that an intruder had broken into Mika's home through a back window, raped the young woman for several hours, then hacked her to death with a knife from her own kitchen. At the time of Mika's murder, her family and Speziale's family lived on opposite sides of the same duplex.

Not only did *Scared Straight!* fail to protect society from Angelo Speziale, Bergen County detectives were unable to solve Michele Mika's murder for more than a quarter century. Without DNA, it's quite likely that Speziale would still be walking the streets and claiming that "...*Scared Straight!* changed my life." However, because New Jersey lawmakers took the crucial, life-saving step of codifying reasonable arrestee DNA collection laws, Speziale is now rotting behind bars. Ironically, after pleading guilty to Michele Mika's murder and receiving a sentence of twenty-five years to life, Speziale was sent to Rahway State Prison.

———•••———

Gary Ridgway and Angelo Speziale are not isolated, anecdotal cases of scientific crime fighting done right. Instead, Ridgway and Speziale represent the myriad of violent criminals who've been identified through DNA collection and held accountable for their crimes. In this sense, the Ridgway and Speziale cases underscore one of the most important truths of modern law enforcement: Unless suspect DNA is connected to crime-scene DNA, there's a strong probability that serious violent felonies will go unsolved. When this occurs, victims are denied justice and the public is placed at risk.

There's no doubt that DNA databases have revolutionized the criminal-justice system in the United States. Where once there were cold cases, now there are predators behind bars. Where once there was reasonable doubt, now there is near-definitive proof of guilt. And where once there were innocent people rotting in prison for crimes they didn't commit, now there are compensation funds for the wrongly convicted. As New York State Supreme Court Justice Joseph Harris put it, "DNA technology could be the greatest single advance in the search for truth, conviction of the guilty, and acquittal of the innocent since the advent of cross-examination." [69]

Mike Frawley concurs with Harris's assessment. As a veteran prosecutor, Frawley views DNA as one of the strongest bridges between indictment and conviction beyond a reasonable doubt. When asked about DNA's role in getting jurors over the cognitive hurdle of reasonable doubt, Frawley was succinct.

"It's huge," Frawley said. "If you've got a case with DNA, it's a big relief because jurors will be so accepting of it. They're not relying on anyone's testimony or believability or credibility. If the DNA matches, then the defendant's story about 'I was never there' is obviously hogwash."

Time and again, Frawley has seen DNA crack violent-crime cases and bring human predators to justice. To this end, Josh Packer isn't the only Ventura County killer to be identified through a booking buccal swab and taken off the streets.

On July 30, 1980, a fifteen-year-old girl named Stacy Knappenberger was found murdered in her Oxnard home. An autopsy revealed that Knappenberger's assailant had raped her, bludgeoned her, bitten her, and then stabbed her to death with a broken glass ashtray. [70] Although the medical examiner recovered semen from Knappenberger's battered body, the semen was of minimal investigative value in 1980 and the Oxnard Police Department was never able to make an arrest in the case.

For more than three decades, Knappenberger's case remained cold and unsolved. Eventually, the semen found in Knappenberger's body was used to create a DNA profile of her killer. Unfortunately, when the DNA profile was entered into CODIS, it didn't register a hit and the investigation into Knappenberger's murder remained stalled.

Finally, just when it appeared that Knappenberger's murderer might escape justice forever, Oxnard detectives received word that a DNA match had been made in the case. As it turned out, DNA from the

Knappenberger crime scene had been matched to a sixty-five-year-old man named Thomas Coalt Young, Jr. Young's DNA ended up in the federal DNA database after he was arrested in 2010 on a sexual-assault charge in Illinois.

After being extradited to Ventura County, Young was tried for and convicted of Knappenberger's murder. Young was sentenced to life without parole on March 15, 2015. He is serving his time at High Desert State Prison in Susanville, California.

Since the dawn of modern law enforcement, solving violent crimes has been a matter of linking suspects to victims, then eliminating suspects who lacked the means, motive, and/or opportunity to commit a given offense. American law-enforcement agencies are good at solving crimes when a clear link exists between victim and offender. Case in point is the murder of Wendy Di Rodio, which occurred less than two weeks after the Faria murders.

On May 25, 2012, nearly three years after Di Rodio was murdered in her parents' Ventura Keys home, an arrest was made in the case. The suspect was none other than Di Rodio's niece, Gina Francesca Drake. The ex-wife of a Ventura police officer, Drake is suspected of entering Di Rodio's bedroom on June 3, 2009, stabbing her aunt to death over an unresolved family issue, then fleeing the scene. As of this writing, Drake is being held without bail at the Pretrial Detention Facility.

By synergizing hard work with tried-and-true investigative techniques, Ventura detectives were able to establish a link between Wendy Di Rodio and her suspected murderer. In many cases, however, such an outcome is not possible. Either the link between the suspect and the victim is unclear to detectives or, in the case of stranger-on-stranger crimes, the link doesn't exist at all. This is where arrestee DNA collection and DNA databases become indispensable variables in the equation of criminal justice.

According to a 2011 report by the Bureau of Justice Statistics, the incidence of stranger homicide rose steadily between 1980 and 2008. In 1980, stranger homicides accounted for just thirty-six percent of all murders in the United States. By 2008, that figure had risen to forty-four percent. [71] Without comprehensive DNA databases and the investigative leads they generate, law enforcement would be unable to identify suspects in many of these cases. Comprehensive DNA databases allow detectives to be proactive—not reactive—in tracking down violent offenders and building solid cases against them. This is particularly important when detectives are searching for highly mobile predators who target strangers.

It's worth noting that, since DNA became an ubiquitous part of the criminal-justice landscape in the early 1990s, American crime rates have plummeted. Between 1980 and 2013, the violent-crime rate in the United States dropped by almost forty percent. [72] Although this decline was attributable to a number of factors, there's no doubt that DNA has played a central role in identifying violent offenders earlier in their criminal careers and taking them off the streets before they achieved maximum carnage. In a study entitled "The Effects of DNA Databases on Crime," author Jennifer Doleac found that "...DNA profiling has a large net probative effect, particularly for young offenders. This result is an incapacitation effect, as those offenders continue to commit more crimes but are caught more frequently (or at least more quickly) when they do."

Elsewhere in her study, Doleac addresses the impact of DNA-database expansion on criminals of all ages.

"Using...data I collected on database size in each state, I find that, between 2000 and 2010, increasing the size of state databases lowered crime rates," Doleac wrote. "The estimated magnitudes imply that expanding databases by 10% would result in 5.2% fewer murders, 5.5% fewer rapes, 6.0% fewer aggravated assaults, 3.7% fewer robberies, 3.4% fewer larcenies, and 8.8% fewer vehicle thefts." [73]

On the surface, Doleac's calculated percentages may not seem all that significant. However, it's important to keep a couple of factors in mind. First, by collecting buccal swabs from every arrestee, states have the ability to expand their DNA databases by much more than a measly ten percent. Second, by an objective standard, five percent fewer murders should never be considered an insignificant figure. Imagine a room filled with 100 murder victims. Now imagine all the mothers, fathers, sons, daughters, and friends who've been devastated by the violent slaughters of their loved ones. Now imagine telling five of the murder victims in that room that they can leave and rejoin their families. According to Doleac's research, states can literally save lives and spare untold amounts of pain to survivors by expanding DNA databases.

Doleac, who is an assistant professor of economics and public policy at the University of Virginia, also addressed the effects of DNA databases on burglary rates in her study. According to Doleac, these effects are difficult to quantify. Doleac wrote that, because biological evidence is rarely left at the scenes of property crimes, few stand-alone burglaries can be solved using DNA databases. [74] Nevertheless, when burglaries are coupled with violent crimes, DNA databases become extremely valuable in generating leads.

The value of arrestee DNA collection and comprehensive DNA databases isn't just recognized within the academic community. Federal law-enforcement leaders have also championed the cause of collecting and cataloging arrestee DNA. In a November 2010 memorandum to federal law-enforcement officials, former U.S. Attorney General Eric Holder wrote, "DNA provides a powerful new tool in the enforcement of federal and state criminal laws and the administration of justice, helping both to bring the guilty to justice and to protect the innocent from mistaken suspicion, accusation, and conviction. As with other forms of identification information that are taken from persons who enter the justice system, including fingerprints and photographs, the value of DNA identification information is maximized by obtaining it at the earliest feasible point in the criminal justice process. Accordingly, the regular collection of DNA samples from federal arrestees and defendants must be a priority." [75]

Research conducted by the FBI supports Attorney General Holder's position. In 2014, the FBI's National Center for the Analysis of Violent Crime published a report entitled *Serial Murder: Pathways for Investigators*. Authored by supervisory Special Agent Robert Morton, crime analyst Jennifer Tillman, and research analyst Stephanie Gaines, *Pathways* explores a variety of topics related to patterns in serial homicide. These patterns include body-disposal strategies, victim selection, and methods of killing. Of particular interest, as it relates to the subject of arrestee DNA collection, is a section in *Pathways* that examines the prior criminal histories of known serial murderers. According to *Pathways*, "A large percentage of offenders had arrest records; however, 78.3% had a record at the time of their first murder versus 88.0% that had a record at the time of last murder." [76] In other words, violent serial predators aren't faceless phantoms who are completely unknown to law enforcement. Instead, violent serial predators are arrested at elevated rates, ensuring that—in a large number of cases—their DNA will be on file when they commit their first murder if arrestee buccal-swab collection is the law of the land. This fact, coupled with the unassailable science of properly handled DNA evidence, points to an incontrovertible conclusion: Collecting DNA from arrestees at the time of booking could, in many cases, identify serial-murder suspects early in their homicidal careers *before* they claim a maximum number of victims. Underscoring this point is the ease with which DNA can be transferred from offender to victim, offender to crime scene, and/or offender to body-dump site. While other identifying information—such as tire tracks and fingerprints—can be easily concealed by violent offenders, DNA is extremely difficult to conceal in its entirety. One tiny drop of blood, saliva, or semen can be amplified by crime-lab personnel and matched to an offender's genetic profile in the database. One flake of dry skin, an errant hair follicle, or an eyelash can be traced to a specific offender. A single microscopic cell that's invisible to the naked eye can be used to link a violent offender to his crimes and stop his reign of terror. In the Faria case, it was saliva droplets on the visor of Josh Packer's motorcycle helmet that helped hang him. These droplets were the byproduct of nothing more than Josh's normal breathing. As Alan Gunn wrote in his exceptional textbook *Essential Forensic Biology*, "Indeed, it is so easy to leave a trail of DNA at a crime scene investigators must wear masks and disposable over-suits and over-shoes to avoid contaminating the location..." with their own DNA. [77]

Not only is crime-scene DNA virtually impossible to conceal in its entirety, DNA-processing technology is evolving by the day. For this reason, as Attorney General Holder aptly pointed out in his 2010 memo, more arrestee DNA profiles will trigger more hits in CODIS, thereby giving detectives the valuable leads they need to identify violent suspects and protect the public.

The statistics contained in *Pathways* suggest that, by expanding arrestee DNA collection, law enforcement can identify future serial offenders more quickly in their criminal careers. In turn, this will spare the lives of potential victims and conserve investigative resources that would otherwise be spent on ongoing serial-homicide investigations. Be that as it may, serial murderers make up only a tiny minority of all violent offenders. As a result, to fully understand the importance of arrestee DNA collection, it's necessary to look at state-level statistics related to *all* violent offenders. These statistics indicate, in no uncertain terms, that violent non-serial offenders also experience high rates of arrest.

In December 2012, the California Department of Justice conducted a study on the state's arrestee DNA collection program, which was an outgrowth of Proposition 69. As part of this study, DOJ analysts examined the criminal histories of arrestees who were linked to unsolved murders, rapes, and robberies through their booking buccal swabs. Analysts found that seventy-nine percent of their subjects had experienced at least one arrest before their buccal swabs were collected. [78] This statistic is extremely significant in light of two other critical facts: 1) it's easy for violent offenders to leave DNA at their crime scenes and 2) violent offenders often claim multiple victims (even if the offenders don't satisfy the technical definition of a serial offender). When all three of these facts—the high incidence of arrest among violent offenders, the high incidence of DNA deposits at violent-crime scenes, the high incidence of multiple crimes by violent offenders—are tied together, the policy implications become obvious: The earlier DNA samples are collected and entered into CODIS, the more victims they will potentially spare. To illustrate this point, let's consider the hypothetical case of offender X.

When X begins his criminal career, he hasn't murdered, raped, or robbed anyone yet. He's just another degenerate in his late teens or early twenties who's committing low-risk burglaries, picking fights, or fencing a few stolen goods in his spare time. X isn't arrested the first or second or third time he commits one of his low-level offenses, but according to the California Department of Justice's study, there's a seventy-nine-percent chance that X will be arrested at some point during his criminal career. If X is arrested in a jurisdiction that collects arrestee DNA, then his buccal swab will be secured during the booking process and his genetic profile will be entered into CODIS.

After he's arrested for his first offense, X will get some probation. If X is like many offenders, probation will do little to satiate his appetite for criminality. X is young and strong and risk prone, so when he gets off probation, he decides to up the ante and commit a rape, pull a robbery, or claim a life. Regardless of which crime he chooses to commit, there's a decent chance that X will leave some type of DNA at the scene of his violent crime. Maybe X accidentally dribbles semen in his rape victim's bed. Maybe X sneezes during his robbery. Maybe X drops the screwdriver he used as a burglary tool at his murder scene, and maybe that screwdriver contains X's touch-DNA on its handle. Or maybe (like Josh Packer) X gets clawed by his murder victim. Whatever the case, if one minuscule fleck of X's DNA is found at the crime scene, it's game over. Because X's genetic fingerprint was collected at the time of his first arrest (along with his actual fingerprints), it won't take two or three or ten or fifty victims before X is linked to his crimes. Instead, X will be identified in short order and taken off the streets. And if X doesn't dribble semen or drop a screwdriver or otherwise leave DNA at the scene of his first violent offense, he'll slip up eventually. As mentioned previously, all it takes is one microscopic dusting of DNA and X's genetic profile can be matched in the database.

With all of that being said, there's a flipside to X's hypothetical case study: If X's first arrest occurred in a jurisdiction that does not mandate the collection of DNA at the time of booking, then X may not be linked to any of his later violent crimes. Let's say X is smart and decides to commit his crimes in disparate law-enforcement jurisdictions. Or let's say X is really smart and decides to target strangers. The probability that X will be linked to his crimes (or that his crimes will be linked at all) diminishes dramatically. The longer society waits to collect X's DNA, the more murders, rapes, and robberies X is allowed to commit.

X is a hypothetical criminal, but he's an ambassador for the scores of real-life violent offenders who are hiding in the shadows, just waiting to pounce on innocent, unsuspecting victims like the Husteds. Fortunately, many American law-enforcement officials and political leaders recognize this reality. In a 2010 interview with *America's Most Wanted*, President Barack Obama was asked whether states should collect buccal swabs from arrestees, thereby expanding the national DNA database. President Obama, who is a former constitutional law professor at the University of Chicago Law School, answered the question directly.

"It's the right thing to do," Obama said. The president added that, by expanding the national DNA database, states can share information more effectively and stop mobile predators more quickly.

"That's how we make sure that we continue to tighten the grip around folks who have perpetrated these crimes," Obama stated. [79]

CHAPTER 25

Although arrestee DNA collection enjoys strong and diffuse support among American political leaders and law-enforcement officials, the practice of collecting buccal swabs at the time of booking is opposed by some members of the academic and policy communities. In 2009, when California began collecting arrestee DNA, the American Civil Liberties Union of Northern California challenged the provisions of Proposition 69 in court. According to the ACLU, arrestee DNA collection "...violates constitutional guarantees of privacy and freedom from unreasonable search and seizure..." and has a "...harmful impact on communities of color." [80]

The ACLU isn't alone in its opposition to arrestee DNA collection on constitutional grounds. On December 2, 2014, just two weeks before Josh Packer plead guilty to the Faria murders, the First Appellate District of the California Court of Appeals dealt a substantial blow to arrestee DNA collection in the Golden State. The blow was delivered as part of the court's ruling in the case of *People v. Buza.*

The facts of the Buza case go like this: In the early

morning hours of January 21, 2009, a San Francisco police sergeant noticed that an arsonist had set fire to a marked squad car. Moments later, a man was seen running away from the burning car, prompting the sergeant and other officers to give chase. The officers eventually cornered the suspect in a wooded area, where he surrendered. The suspect's name was Mark Buza. After finding oil and matches in Buza's backpack, officers arrested Buza and booked him on felony charges of arson and vandalism. In accordance with state law, Buza was asked to provide a DNA sample during the booking process. When Buza refused, he was charged with an additional misdemeanor count of refusing to provide a biological sample.

On April 30, 2009, a jury convicted Buza on all charges, including failure to provide a DNA sample at the time of booking. Buza's torch job, as well as the related charges, earned him a year and four months in state prison. It was from his prison cell that Buza appealed his conviction on the DNA charge. According to Buza's appellate attorneys, the statute requiring him to provide a buccal swab at the time of booking was unconstitutional.

Although the U.S. Supreme Court had upheld the constitutionality of arrestee DNA collection in the case of *Maryland v. King*, Mark Buza prevailed in his state-level appeal. [81] As part of its ruling in Buza's case, the three-judge panel of the First Appellate District pointed out that Maryland authorities only collected DNA from arrestees who were taken into custody for "serious felonies," whereas the California collection statute applied to all felony arrestees. In the end, the First Appellate District held that, because privacy is an inalienable right under the California Constitution, the state's compulsory DNA-collection statute was unlawful.

After the First Appellate District handed down its ruling in *Buza*, California law-enforcement agencies were forced to suspended their cataloging of arrestee DNA samples. As a result, if Santa Barbara County detectives had arrested Josh Packer for the Thrifty robbery on December 3, 2014, instead of January 14, 2010, Josh's DNA would not have been collected at the time of booking and the forensic link to the Faria murders would not have been established.

Not every opponent of arrestee DNA collection predicates his opposition on a constitutional rationale. Some opponents of arrestee DNA collection are concerned about potential forensic processing errors in crime labs. In an excellent piece entitled "The Myth of Infallibility," author William C. Thompson examines the many ways in which substandard lab protocols, sample contamination, false-positives, police misconduct, and lax crime-lab management can imperil a defendant's right to a fair trial. Thompson, who is a professor in the Department of Criminology, Law, and Society at the University of California-Irvine, explores cases in which unclean laboratory equipment, spilled samples, misinterpretation of test results, cross-contamination, mislabeling, and interpersonal relationships between crime-lab personnel and detectives led to inaccurate DNA identifications and/ or wrongful convictions. According to Thompson, expanding DNA databases through the collection of arrestee DNA could exacerbate these problems, especially in cases of familial DNA searches.

In "The Myth of Infallibility," Thompson makes several solid points about the potential pitfalls of poorly handled or unethically processed DNA samples. Thompson also makes a strong case for establishing a National Institute of Forensic Science, which would serve as a central clearinghouse for all criminal DNA samples in the United States. Thompson posits that a National Institute of Forensic Science could eliminate—or at least mitigate—bias in DNA processing and neutralize many of the problems that are endemic to local crime labs. These problems, according to Thompson, include a lack of uniform processing standards and poor quality controls. Thompson argues that a National Institute of Forensic Science could enhance the probability that DNA samples will be handed properly and that justice—real justice—will be served in a maximum number of criminal cases.

Though Thompson raises many legitimate concerns about America's extant system of DNA processing, almost all of his concerns are procedural in nature. If sample contamination, low-quality processing standards, and internal bias are widespread problems in our nation's crime labs, then, as a society, we have the ability to correct these problems. However, the mere existence of procedural problems doesn't diminish the crime-fighting, life-saving potential of comprehensive DNA databases. As stated in the previous chapter, the full potential of these databases can only be realized when DNA is collected early in an offender's criminal career. In this sense, eliminating arrestee DNA collection because of isolated, lab-based procedural problems is akin to throwing the baby out with the bathwater.

It should be noted that Thompson is not averse

to arrestee DNA collection on scientific grounds. At no point in "The Myth of Infallibility" does Thompson argue that arrestee DNA screening—when performed properly—is a flawed science. Instead, Thompson writes that "I agree that...DNA testing rests on a stronger scientific foundation than most other scientific disciplines..." [82] Moreover, in the course of his research, Thompson found only three cases in which innocent people were convicted due to false DNA matching (which resulted from procedural errors), but were later exonerated through retesting of their DNA. [83] This raises a critical question: Should three cases out of hundreds of thousands prevent us from harnessing the full potential of technology that can identify hard-to-catch violent offenders, protect communities, and save lives?

While "The Myth of Infallibility" fails to rebut the assertions of arrestee DNA proponents, Thompson writes convincingly about the need for uniform DNA processing standards within crime labs. High-quality processing standards and the accuracy of suspect identifications should always be paramount concerns. In this regard, DNA screening should not be an end in itself. CODIS hits should be used to generate investigative leads and identify suspects, not establish guilt beyond a reasonable doubt. Once a CODIS hit is made, detectives should do everything in their power to eliminate the matched suspect before making an arrest. Then, if an arrest is made, the defendant must have the ability to challenge the DNA evidence in court. Simply put, the crime-fighting potential of DNA will only be realized if it is equitably balanced with a defendant's presumption of innocence. Because "The Myth of Infallibility" emphasizes the need for exemplary DNA processing standards and stringent protections for all criminal suspects, Thompson's overarching point hits its mark.

———————— ••• ————————

Elizabeth Joh, a professor of criminal procedure at the University of California-Davis School of Law, opposes arrestee DNA collection on different grounds than Thompson. In an article entitled "Should Arrestee DNA Databases Extend to Misdemeanors?," Joh focuses on three issues surrounding the debate over arrestee DNA collection: police discretion, cost, and racial bias within the criminal-justice system.

Insofar as police discretion is concerned, Joh worries that mandating the collection of buccal swabs from misdemeanor arrestees could lead to abuses of authority by sworn law-enforcement officers. Specifically, Joh worries that law-enforcement officers might begin making specious arrests to increase the number of reference samples in CODIS. As Joh writes in her article, "Discretion is an unavoidable aspect of police work. The police make arrests—or choose not to—for many reasons other than law enforcement. The blunt instrument of arrest may be used as a tactical end in itself: an immediate imposition of forcible control with little thought given to the ultimate disposition of a case." [84]

It's true that a small percentage of law-enforcement officers abuse their power, and to this end, Professor Joh's point is well taken. However, for better or worse, society grants law-enforcement officers a certain amount of discretionary latitude when making arrests. This latitude is the price we pay for living in a world that's policed by imperfect human beings. Despite the fact that some law-enforcement officers abuse their authority—and despite the fact that honest, virtuous officers make errors from time to time— we allow the government to collect many forms of personal information (name, address, Social Security number, driver's license number) and physical data (race, height, weight, eye and hair colour, tattoo descriptions, mugshots, fingerprints) from felony and misdemeanor arrestees. In many cases, the arrestee's personal information and physical data are maintained indefinitely in government databases.

So what makes DNA different from all the other information that's collected in the name of public safety when an arrestee is booked? After all, as the Faria case demonstrates, DNA has the potential to generate valuable investigative leads and take dangerous offenders out of circulation. Is isolated police misconduct really sufficient grounds for underutilizing a powerful public-safety tool like CODIS?

To get a better understanding of these questions, I contacted Professor Joh directly. At the beginning of our conversation, I asked Professor Joh whether spurious arrests by a few bad cops should prevent us from collecting DNA that might identify violent offenders and save lives. I pointed out that, despite the shameful realities of police misconduct, we allow law-enforcement agencies to collect fingerprints from felony and misdemeanor suspects at the time of booking.

"Haven't we set a precedent by allowing the police to collect fingerprints from arrestees?" I asked. "I mean, how are fingerprints substantively different from DNA?"

"I think there are important differences between fingerprinting versus taking a biological sample from someone that contains the entirety of your DNA then extracting an analysis from it," Professor Joh told me. "Those are two very different things. And, if we're thinking about—not just cost—but fairness and privacy, would we feel comfortable with everyone providing a fingerprint for criminal-justice purposes?"

Professor Joh went on to point out that, after the terror attacks of September 11, 2001, a proposed national identification card was roundly rejected by the American public. According to Professor Joh, this rejection indicated that Americans are averse to giving personal information—which she'd extrapolated to include fingerprints and arrestee DNA—to the government.

Comparing the proposed national identification card to the collection of arrestee fingerprints and DNA struck me as problematic for a couple of reasons.

First, the national identification card would've applied to every American citizen, whereas fingerprint and DNA collection by the police would only apply to arrestees. In all of my research, I couldn't find a single instance of a government official or law-enforcement leader arguing that fingerprinting or DNA collection (for law-enforcement purposes) should be expanded to the general public. As a result, comparing arrestee fingerprinting and DNA collection to the national identification card was a case of comparing apples and oranges.

Second, motorists in most states are already required to provide some combination of fingerprints in order to receive driver's licenses. In California, motorists are required to provide an index fingerprint and a thumb print to the Department of Motor Vehicles. Until the spring of 2015, the State of Texas required residents to provide *all ten* fingerprints in order to receive a driver's license. [85] Ostensibly, state motor-vehicle departments don't collect fingerprints for law-enforcement purposes. However, there's no way for the average individual to know how her or his prints are being used once they're collected by the DMV. The fact that citizens have not revolted against DMV fingerprinting points to a very distinct probability: reasonable data collection is not opposed by the majority of American citizens. Furthermore, American job applicants are routinely asked to give blood, urine, and hair-follicle samples as part of pre-employment drug screening. Again, widespread opposition to these intimate biological collections has never materialized, suggesting that most Americans grasp the pragmatism of reasonable collections.

Next, I asked Professor Joh about privacy concerns related to arrestee DNA collection. Her reasoning on this point was much easier to follow. Professor Joh pointed out that, instead of extracting DNA profiles from arrestee buccal swabs and entering the profiles into CODIS, many states maintain actual biological samples for indefinite periods of time.

"The (DNA) profile itself is just an electronic file that won't tell you much other than (the suspect's) pure identity," Professor Joh said. "But the sample, as people who watch TV and movies know, can give all sorts of rich information, not just about ourselves, but people who are related to us and so-called familial searches. This raises privacy concerns."

In its *Maryland v. King* ruling, the U.S. Supreme Court made clear that collecting arrestee DNA is constitutional. However, the Maryland statute made specific provisions for automatically expunging DNA from its offender database. Though federal law requires states that participate in CODIS to establish expungement procedures for arrestee DNA samples, no automatic-expungement provisions exist in several states, including California. This is an issue that troubles Professor Joh, and she makes a strong case for why automatic-expungement provisions are necessary.

When we finished discussing automatic expungement and privacy concerns, Professor Joh and I moved into the issue of funding. Professor Joh worries that the costs associated with collecting, processing, and screening arrestee DNA might force states to cut spending on more important law-enforcement priorities.

"The larger cost issue has to do with the finite resources any state has and whether they're going to use that to collect and process new samples or they're going to go through the very large backlog of rape kits that exists," Professor Joh told me. "That can be much more beneficial than simply collecting more and more and more (arrestee) samples."

In response to this I asked, "What would you say to the people who believe that the DNA extracted from those old rape kits is only as good as the arrestee profiles to which it can be compared?"

Professor Joh cited research that showed "...in terms of pure dollars saved and benefit in terms of cases solved, each additional arrestee DNA sample doesn't yield as much as just going through the old outstanding forensic samples and seeing if there are matches within the existing database."

Professor Joh was absolutely correct on this point. In a 2013 study entitled "Collecting DNA at Arrest: Policies, Practices, and Implications," The Urban Institute found that processing forensic samples (rape kits) yields more CODIS hits than processing offender samples.

"While the analysis of (the National DNA Index) data indicates that including more offender profiles has a significant, positive effect on investigations aided (for every 1,000 *offender* profiles, 8 investigations are aided), increasing the number of forensic profiles in CODIS has a much larger, significant, positive effect on investigations aided (for every 1,000 forensic profiles, 407 investigations are aided)," the report states.

However, The Urban Institute's report goes on to point out that, "...it is also important to consider the relative costs—in its FY 2012 solicitation, the Department of Justice's DNA Backlog Reduction Programs' reimbursement rate for analyzing forensic evidence is, on average, $1,000 per case, and $40, on average, for each offender profile analyzed and uploaded to CODIS." [86]

When considering the relative cost-benefit of arrestee DNA collection, it's worth noting the findings of Jennifer Doleac's study. Doleac found that arrestee DNA collection is highly cost effective *over the long term*. According to Doleac, most of the long-term savings associated with arrestee DNA screening involve the prevention of new crimes. When crimes are prevented, states save money on investigative costs, court costs, defense and prosecution costs, appellate costs, and other high-dollar expenses associated with the administration of justice.

"In 2010, 761,609 offender profiles were uploaded

to CODIS. At $40 apiece, this cost the state and federal governments approximately $30.5 million, but saved $15.3 billion by preventing new crimes," Doleac wrote in her report. [87]

Doleac's findings raise an important economic question: As a society, should we take the long-view or the short-view when it comes to spending on arrestee DNA collection? In the short-term, there's no doubt that increasing staff levels at crime labs, improving quality controls at crime labs, and upgrading crime-lab equipment will be very expensive. However, according to Doleac's calculations, the long-term savings—both in terms of dollars saved and victims spared—will more than offset these initial investments.

While Doleac's study suggests that arrestee DNA collection will be highly cost-effective over the long-term, Professor Joh raises a valid point about spending priorities. As Professor Joh pointed out, states have limited financial resources, and difficult decisions must be made regarding the delegation of those resources. Should public funds be spent clearing up rape-kit backlogs? Or should public funds be spent on processing and cataloging buccal swabs from arrestees like Josh Packer, whose violent criminal offenses might be completely unknown to law enforcement?

Ultimately, this debate might be resolved best through analogy: If the owner of a Major League Baseball franchise is attempting to put together a world-class team, he doesn't invest all his money in a great hitting line-up. Driving in runs is important, but those runs are only significant if the team's pitching roster can stop the opposing team from scoring runs. The goal is to put together a team that's both great at the plate and great from the mound—some combination of the Big Red Machine and the '66 Dodgers pitching rotation.

The same is true for DNA cataloging. Public resources need to be balanced in such a way that rape-kit backlogs are being cleared at the same time that new arrestee profiles are being processed into the system. Fortunately, California Attorney General Kamala Harris has proven that such a balancing act is achievable. Since taking office in 2011, Attorney General Harris has made arrestee DNA collection and processing a top priority. Under Attorney General Harris's leadership, a mountainous backlog of unprocessed rape kits has been cleared, tens of thousands of new arrestee DNA profiles have been processed into the system, and California's DNA database has been expanded to more than 2.4 million samples. Every month, these samples register at least 500 hits in criminal cases. [88]

When it comes to arrestee DNA collection, Professor Joh isn't just concerned about police discretion and financial costs. Like the ACLU, Professor Joh worries that widening the DNA-collection net will "... have a detrimental impact on communities of color." [89] To this end, Professor Joh points out that some racial minorities are disproportionately represented in CODIS. According to Professor Joh, these racial disparities are problematic because law enforcement uses crime-scene DNA to perform familial searches within CODIS. Such searches allow law enforcement to locate, not just specific offenders within the DNA database, but blood relatives of those offenders.

When I asked Professor Joh about the issue of

racial disparities in CODIS, I mentioned that racial disparities also exist in Uniform Crime Report statistics. These statistics, which are compiled annually by the U.S. Justice Department, indicate that blacks commit a disproportionate amount of crime in the United States. For example, despite making up just thirteen percent of the American population, blacks committed more than half the murders in the U.S. between 1976 and 2005. [90] In addition, UCR statistics reveal that blacks commit assault and robbery at elevated levels. According to the FBI, blacks committed thirty-three percent of all aggravated assaults and fifty-six percent of all robberies in 2014. [91] These numbers reflect long-term violent-crime trends in the U.S. With these statistics in mind, I asked Professor Joh if it didn't make sense that blacks are overrepresented in CODIS.

"I think anytime in a democratic society we have law enforcement focus or resources disproportionately focused on certain groups we worry that they unfairly bear the cost of government scrutiny," Professor Joh said. "That's something that should be a concern, period. Not just in the DNA collection context, but just in how heavily some groups or some communities are watched and surveilled. Many of our policing policies are highly discretionary, so this is in the larger context of what it means to have police in a democratic society."

In other words, police focus more attention on minority communities, not because there's more crime in those communities, but because police are unfairly targeting those communities. Therefore, according to Professor Joh, it's possible that minorities are arrested at higher rates and end up overrepresented in law-enforcement DNA databases.

Frankly, this was hard for me to swallow.

"Why would the police arbitrarily choose to focus on minority communities?" I wondered. "Are there really that many racist cops out there? And even if there are that many racist cops out there, do they really care more about arresting innocent minorities than they do about suppressing crime and keeping their jobs? After all, if police officers are wasting time on spurious arrests and the associated paperwork, they don't have time to apprehend real criminals. In turn, this would lead to rising crime rates, which would lead to bad press, which would thwart the upward mobility of officers and the supervisors to whom they answer. Are all of these people—including the minority officers and minority supervisors and minority chiefs of police—so rabidly racist that they care more about targeting innocent minorities than they do about their jobs, pensions, families, and livelihoods?"

As I contemplated Professor Joh's notions about racial bias within the American law-enforcement establishment, I decided to play devil's advocate with myself.

"Assuming that local law-enforcement agencies really are as unfair as Professor Joh insinuated, why would the U.S. Justice Department go along with it?" I wondered. "Why would Justice publish crime statistics in the Uniform Crime Report that reflect biased, racist policing practices? After all, the U.S. Justice Department has been run by black attorneys general for nearly a decade and racial arrest statistics haven't budged. Do Eric Holder and Loretta Lynch really care more about protecting racist cops, perpetuating negative minority stereotypes, and reporting erroneous crime statistics than they do about preventing crimes and protecting communities?"

Then I thought about Professor Joh's contention that law-enforcement resources are "...disproportionately focused on certain groups."

"Are the police focusing on certain racial groups or are the police focusing on high-crime areas where certain racial groups tend to live?" I wondered. "And if law enforcement is focusing more attention on high-crime areas, is this really a bad policing model?"

In considering these questions, I thought about two disparate Los Angeles neighborhoods: Pacific Palisades and Watts. Pacific Palisades is populated almost exclusively with upper-middle-class whites. Watts is populated almost exclusively with low-income blacks and Latinos. Pacific Palisades is a laid-back, low-crime beach community on the far-western edge of the city. Watts is a crime-ridden southside ghetto where anomie is the rule, not the exception. With these realities in mind, should the Los Angeles Police Department really delegate the same quantity of resources to the Palisades that it does to Watts? According to what logic would such an allocation of police resources make sense? And, if the LAPD did shift resources out of Watts and into the Palisades, wouldn't the residents of Watts start complaining about a lack of police protection in their community, delayed response times, and rising crime rates? As far as I could tell, Professor Joh's contention that police resources are "...disproportionately focused on certain groups..." places law enforcement in an impossible bind: The police are damned if they crack down on illegal activity in high-crime minority communities and they're damned if they don't.

To buttress her contention that elevated minority arrest rates are the result of unfair policing practices,

Professor Joh told me about a study that was conducted in the State of New Jersey. According to Professor Joh, the study found that law-enforcement officers stop black and Latino motorists at higher rates than motorists of other races. On the surface, this study seems to confirm that systemic racial discrimination exists within the American law-enforcement establishment (or at least New Jersey's law-enforcement establishment). However, the New Jersey study proves nothing of the sort. After all, it's one thing for a police officer to stop a minority motorist for "driving while black." It's another thing for a police officer to frame an innocent black person for assault, robbery, or murder. Felony arrests require witnesses and evidence and actual victims. If the UCR statistics regarding elevated levels of black violent crime are truly flawed, then how did police come up with the witnesses, evidence, and victims to justify the arrests of all those innocent blacks?

When considering this question, it's important to remember that most crimes in the U.S. are intraracial, meaning that crime victims are usually victimized by someone of their own race. [92] If the UCR statistics are the result of racially biased policing, then how did thousands upon thousands of racist cops talk black community members (who are the most frequent victims of black criminals) into bearing false witness against members of their own race? Just imagine the conversations that would need to occur to justify all of those supposedly unfair, racially motivated arrests by bad cops.

"Listen," the racist officer would say to the black robbery victim. "We know it was a white guy who ripped you off, but we'd really appreciate it if you'd just say that you were robbed by a black guy. Can you dig it?"

Or, while speaking with a black witness about the murder of a black victim, the racist officer might say, "Look, I know you're tellin' me that you saw some Asian grandmothers pull this drive-by, but it'll make our jobs a lot easier if we can just arrest some young black guys. Would you mind changing your story and saying that the shooters were black?"

In the end, the New Jersey traffic-stop study does nothing to prove that elevated arrest rates among blacks are the byproduct of widespread police racism. More importantly, the traffic-stop study does nothing to undercut the case for arrestee DNA collection. There's no doubt that racial profiling is an odious practice. However, looking at the traffic-stop study and concluding that racism is endemic to all facets of American police culture is like looking at an unsightly mole on your arm and concluding that you have malignant melanoma raging through your body. Or, as it relates to the issue of arrestee DNA collection, it's like seeing an unsightly mole on your arm, jumping to the conclusion that you have malignant melanoma, and stopping your daily jogs through the park so you can shield yourself from sunlight—even though the jogging optimizes your overall health.

Toward the end of my conversation with Professor Joh, it occurred to me that UCR arrest statistics reflect other types of demographic disparities as well. Specifically, American males are arrested at significantly higher rates than American females. Should we stop collecting buccal swabs from male arrestees until an equality of gender outcomes is achieved in arrest statistics?

"When you talk about disproportionate (racial) representation in the databases, do you have any concern that men are disproportionately represented in these databases?" I asked Professor Joh. "Do you have the same concerns there that you do about racial minorities?"

"Those are two different questions," she answered. "I think, in general, men far outnumber women in the criminal-justice system. But to look at it another way, when I talk about racial disproportion, people are typically concerned about the disproportionate representation of, let's say, African-American men. So yes, I suppose, to your question. But I don't think there's ever been any dispute that men in general constitute most of those who are in the criminal-justice system. I don't think that's a particularly controversial point."

"But if men are disproportionately represented and you accept those numbers, why not accept the numbers as well that African-Americans are disproportionately represented and that both groups of statistics regarding arrests and incarcerations are either accurate or they're not accurate?" I asked. "How do you disentangle those?"

Professor Joh hesitated for a long second, then began to answer.

"I think the first proposition about the gender distinction in criminal justice is not something I've looked at at all, but my general awareness there is that there's been a long-standing support for the fact that males tend to engage in criminal offending more than women. And particularly younger men than older men," she said. "I think there's much more dispute and controversy about enforcing the criminal law against certain racial groups. You'll get much less consensus on that. Does that make sense?"

"Sort of," I answered. "But I don't really know where people would be drawing their opinions from besides statistics. I mean, if it's just completely arbitrary and one opinion on that subject would be just as legitimate as the next—"

Professor Joh jumped in and attempted to reexplain.

"I don't think anyone is saying, well, the police departments are targeting men but they're not targeting women and that's unfair. We've known for decades that offending patterns are such that it's typically men more than women who are involved with offending," she said. "I think it's much more subject to dispute to say, well, it's okay for African-Americans to be overrepresented in the criminal-justice population because they are offending in higher numbers."

Professor Joh asked me if I understood. I told her that I did not. Using a slightly different phraseology, she re-explained the same concept. When she was finished, she again asked me if I understood. I relented and said that I did. However, my answer was only half honest.

I understood what Professor Joh was saying about social attitudes. Few people would argue that males are overrepresented in the criminal-justice system because of gender discrimination. On the other hand, many people *feel* that blacks are victims of systemic police bias and end up overrepresented among arrest statistics. To this end, I understood completely what Professor Joh was saying. In fact, I agreed with her assessment of how the public *feels* about these issues.

However, my understanding of Professor Joh's position started to break down when it came to the public-policy angle. Should policies related to arrestee DNA collection be based on cold, hard, objective statistics? Or should DNA-collection policies be based on how people *feel* about matters pertaining to racial arrest rates?

There's no doubt that minorities are sometimes unfairly targeted by unscrupulous, racist police officers. It's tragic when this happens, but is it prudent to eliminate arrestee DNA collection until an equality of outcomes is achieved in racial arrest statistics? Would such an approach really enhance public safety, save lives, or make the world a better place? Data from the National Registry of Exonerations, which is operated jointly by the University of Michigan Law School and the Northwestern University School of Law, indicates that the answer to both questions is no. In fact, when it comes to exonerations, statistics indicate that blacks are the overwhelming beneficiaries of law-enforcement DNA screening.

According to the National Registry of Exonerations, as of July 2015, blacks make up forty-eight percent of homicide exonerations due to DNA, sixty-one percent of sexual-assault exonerations due to DNA, and forty-seven percent of all criminal exonerations due to DNA. [93] Despite the fact that whites comprise a much larger percentage of the American population than blacks, child sex abuse was the only crime for which whites were more likely to be exonerated through DNA than blacks. This points to an unavoidable conclusion: DNA collection doesn't harm innocent blacks and "communities of color," it actually helps them.

By collecting arrestee DNA at the time of booking and entering genetic profiles into CODIS, we can enhance the probability that guilty suspects will be identified and that innocent people of all races will be spared the horror of wrongful conviction. After all, when DNA is handled and processed properly, it takes much of the guesswork out of criminal investigations and criminal prosecutions. And, according to the National Registry of Exonerations, no group benefits more from this than blacks.

Professor Joh did not convince me that arrestee DNA collection is a flawed social policy. However, there's no denying that the broad brushstrokes of Professor Joh's arguments are sound. As a society, we should be concerned about police discretion, government spending, and racism within the justice system. In fact, when it comes to racism in the justice system, we should be more than concerned; we should be vigilant about rooting out racist cops, making victims of racially motivated arrests whole, and preventing racially motivated arrests in the future. In addition, Professor Joh is absolutely correct about the need for caution when it comes to arrestee DNA collection. As responsible and conscientious citizens, we should ask tough questions when our government wants to collect our most intimate biological data.

Unfortunately, the issues surrounding arrestee DNA collection are not so cut and dry. As Professor Joh readily admits, it's impossible to prove what's going through an officer's mind when she or he decides to arrest a suspect. Also, in a nation of 320 million people, we're never going to achieve a perfect equality of outcomes when it comes to racial arrest statistics.

Be that as it may, the government plays a vital role

in ensuring public safety. Like it says on the side of every marked police vehicle in the city of Los Angeles, two of the government's principal responsibilities are "To Protect and To Serve" citizens. Police officers are imperfect people, crime labs are imperfect places, and DNA databases are imperfect tools (if samples are not processed properly), but that doesn't mean these cornerstones of our public-safety apparatus should be underutilized.

Our society has reached a crossroads and we're now confronted with a critical, epoch-defining question: What price are we willing to pay to live in a safe society where life is not solitary, poor, nasty, brutish, and short?

There's a price involved with placing reasonable trust in law enforcement.

There's a price involved with upgrading, staffing, and ensuring quality controls within crime labs.

There's a price involved with acknowledging the uncomfortable realities of crime statistics.

Are these prices so high that we're willing to eschew scientifically sound technology that can save lives, free innocent people from prison, and safeguard other innocent people from wrongful conviction?

Perhaps Mike Frawley provided the best answer to this question when he posed a rhetorical question to me after Josh Packer's sentencing.

"What price can you place on being a victim?" Frawley asked.

CHAPTER 26

Such of downtown Camarillo, nestled along a broad, sunny hillside, is Conejo Mountain Memorial Park. The burnished slopes of the Santa Monica Mountains enclose the cemetery on two sides, giving it a feeling of intimacy, solitude, and tranquility. The road from the freeway to Conejo Mountain winds past several small office parks and residential neighborhoods. As one nears the memorial park, the office buildings and neighborhoods fall away, and the road is enveloped by rich, loamy farmland. Acres of yellow-dotted lemon trees, crimson-dappled tomato plants, and luscious avocado bushes stretch out in perfect rows in all directions. The vibrant colours of the crops create a powerful contrast with the beige backdrop of the mountains.

The sky was softening to a deep, early evening blue as I drove through Conejo Mountain's gates, looped around to the back quadrant of the cemetery, and began walking toward the headstone. It was a sweltering summer evening and heat waves trembled in the air as I wound through the rows of marble slabs.

Finally, I found the headstone I was seeking. The left side of the stone read as follows:

Beloved Daughter, Sister, Wife and Mother
Davina Marie Husted
July 31, 1966 - May 20, 2009

The right side of the headstone was even more laconic in its wording:

Our Precious Baby
Grant Husted
May 20, 2009

Below the names were the words "We Will Love You Forever." A rose was emblazoned in the upper left corner of the headstone beside Davina Husted's name. Two small rabbits were etched into the stone's lower right corner beside Grant's name. Davina's father, David John Deboni, was buried a few feet away. Brock Husted had been laid to rest elsewhere.

As I stood in front of the gravestone, images flashed through my mind. In pictures taken during her lifetime, Davina Husted looked so poised, so happy, so alive. When I studied those pictures, I couldn't detect a trace of subterfuge or cynicism in her features. Davina Husted had radiated a genuine warmth that was difficult to reconcile with the fate that had claimed her life. Gazing down at her gravestone, I was left with many questions and almost no answers.

I was hoping that a trip to Conejo Mountain might give me some type of visceral insight into the Faria murders. Instead, standing in front of Davina and Grant Husted's grave filled me with a hollow, empty sadness. As the sun dropped lower behind the mountains and shadows crept across the valley, images from the crime-scene photos began to encroach on my thoughts. I recalled the chaotic disarray of the Husteds' bedroom, the gore-drenched butcher knife, and the way Davina Husted's frozen arm curled up protectively in front of her bloodied face. A loving mother, who was on the verge of giving birth for the third time, had been stabbed to death in her own bedroom. Her hard-working husband had perished beside her. They were both forty-two years old. Their children needed them. They had their whole lives ahead of them.

Almost an hour passed. Eventually, as I studied the headstone and absorbed the near-total silence of Conejo Mountain, a sense of foreboding began to consume my thoughts. With the sun dropping quickly and the landscape fading to black, I returned to my car, drove back to the freeway, and made my way toward Ventura.

During the drive, in an attempt to escape the darkness that was settling on my psyche like a weight, I tried to think of a single word that encapsulated the malignant enormity of the Faria case. Finding single words to describe complex, multifaceted phenomena was a coping mechanism I'd used since I was a teenager. Somehow, distilling a profound, unfathomable complexity down to a single, all-encompassing descriptor made it easier to pick apart the descriptor's definition, dissect the larger problem, examine each of its constituent parts, and reach a logical conclusion. Unfortunately, after racking my brain for twenty minutes, I was unable to think of a single word that captured horrific breadth of the Faria case. By the time I exited the freeway and parked on a quiet side street in downtown Ventura, I'd concluded that, perhaps, no single word was capable of describing the Faria case as a whole. It was at that point that I exited my car and began wandering and thinking.

The Faria murders were horrendous crimes by any measure, but at the same time, they revealed some important truths about life in contemporary America. The Faria murders underscored the importance of keeping one's home secured at all times. The Faria murders illuminated the crime-fighting potential of arrestee DNA collection and DNA databases. And the Faria murders proved that caring for and protecting children—all children—is a societal concern. As I weaved through the evening crowd on Main Street and ruminated about these issues, I passed a shop called Child Abuse and Neglect Thrift Store. It was around that time that my thoughts shifted to Josh Packer.

In late July 2015, Josh was transferred from the Medical Facility at Vacaville to the California Health Care Facility in Stockton. Although I'd spent untold hours talking with Josh's mother and researching his life, I realized that I was no closer to having a definitive explanation for the Faria murders. Nevertheless, I was sure of one thing: Josh Packer's propensity for violence didn't crystalize in a vacuum. Instead, it was fostered through a lifetime of abuse, neglect, indifference, sexual perversion, unmet needs, and toxic influences. Josh Packer wasn't born bad. To the contrary, Josh possessed many fine qualities: he was good at making friends, he was a hard worker and a reliable employee, he stuck up for himself, and he never allowed his terrible childhood to transform him into an excuse-making whiner. From what I could tell, Josh never asked for much out of life. In fact, when Josh was a boy, it appeared that he never wanted anything more than what every child has a right to expect: a safe and stable home, loving and protective caretakers, and an environment that nurtures positive moral and intellectual development. Josh Packer was denied these things. Society failed to intervene effectively on his behalf. The Husteds paid the price.

The last sliver of sun sank below the horizon as I continued to wander the bustling streets of Ventura. Lights began to twinkle in the hills above the city and my thoughts turned to Josh's sentencing. Although I'd missed the actual hearing, I'd watched news coverage of the sentencing online. Thinking back on that news coverage, a statement by Judge Murphy stood out in my mind.

In pronouncing sentence, Judge Murphy referred to Josh as "...the worst of the worst." [94] While I respected Judge Murphy's authority, her "worst of the worst" remark had, in my opinion, missed the point. There was no denying that Josh was a hardcore criminal who had committed nightmarish crimes. However, by what objective standard did Josh's actions in Faria make him the worst of the worst?

Were Josh's crimes worse than the Columbine High School massacre? Were Josh's crimes worse than the 9/11 terror attacks? Were Josh's crimes qualitatively worse than the litany of other grisly murders that have taken place in Ventura County over the past half century? For that matter, how do Josh Packer's crimes compare with the actions George W. Bush and his cabinet? The former president and his cabinet launched the Iraq War based on intelligence they knew was flawed, and the needless havoc they caused was absolutely catastrophic. The Iraq War plunged two Middle Eastern nations into civil war, inflamed the anger of jihadists around the globe, and led to the burning, maiming, beheading, disfigurement, blinding, torture, and psychological destruction of countless human beings. According to the most recent estimates of the Iraq Body Count Project, the needless carnage of Bush's war ended the lives of more than 220,000 Iraqi civilians and allied troops. What were those lives worth? How many fathers, pregnant mothers, and fetuses were obliterated by the political grandstanding, pathological arrogance, and unforgivable incompetence of the Bush Administration? How many families were left traumatized by the psychopathic temerity and abject stupidity of America's political leaders? Were the impulsive actions of a profoundly damaged nineteen-year-old security guard in Faria really worse than the actions of a privileged president, who used his Andover-Yale-Harvard Business School pedigree to launch a pointless, bloody, multi-trillion-dollar war?

Murder is always atrocious, but as I walked through the waning twilight of downtown Ventura and reflected on the relative scale of human degeneracy, Judge Murphy's "worst of the worst" comment struck me as totally lacking in both purview and proportionality. Of course the Faria murders made Josh Packer "the worst of the worst" in the eyes of the victims' family members. However, if the only criteria for gauging the severity of a criminal's actions are the subjective feelings of the victims' family members, then every murderer is the worst of the worst and the term loses all meaning.

Maybe Judge Murphy understood all of this and decided to make her "worst of the worst" statement anyway. Perhaps, in making her "worst of the worst" statement, Judge Murphy was speaking only of the defendants who've passed through her courtroom over the years. Or maybe Judge Murphy was doing her best to placate the victims' family members and provide them with a sense closure. If the latter was true, then Judge Murphy's intent was laudable. Whatever the case, it seemed that Judge Murphy had missed a tremendous opportunity to offer a nuanced commentary, not only on the issues raised by Josh Packer's life, but on the broader implications of the Faria case.

Here's what another judge might've said at the sentencing: "Josh Packer, when I look at you and think about the horrors you endured as a child, I can hardly find the words to express my profound sympathy and sadness. You endured traumas that no child should ever suffer. You were abandoned, you were neglected, and you were sexually abused. You were maimed, you were beaten, and you were exposed to atrocious adult influences. The cumulative psychological damage you've suffered is more than our best medical doctors can begin to quantify. As a society, we need to take real, aggressive, and proactive steps to ensure that what happened to you never, ever happens again.

"At the same time, your horrible upbringing doesn't mitigate your culpability in these crimes. Your moral compass was warped by your aberrant childhood, but when you went to Faria on the night of May 20, 2009, you understood the difference between right and wrong. You knew it was wrong to rob, you knew it was wrong to commit sexual assault, and you knew it was wrong to murder. The wrongness of your crimes was not beyond your range of comprehension. When you arrived at the Husted home, you had a choice to make: Do I violate the law or do I not violate the law? This ability to make choices is the bedrock of humanity; it's what separates us from animals. As humans, we have the ability to make rational choices. You chose to break the law.

"In pronouncing sentence on you today, I'm sending a message that burglary and robbery and sexual assault and murder will not be tolerated in our society. If an individual makes the choice to behave like an animal, then, as a society, we'll utilize our best technology and our best resources to hunt that person down like an animal. Make no mistake about it: Those who *choose* to commit crimes will be identified, brought to the bar of justice, and held accountable for their decisions."

Eventually, I walked out of the downtown core, across the railroad tracks, and onto the Ventura Pier. As I made my way down the length of the Pier, the traffic noises of the city fell away and the rolling hiss of the waves filled my ears. When I reached the end of the Pier, I stopped, turned around, and faced the city. The wind howled and the coastline sparkled.

Standing at the end of the Pier, with the blackness of the sea and the sky all around me, thoughts of the Faria murders flooded my mind. I thought of the pain, the grief, and the tragedy. I thought of the missed opportunities, the squandered potential, and the eternal devastation. Gazing down at the water, I suddenly realized that there was a single word that encapsulated the totality of the Faria case. The word was paradox.

It was a paradox that the Husteds' everyday safety and comfort blinded them to the importance of home security, thereby facilitating Josh Packer's crimes.

It was a paradox that society would spend tens of thousands of dollars a year to keep an adult Josh Packer in prison, yet the same society would only spend pennies when Josh was a troubled child who was desperately in need of help.

More than anything, it was a paradox that the Faria crimes—crimes that had scarred the victims' families forever—had the potential to spare other families pain by highlighting the life-saving potential of arrestee DNA collection.

Leaning against the Pier's railing, I stared out across the water. The lights of the Gold Coast glittered like diamonds on top of the waves. It was hard to believe that a world filled with such beauty, such wonder, and such promise could also be filled with such horror. For a brief second, as the lights sparkled on top of the water and the sounds of distant laughter echoed from the beach, the horrors of humanity receded from my mind. In that moment, the infinite potential of the universe—with all of its equity and rationality and benevolence—seemed to hover within reach. Then, without warning, the wind shifted, the sea began to roil, and a black wave rolled in from the deep.

In an instant, the lights were gone.

NOTES

(i) Catalano, S. (2010, September). *Victimization During Household Burglary.* Bureau of Justice Statistics, p. 2.

(ii) Catalano, S. (2010, September). *Victimization During Household Burglary.* Bureau of Justice Statistics, p. 6.

(iii) Analysis of Uniform Crime Report clearance data, 2004-2014.

(iv) Federal Bureau of Investigation. (2009). Crime in the United States 2009 — Expanded Homicide Data Table 7. <https://www2.fbi.gov/ucr/cius2009/offenses/expanded_information/data/shrtable_07.html> Accessed October 2, 2015.

(1) Geberth, V.J. (2010). *Sex-Related Homicide and Death Investigation: Practical and Clinical Perspectives, 2nd Edition.* Boca Raton, FL: CRC Press, p. 176.

(2) Federal Bureau of Investigation. (2015). Uniform Crime Report Data Table: Ventura County Sheriff's Department Violent Crime Rate, 1998-2008. <http://www.ucrdatatool.gov/Search/Crime/Local/RunCrimeJurisbyJuris.cfm>. Accessed April 3, 2015.

(3) Pearl, M.S. (2007, November/December). Home on the Range. *California Homes*, 106-111.

(4) Covarrubias, A. (2003, November 23). At 91, He Has a Lot on the Bean. *Los Angeles Times*, B1.

(5) Barlow, Z. (2009, May 21). Husteds remembered as lively and loving. *Ventura County Star*, A1.

(6) Ventura County District Attorney's Office. (2015, February 2). *State of California v. Joshua Packer*. Statement in Aggravation, p. 12.

(7) Scheibe, J. (2009, May 28). Detectives believe killer targeted Faria Beach pair. *McClatchy-Tribune Business News*. <http://search.proquest.com/docview/455826630?accountid=11124>.

(8) Federal Bureau of Investigation. (2010, September). Uniform Crime Report — Crime in the United States, 2009.

(9) Gamboa, R. (2010, January 19). Report of Arrest — Case Number 09-15577. Santa Barbara County Sheriff's Department, p. 4.

(10) Tilley, N. (2009). *Crime Prevention*. New York: Routledge, p. 19.

(11) Gamboa, R. (2010, January 19). Report of Arrest — Case Number 09-15577. Santa Barbara County Sheriff's Department, p. 5.

(12) Reagan, N. (1983, January). Let's Get Our Kids Off Drugs. *Ladies' Home Journal*, 44-46.

(13) Fager, W.M. (2002). *Straight Foundation, Inc. — The Shell Company: Piercing the Corporate Veil*. <http://www.thestraights.net/financial/st-fdn-piercing-veil.htm>.

(14) Balko, R. (2002, May 23). *Drug War Casualties*. Fox News. <http://www.webdiva.org/fox/>.

(15) Ventura County Superior Court. (1993, December 28). Income and Expense Declaration of Petitioner Terri L. Packer — Case Number D210512, p. 3.

(16) Wolcott, H. (1998, July 20). 4 Fugitives Sought by Sheriff's Department. *Los Angeles Times*, B3.

(17) Ganier, S. (2000, January 28). Suspension Report — E.P. Foster Elementary School. Ventura Unified School District.

(18) Sims-Schneider, K. (2002, June 6). Detail Behavior — Committed Sexual Harassment. Ventura Unified School District.

(19) Tallakson, L. (2002, April 25). Detail Behavior — Battery/Caused Physical Injury. Ventura Unified School District.

(20) Castro, L. (2002, May 24). Detail Behavior — Committed Sexual Harassment. Ventura Unified School District.

(21) Castro, L. (2002, June 4). Detail Behavior — Committed Sexual Harassment. Ventura Unified School District.

(22) Sims-Schneider, K. (2002, June 6). Detail Behavior — Physical Injury. Ventura Unified School District.

(23) Kelsch, E. (2002, August 12). Detail Behavior — Harassment/Engaged in Intimidation. Ventura Unified School District.

(24) Etter, N. (2002, August 14). Suspension Report — De Anza Middle School. Ventura Unified School District.

(25) California School Ratings. <http://school-ratings.com/school_details/56726526062152.html>. Accessed March 31, 2015.

(26) Ventura County District Attorney's Office. (2012, July 19). State of California v. Joshua Packer. Interview Summary, p. 1-2.

(27) Ventura County District Attorney's Office. (2013, July 30). State of California v. Joshua Packer. Interview Summary, p. 1-3.

(28) Sutherland, C. (2006, January 25). Arrest Report — Case Number 06-01234. Ventura Police Department.

(29) Hester, B. (2011, March 7). Major Crimes Interview — 4RB Number 090012515, Narrative/Supplemental Report. Ventura County Sheriff's Department.

(30) Frawley, M. (2011, July 8). State of California v. Joshua Packer. Interview, p. 3.

(31) Snow, A. (2007, June 11). Arrest Report Narrative — Case Number 07-08851. Ventura Police Department, p. 2.

(32) Snow, A. (2007, June 11). Arrest Report Narrative — Case Number 07-08851. Ventura Police Department, p. 2.

(33) Eltz, M. (2009, April 27). Probable Cause Declaration — Declaration Number 14892. Ventura Police Department.

(34) Personal communication. (2015, May 27). Commander Sam Arroyo, Ventura Police Department.

(35) Gamboa, R. (2010, January 19). Report of Arrest — Case Number 09-15577. Santa Barbara County Sheriff's Department, p. 5-6.

(36) Gamboa, R. (2010, January 19). Report of Arrest — Case Number 09-15577. Santa Barbara County Sheriff's Department, p. 6.

(37) Frawley, M. & Sabo, A. (2011, January 11). *State of California v. Joshua Packer.* Interview with Ryan Deleon, p. 2.

(38) Eltz, M. (2009, December 11). Traffic Collision Report — Case Number 09-16779. Ventura Police Department, p. 2.

(39) Gamboa, R. (2010, January 19). Report of Arrest — Case Number 09-15577. Santa Barbara County Sheriff's Department, p. 6-7.

(40) Gamboa, R. (2010, January 19). Report of Arrest — Case Number 09-15577. Santa Barbara County Sheriff's Department, p. 8.

(41) Hamilton, D. (1989, September 14). Woman Guilty of Murder in State's First Case Based on Genetic Evidence. *Los Angeles Times*, 3 and 27.

(42) Samuels, J., Davies, E., Pope, D., & Holand, A. (2012, June). Collecting DNA From Arrestees: Implementation Lessons. *National Institute of Justice Journal, 270*, p. 19.

(43) Ingram, C. (2002, September 18). Davis Signs 2 Key Measures Against Crime. *Los Angeles Times*, B8.

(44) Slater, E. (2004, November 9). State Lends a Strong Hand to Crime-Fighting With DNA. *Los Angeles Times*, A1.

(45) *Haskell v. Brown*, 677 F.Supp.2d 1187 (N.D. Cal. 2009).

(46) Schierman, W. (2010, April 14). Supplemental Arrest Report — 4RB Number 090012515. Ventura County Sheriff's Department, p. 1-2.

(47) Ventura County District Attorney's Office. (2015, February 2). *State of California v. Joshua Packer*. Statement in Aggravation, p. 14.

(48) Ventura County District Attorney's Office. (2015, February 2). *State of California v. Joshua Packer*. Statement in Aggravation, p. 21-22.

(49) Jauregui, E. (2010, August 16). Jail Incident Report — Report Number 111835. Ventura County Sheriff's Department, p. 1.

(50) Jauregui, E. (2010, August 16). Jail Incident Report — Report Number 111835. Ventura County Sheriff's Department, p. 2.

(51) Hernandez, R. (2011, April 4). Murder suspect in court on 3 unrelated charges. *Ventura County Star*, A1.

(52) Gens, M. (2009, August 11). Crime Report — Case Number 09-06756. Ventura Police Department.

(53) Ventura County District Attorney's Office. (2015, February 2). *State of California v. Joshua Packer.* Statement in Aggravation, p. 20.

(54) Ventura County District Attorney's Office. (2015, February 2). *State of California v. Joshua Packer.* Statement in Aggravation, p. 21.

(55) Hernandez, R. (2010, September 3). Packer had hand cut, says affidavit. *Ventura County Star*, A1.

(56) Ventura County District Attorney's Office. (2015, February 2). *State of California v. Joshua Packer.* Statement in Aggravation, p. 21.

(57) Hester, B. (2011, February 23). Major Crimes Interview — 4RB Number 090012515, Supplemental Report. Ventura County Sheriff's Department, p. 1.

(58) Hester, B. (2011, February 23). Major Crimes Interview — 4RB Number 090012515, Supplemental Report. Ventura County Sheriff's Department, p. 1.

(59) Hester, B. (2011, February 24). Major Crimes Interview — 4RB Number 090012515, Supplemental Report. Ventura County Sheriff's Department, p. 2.

(60) California Supreme Court. (2014, December 11). *Joshua Packer v. Ventura County Superior Court.* Opinion Number S213894, p. 2.

(61) California Supreme Court. (2014, December 11). *Joshua Packer v. Ventura County Superior Court.* Opinion Number S213894, p. 8.

(62) *Pier'Angela Spaccia v. Los Angeles County Superior Court,* 209 Cal.App. 4th 93 at p. 112.

(63) California Supreme Court. (2014, December 11). *Joshua Packer v. Ventura County Superior Court.* Opinion Number S213894, p. 11.

(64) Wagstaff, E. (2014, July 16). Here are the 13 men executed by California since 1978. *Los Angeles Times,* B3.

(65) Ventura County Public Defender's Office. (2014, January 21). *Joshua Packer v. Ventura County Superior Court.* Opening Brief on the Merits, p. 9.

(66) Prothero, M. & Smith, C. (2006). *Defending Gary.* San Francisco: Jossey Bass, p. 83.

(67) Prothero, M. & Smith, C. (2006). *Defending Gary.* San Francisco: Jossey Bass, p. 85.

(68) Lilienfeld, S.O., Lynn, S.J., Ruscio, J., & Beyerstein, B.L. (2010). *50 Great Myths of Popular Psychology: Shattering Widespread Misconceptions About Human Behavior.* Malden, MA: Wiley-Blackwell, p. 225.

(69) Kirby, L.T. (1992). *DNA Fingerprinting: An Introduction.* New York: Oxford University Press.

(70) Chawkins, S. & Winton, R. (2012, September 8). DNA match leads to arrest in 1980 Oxnard slaying. *Los Angeles Times,* B1.

(71) Cooper, A. & Smith, E. (2011, November). Homicide Trends in the United States, 1980-2008. *Bureau of Justice Statistics-NCJ 236018,* p. 16.

(72) Chettiar, I.M. (2015, February 11). The Many Causes of America's Decline in Crime. *The Atlantic*. <http://www.theatlantic.com/features/archive/2015/02/the-many-causes-of-americas-decline-in-crime/385364/>.

(73) Doleac, J.L. (2015, January). *The Effects of DNA Databases on Crime*, p. 5.

(74) Doleac, J.L. (2015, January). *The Effects of DNA Databases on Crime*, p. 5.

(75) Holder, E.H. (2010, November 19). Memorandum—DNA Sample Collection from Federal Arrestees and Defendants, <http://www.justice.gov/sites/default/files/ag/legacy/2010/11/19/ag-memo-dna-collection111810.pdf>.

(76) Morton, R.J., Tillman, J.M., & Gaines, S.J. (2014). *Serial Murder: Pathways for Investigators*. National Center for the Analysis of Violent Crime, p. 14-15.

(77) Gunn, A. (2009). *Essential Forensic Biology, 2nd Edition*. Hoboken, NJ: Wiley, 3-1.

(78) State of California — Office of the Attorney General. (2012). <https://oag.ca.gov/sites/all/files/agweb/pdfs/bfs/arrestee_2013.pdf?>

(79) Walsh, J. (2010, March 4). *America's Most Wanted*. Los Angeles: Fox.

(80) American Civil Liberties Union of Northern California. (2014, December 3). *Haskell v. Harris*. <https://aclunc.org/our-work/legal-docket/haskell-v-harris>.

(81) Emery, S. (2014, December 10). Just a quick swab for DNA? Not so fast, California courts say. *Orange County Register*, A1.

(82) Krimsky, S. & Gruber, J. (Eds.). (2013). *Genetic Explanations: Sense and Nonsense.* Cambridge, MA: Harvard University Press, p. 228.

(83) Krimsky, S. & Gruber, J. (Eds.). (2013). *Genetic Explanations: Sense and Nonsense.* Cambridge, MA: Harvard University Press, p. 233.

(84) Joh, E.E. (2015). Should Arrestee DNA Databases Extend to Misdemeanors? *Recent Advances in DNA and Gene Sequences, 8* (2), 3.

(85) McCraw, S. (2014, September 3). Why DPS takes all 10 fingerprints when you get your driver's license. *Dallas Morning News*, A7.

(86) Samuels, J.E., Davies, E.H., & Pope, D.B. (2013, May). *Collecting DNA At Arrest: Policies, Practices, and Implications—Final Technical Report.* The Urban Institute-Justice Policy Center, p. 80.

(87) Doleac, J.L. (2015, January). *The Effects of DNA Databases on Crime*, p. 18.

(88) Personal communication. (2015, March 9). Kristin Ford, Press Secretary for the California Department of Justice.

(89) Joh, E.E. (2015). Should Arrestee DNA Databases Extend to Misdemeanors? *Recent Advances in DNA and Gene Sequences, 8* (2), 1-6.

(90) Cooper, A. & Smith, E. (2011, November). Homicide Trends in the United States, 1980-2008. *Bureau of Justice Statistics-NCJ 236018*, p. 12.

(91) Federal Bureau of Investigation. (2014). Crime in the United States 2014 — Data Table 43A. <https://www.fbi.gov/about-us/cjis/ucr/crime-in-the-u.s/2014/crime-in-the-u.s.-2014/tables/table-43>. Accessed June 5, 2015.

(92) Cooper, A. & Smith, E. (2011, November). Homicide Trends in the United States, 1980-2008. *Bureau of Justice Statistics-NCJ 236018*, p. 13.

(93) National Registry of Exonerations. (2015). <https://www.law.umich.edu/special/exoneration/Pages/ExonerationsRaceByCrime.aspx>. Accessed July 17, 2015.

(94) Hernandez, M. (2015, February 6). Joshua Packer gets life without parole for Husted killings. *Ventura County Star*, A1.

29427155R00236

Made in the USA
San Bernardino, CA
23 January 2016